"O" LEVEL
ENGLISH LAW

A THOUSAND YEARS OF ENGLISH LAW

Some important dates

Monarch		
Alfred	{ 871 899 }	890 Laws of King Alfred
		900
		1000
Canute	{ 1016 1035 }	1029 Laws of King Canute
William I	{ 1066 1087 }	1066 Battle of Hastings 1086 Domesday Book
		1100
Henry II	{ 1154 1189 }	Emergence of Court of Exchequer Emergence of Court of Common Pleas
		1200 1215 Magna Carta
Edward I	{ 1272 1307 }	Emergence of Court of Kings Bench
		1300 Emergence of Court of Chancery Emergence of the Court of Admiralty
		1400
		1500
Henry VIII	{ 1509 1547 }	1535 Statute of Uses
		1600
James I	{ 1603 1625 }	1616 James I decided in favour of equity Development of Trusts
		1700 Great era of equity
		1800
Queen Victoria	{ 1837 1901 }	1857 Court of Probate Established Court of Divorce Established 1875 Old courts abolished; Supreme Court established
		1900 1907 Court of Criminal Appeal set up
George V	{ 1910 1936 }	1925 Reform of the Land Law
Queen Elizabeth II	{ 1952	1966 Court of Criminal Appeal abolished and combined with Court of Appeal 1973 United Kingdom joined Common Market, European Court given jurisdiction.

"O" LEVEL ENGLISH LAW

FOURTH EDITION

By

D. M. M. SCOTT

LL.B. (London), Dip. Air Law

Solicitor; Chief Examiner to the Institute of Legal Executives; Vice President of the International Institute of Legal and Administrative Terminology, Berlin; Chargé d'enseignement to the Centre Universitaire, Luxembourg.

LONDON

BUTTERWORTHS

1981

England   Butterworth & Co (Publishers) Ltd
88 Kingsway, London WC2B 6AB

Australia   Butterworths Pty Ltd
271–273 Lane Cove Road, North Ryde
Sydney, NSW 2113
Also at Melbourne, Brisbane, Adelaide and Perth

Canada   Butterworth & Co (Canada) Ltd
2265 Midland Avenue, Scarborough
Toronto, M1P 4S1

Butterworth & Co (Western Canada)
409 Granville Street, Ste 856
Vancouver BC, V6C 1T2

New Zealand   Butterworths of New Zealand Ltd
33–35 Cumberland Place, Wellington

Singapore   Butterworth & Co (Asia) Pte Ltd
Crawford Post Office Box 770, Singapore 9119

South Africa   Butterworth Publishers (Pty) Ltd
Box No 792, Durban

USA   Mason Publishing Co
Finch Building, 366 Wacouta Street
St Paul, Minnesota 55101

Butterworth (Legal Publishers) Inc
15014 NE 40th, Ste 205, Redmond, Washington 98052

Butterworth (Legal Publishers) Inc
381 Elliot Street, Newton, Upper Falls
Massachusetts 02164

First Edition	Aug. 1967
1st Reprint	Aug. 1969
2nd Reprint	Jan. 1970
Second Edition	Oct. 1971
1st Reprint	Oct. 1972
2nd Reprint	Jan. 1974
Third Edition	May 1976
Reprinted	Sept. 1977
Fourth Edition	June 1981
Reprinted	July 1983

ISBN—0 406 65305 4

Printed in Great Britain by Thomson Litho Ltd., East Kilbride, Scotland.

To

ANNE-MARIE,
KATERI,
ALICIA
and
CHRISTIANE

Preface

One of the more evident developments in our national life over the past few years has been an increasing awareness of the importance of law in the life of the ordinary citizen, together with improved access to legal remedies. Law centres have been established in many areas, divorces may be obtained by post without charge by those unable to afford court fees and industrial tribunals deal with large numbers of workers bringing proceedings for unfair dismissal and similar grievances. Since the first edition was published the number of people involved in the administration of law has substantially increased. All these developments make the study of law in schools of increasing relevance and importance as part of a general education.

The main features of legal development since the last edition have been the changes in the matrimonial jurisdiction of magistrates' courts, the growing importance of industrial tribunals and the increasing influence of European Community law.

Once again, I must thank my publishers for their assistance and understanding.

April 1981   D.M.M.S.
                                                           Lenningen,
                                      Grand Duchy of Luxembourg.

Contents

CHAPTER 4—THE COURTS OF LAW

CHAPTER 5—THE PERSONNEL OF THE LAW

CHAPTER 10—CRIMINAL LAW

CHAPTER 11—THE LAW OF TORT

CHAPTER 12—THE LAW OF CONTRACT

CHAPTER 13—SOME IMPORTANT CONTRACTS

INDEX

ILLUSTRATIONS

Table of Cases

Note.—For an explanation of the system of law reports and report references see pp. 31–36 of this book. A comprehensive list of abbreviations may be found at the beginning of Vol. 1 of *Halsbury's Laws of England* (4th Edn.) or Vol. 1 of *Halsbury's Statutes of England* (3rd Edn.).

Chapter 1

The Meaning and Classification of Law

THE BRITISH CONSTITUTION

England, Wales, Scotland and Northern Ireland together constitute the United Kingdom which is a single independent country (or state, to use a legal term). The rules that lay down how the state's institutions of government and administration are to be organised and operated are collectively called "the Constitution". Every person in the country is directly affected by the Constitution because it is the basis of certain important factors in our national life. Among these factors are, firstly our freedom to choose a government we want and to dismiss it when we no longer wish to be ruled by it, secondly our personal liberty, and thirdly our system of law which exists to regulate behaviour and to rectify injustices.

The British Constitution as it is usually called, differs from the Constitutions of foreign states in one important respect. Foreign Constitutions are nearly all "written" which means that the rules of the Constitution and structure of government are set out in a document and may often include a number of fundamental rights granted to citizens. The British Constitution is said to be "unwritten" because there is no single document that contains all its rules. In fact some of the rules of the British Constitution are written down (although in many different documents) while others are not.

It might be thought that a foreigner with an easily accessible document guaranteeing his rights would be in a better position than a British subject with no such document to turn to, but this is

1

not the case, because however near to perfection the Constitution of a state may be on paper, there can be no good government or personal freedom unless the working of the Constitution is in the hands of rulers, judges and administrators who will operate the Constitution honestly and impartially and be prepared to put the interests of the state before their own. It may be said that the British system, with its rather vague Constitution, its honest civil service and its incorruptible judges compares favourably with some foreign systems where a written Constitution guaranteeing every conceivable right is in practice daily violated by a powerful government.

The governing of a country involves the performance of three main functions; these are: (i) making law; (ii) ruling according to the law, and (iii) judging violations of the law. The British constitution in relation to these functions has evolved gradually in the course of history, and we must consider in outline the rules that have been developed. In relation to the making of the law, it should be appreciated that whichever person or group performs this function, will be supreme in the state, so that, not surprisingly, the present position, has been reached only after many bitter struggles. One important turning point was the Bill of Rights (1688) whereby the power of the King to pass laws without consulting Parliament was lost. Another was reached with the great Reform Act of 1832, which much increased the number of men allowed to vote. A third important development was the passing of the Parliament Act 1911, which reduced the power of the House of Lords.

The Monarchy and Parliament

Today the supreme power in the state is vested in the Queen in Parliament, that is to say, the Queen, the House of Lords, and the House of Commons acting together. This group of people is free to make, repeal, or change any law. The Queen acts on her own behalf and has the right to do this because she is the daughter of our previous monarch, King George VI, and in the line of succession laid down by the Act of Settlement 1701. The members of the House of Lords speak on behalf of themselves in the House.

and hold their rank, either by inheritance, or because they have been raised to the peerage by the Queen. The members of Parliament, who sit in the House of Commons are in a different position. They are representatives of the common people, and are elected to their positions by the voters. Neither the Queen nor the members of the House of Lords are entitled to vote, but nearly all the common people who are over eighteen are entitled to do so, except certain criminals and mentally disordered persons. The principle is "one man, one vote".

The Cabinet

At one time the King ruled alone or with the help of advisers whom he chose himself. Nowadays we have the Cabinet system, which works in the following way. After a general election, at which the people are able to choose their members of Parliament to serve for a maximum of five years, the Queen will select the leader of the largest party in the House of Commons to be her Prime Minister, and he will choose the most suitable members of his party to head the various government departments as Ministers. About a score of the more important Ministers will be invited by the Prime Minister to become members of the Cabinet. This is a committee that meets usually in the Cabinet Room at No. 10 Downing Street, the Prime Minister's official residence. Nearly all the most important political decisions are taken by the Cabinet, and it is normally the Cabinet that decides what changes should be made in the law, and takes the first steps towards new Acts of Parliament (laws passed by the Queen in Parliament) or statutes, as they are also called. The country is ruled on behalf of the Queen, and in the name of the Queen, by the Government, and it is for this reason that the Prime Minister, and the other ministers are collectively known as "Her Majesty's Government". Sometimes they are just called "the Government". The Queen is said to be a constitutional monarch, which means that she must carry out her part of the task of governing the country without opposing the will of the people as expressed by their votes at a general election, and as put into practice by the Cabinet. She is consulted by the Prime Minister on all major political issues, and has a number of important duties to perform, including giving her assent to laws passed by the two Houses of Parliament (see p. 30).

The Judiciary

To judge violations of the law is the function of the judges and they have a special place in our constitution. They are appointed by the Queen acting on the advice of the Prime Minister or in some cases, the Lord Chancellor. At one time the judges were liable to be dismissed by the King if they came to decisions with which he disagreed, but since the Act of Settlement 1701, they have held office during good behaviour, and a judge of a superior court may be dismissed only if both Houses of Parliament make a request for his removal to the Queen. This has not happened since the Act was passed. They retire at the age of 75. The judges, whose tradition of learning and impartiality commands great respect, are able to carry out their duties without fear of government interference, and do not hesitate to decide cases against the government if they find that the law requires this.

Sources of the Constitution

The constitution, has been built up from three sources, namely Acts of Parliament, decisions of the judges and conventions of the constitution. A convention of the constitution is a rule that is always followed in practice but which could not be enforced by a law court because it is not strictly a part of the law. For example there is no Act of Parliament or decision of any judge laying down how the Prime Minister shall be chosen. The only rule on the subject is a convention of the constitution which grew up as our Parliamentary system developed, and, as we have seen it provides that the Queen shall choose the leader of the largest party in the House of Commons.

Although statutes are the highest form of law, and overrule any other laws that conflict with them, relatively few statutes were passed before the nineteenth century, so that there are many matters on which the statutes are silent. Other rules of law are therefore necessary, and, in fact, the greatest part of our law has been made by the judges. This is so because ever since the twelfth century the judges have been empowered under the constitution to declare what they find to be the law in particular cases coming before them. The importance of this is mentioned below.

Even though the United Kingdom is a single state with one constitution and a Parliament that can pass statutes applying to the whole, or to any part of it, the law is not the same everywhere. England and Wales have the same system of law which, as we shall see is called the common law. Northern Ireland has a very similar system, while Scotland has a rather different system of its own that has been influenced by the law of ancient Rome. In this book we are concerned only with the law of England and Wales.

WHAT IS MEANT BY LAW?

It is not difficult to recognise law when we encounter it, but to define "law" exactly is a task that is so hard as to be almost impossible. In its wider meaning the word law conveys the idea of a set of rules that must be obeyed, such as the laws of cricket or the law of gravity. We are here concerned only with the law of the state and to get closer to the exact meaning of law, we must seek a more restricted definition. The problem would seem to be a relatively simple one, but in fact men have been thinking and writing about the matter for over two thousand years without coming to any universally acceptable definition. By asking what is meant by law, we are launching ourselves on an enquiry into that branch of knowledge which is called jurisprudence, and which consists of speculating and writing about problems connected with the law. Jurisprudence is one aspect of the wider study known as philosophy, which is concerned with examining the fundamental things of life. There are many questions to which everybody would like precise replies, and philosophy provides numerous and conflicting answers to some of them. Such problems as why do we live on this tiny planet apparently alone in the universe; what is the nature of God; why do we have good and evil, and where is mankind going, have exercised the minds of philosophers from the beginnings of civilisation.

Of the many theories about law, the oldest is probably the natural law theory that originated in the thinking of the Greek philosophers some four centuries before the birth of Christ. This theory, which is still accepted in various forms, says that there is a kind of perfect justice given to Man by Nature, and that laws made by men should conform as closely as possible to it. Another view of law was put forward by the nineteenth century German jurist, Savigny, whose theory was supported by a group of philosophers known as the "Historical School". He contended that the law which grows up in a country represents the spirit of the people or "volksgeist", as he called it in German. Two of the more important English jurists are John Austin who lived in the eighteenth and nineteenth centuries, and Sir John Salmond who lived in the nineteenth and twentieth centuries. Austin who was the founder of "Analytical school" of jurisprudence took the view that law is a command issued by a superior (the state) to an inferior (an individual), and enforced by punishments (or sanctions as Austin called them). Salmond defined law as "the body of principles recognised and applied by the state in the administration of justice". Austin's suggestion has the weakness that it does not account satisfactorily for law made by the judges. On the whole Salmond's definition is probably the most useful for practical purposes.

The State

Both Austin's and Salmond's definitions of law use the expression "state". As we have seen this word is used as an equivalent to "country", but it is necessary to define it a little more closely. A state must have an area of land under its domination, and this area must be controlled by a government having the ability to make those who live within its territory obey its decisions. It is not enough in itself that there is an area of land in which people live. Thus, for example there are a number of men living in the Antarctic continent, but that territory is not a state, since the various groups of scientists who live there owe their loyalties to the different states that have sent them. Similarly it is not enough to have a body of people of the same race and speaking a common language. This is well illustrated by the case of the state of Israel. Before 1947 there was of course a clearly defined race of Jewish people with a common language, but it was not until the British left Palestine in 1947 that a Jewish state came into existence. This came about when the Jews occupied a defined area of land, and became able to control the inhabitants of that territory through a government.

A state is a community or association of human beings, but it differs from other communities or associations in that membership is compulsory. This means that anybody within the confines of the state must submit to the laws of the land or find the state taking action against him. Foreigners, for example cannot come to England and expect to be allowed to block up a narrow road with a motor-coach for days, just because they do not have our nationality. As long as they are within our borders they must respect our laws. In the same way, an Englishman or a Welshman cannot opt out of the rules, and the man who, on receiving an income tax demand for the first time replied "your scheme is interesting, but I do not wish to join it", received a sharp reply.

WHY LAW IS NECESSARY

Law is not necessary to a hermit living alone on an island. It is when a community develops that rules appear. That is one of the aspects of the natural order: even herds of deer and other animals accept a hierarchical system based on force. In primitive communities rules develop from the way of life that geographical and climatic circumstances compel the community to lead. In a desert community there will, and must, be strict rules about conservation of drinking water, while in the most northerly latitudes, laws relating to reindeer are essential. These rules concern the survival of the community against the onslaught of nature, but internal rules also become necessary to regulate such matters as who shall be allowed to intermarry, and who shall be entitled to inherit the property of a deceased person. The more civilised a community becomes, and the greater the industrial and scientific progress it makes, the more laws it must have to regulate the new possibilities it is acquiring.

In the course of time, communities impinge on one another

and here we have the beginning of a need for international law, by which the relationships of nations are governed. In every community there are those with anti-social ideas and rules of criminal law grow up to restrain these individuals from inflicting too much harm on the remainder of the community. Some laws do harm, others do good, while many do both good and harm. Sometimes it is necessary to have a rule where it matters not what the rule is, provided it is followed. An example is the rule of the road. As long as everybody does the same thing on the same road, it does not matter whether people drive on the left or on the right.

Some laws, such as those dealing with obsolete matters, are unnecessary. Some laws are not strict enough, others may be too strict. An example of this is seen on p. 123 in connection with juries which refused to find people guilty of offences that carried the death penalty for minor transgressions. However, it must be admitted that law, although imperfect, is necessary in society. It is doubtful whether it will ever reach perfection. Even with the best will in the world, those who make laws cannot be sure how a new law is going to work. Then there is the difficulty of keeping the law up to date, and hand-in-hand with this problem is that of making the law certain, so that everybody can be sure of what it says. The more often the law is changed in order to bring it up to date, the less certain it becomes, and the more often people have to consult their lawyers.

Anarchism

We have so far been considering the experience of mankind, which has led to a belief in the necessity for law. It should be said however , that although a majority of people today continue to look on law as necessary, there are some who hold quite different views. These are the adherents of the political theory called anarchism, a word that means, literally, no rule. Not all anarchists have the same beliefs, but in general they hold that there is no necessity for a central government, and some have expressed the belief that a time may come when our present system of society is overthrown and replaced by a better one in which law, being unnecessary, will wither away.

How the law affects the life of the people

The effect of the law on ordinary people can be compared with the work of the fire brigade. In the ordinary course of events people do not think about the fire brigade, but its influence is always present. Buildings are erected in accordance with the advice of a fire safety officer; there are carefully prepared plans to deal with large conflagrations, and the public has a sense of safety. If, despite all precautions, a fire breaks out, the brigade will be called to a physical confrontation with the blaze, which it will extinguish by force of water and chemicals. In a similar way most people think very little about the law, but it is continuously in operation, influencing their lives. Goods are sold, couples get married, people hold processions, and companies are formed; the law lays down rules in respect of all these matters, but if things are done in the usual way, there is little reason to worry. In the normal course of events people only begin to think about the law when some uncertainty or difficulty arises. This is understandable, although a person who begins to look into his legal situation after trouble has arisen, may find that he is acting too late.

Every aspect of human life has some rules of law affecting it, from the Social Security Act 1980, which makes provision for regulations under which on the arrival of a baby its mother shall be entitled to a cash grant of £25 to start it off in life, to the rules for deciding the meaning of wills. Nobody need know about all the law that affects him, but it is wise to discover whether there are any particular rules that lay duties upon oneself or any laws that give one protection. Examples may be found in the chapters that follow.

The community and the legal profession are concerned mainly with the everyday business of life, and only in exceptional cases do people have to start thinking in terms of a court of law. A law court is the legal equivalent of a fire-engine: it is called into play when, for some reason things have gone wrong. Court proceedings are expensive, and generally disputes between people only come to court if there are disputing parties too firmly entrenched for either of them to give way. Although the courts are actually used only by a very small proportion of those entitled to their services, the fact that they are available to give justice when things go wrong gives the public a permanent feeling of confidence, and makes potential wrongdoers think twice before causing any harm.

THE CLASSIFICATION OF LAW

Public Law

Law may be divided into two main types, public law and private law. Public law concerns the whole community and everybody is affected by it. The two branches of public law are constitutional law and criminal law. Constitutional law is a part of the British constitution. It consists of those constitutional rules that are laid down in statutes and judicial decisions, but does not include conventions of the constitution because, as we have seen, the latter are not rules of law. Among the matters coming within the scope of constitutional law are the following: the functioning of Parliamentary Ministers and their powers, civil liberties (see Chap. 9), the right to vote, local government, and relationships with Commonwealth countries. Most disputes involving constitutional law are settled in the ordinary civil or criminal courts (see below), but there are occasions when a court concerned exclusively with constitutional law is used. For example an allegation of bribery at a parliamentary election would be tried before a specially convened election court.

Criminal law is derived partly from statute and partly from judicial decisions. It is concerned with the suppression of behaviour that disturbs the peace or well-being of the community; its main objects are to punish criminals and to deter others from crime. Criminal law is administered in the criminal courts. A discussion of criminal law and criminal courts will be found in later chapters.

Private law (also called Civil Law)

Private law covers a wider field than public law and is concerned mainly with the rights and duties of individuals towards each other rather than towards the state. It is applied in the civil courts. There are many branches of private law; the following are some of the more important.

The law of contract.—This branch of the law lays down the conditions on which agreements made between two or more persons are to be treated as legally binding. See Chap. 12.

The law of tort.—This lays down the rules whereby a person may recover damages (a sum of money) from anyone who has injured him or his property. See Chap. 11.

Family law.—This governs such matters as marriage and divorce as well as the rights of parents and children. See Chap. 14.

The law of succession.—This lays down rules concerning inheritance of property. See Chap. 14.

The law of trusts.—This is concerned mainly with the situation where one person is entrusted with property to hold and administer for the benefit of another (see p. 19).

Double Liability for Wrongdoing

In connection with the classification of law there is an important point to be borne in mind. This is that a wrongful act may fall under two headings. For example if Jack runs down Alice while driving his car in a dangerous manner this will be at the same time a crime, since it is forbidden in the interests of the community, and also a tort, because it has hurt Alice in particular. The outcome of such an incident may well be that Jack has to appear before two courts: a criminal court that can send him to prison or order him to pay a fine to the state, and also a civil court that can order him to pay compensation to Alice.

There are various combinations of wrongdoing that can occur, and the combination of crime and tort is just one of them. A wrongful act could, for example be both a breach of contract and a tort, although here only an appearance in a civil court would ensue. On the other hand some types of wrongdoing fall into only one category.

HOW WE KNOW THE LAW

As we shall see the law is derived mainly from the decisions of the judges, from Acts of Parliament, and from regulations laid down by such authorities as a county council, under power derived from Parliament. To find the law we need to look at the appropriate books. As far as books are concerned, it is a feature of our law that the great majority of the books on law are produced not by the Government, but by private persons. This has always been the case.

Reference Books

If anybody, but in particular a lawyer, wants to find out the present law on a particular point, he would probably turn first to a large encyclopaedia called *Halsbury's Laws of England* (named after a famous judge who was its first editor), where he will start by looking up the subject in the alphabetical index. This work is sometimes to be found in the reference section of public libraries. *Halsbury's Laws* are likely to have a section on the subject in question and copious footnotes that relate to Acts of Parliament, regulations and decisions of the judges. In order to follow up all the details of the law it may be necessary to turn to the books indicated in the footnotes, but first something else must be done. The law is changing all the time, and it does not take long for any law book to begin getting out of date. *Halsbury's Laws* is so expensive, however, and takes so much time to prepare that new editions must necessarily be infrequent, and so the publishers produce an annual volume noting all the changes that have taken place since the last edition was published. This volume is cumulative and so gets larger every year. Only the latest volume is of any real use. After having looked in *Halsbury's Laws* therefore, the lawyer must take note of any recent changes shown by the supplement.

He will then turn his attention to any Acts of Parliament which may be relevant. The Government bookshops that are operated by Her Majesty's Stationery Office in London, Cardiff, and other towns all sell official (or "Queen's Printer's") copies of Acts of Parliament. The difficulty here is that Acts are sometimes amended by later Acts, but the Government bookshops go on selling them in their original form. It is better, then, very often to turn to another encyclopaedia called *Halsbury's Statutes of England*, where the amended versions of Acts of Parliament can be found. Again there is an annual supplement and periodical service. Should there be any regulations of the type mentioned above these may be found in *Halsbury's Statutory Instruments* and its periodical service.

Next comes the task of tracing the judges' decisions. These are found in volumes known as "law reports" (see p. 31) which stretch back nearly four centuries. One must go to a law library to find the earlier reports but most lawyers will have their own copies of the most recent volumes.

If after all this, it is still not clear what the law is, for example because no statute and no decision of any judge has dealt with the point in question, the lawyer may then turn for help to articles on the subject published in legal journals. If he receives no assistance from these, he may even look up law books and law reports of other countries in the Commonwealth, Scotland, the Republic of Ireland, South Africa, or the United States. These are the countries whose laws are most like ours. If a point of European Law is concerned he may look in a law book written by an author in one of the other countries of the European Community (see p. 24). Very little help is to be expected from looking any further.

In addition to the works mentioned the lawyer may turn to textbooks specialising in the field of law for opinions of authors, and by this time he is likely to know as much as anybody. He will then be in a position to advise his client, or address a judge in court on what he considers the law to be. Of course we have been considering an extreme example, and in most cases the point of law is much more easily come across. Indeed lawyers carry a great deal of law in their heads and will be able to settle the more common points without reference to any book. If there is a court case, and despite all their efforts, neither side nor the judge can find any previous law on the point at issue, then the judge must make a new decision, and lay down the law for the first time. This will then be recorded in the law reports for future use (see p. 27, below).

Interpretation of the Law

It should be mentioned that if a law is to be just, it should be certain, which means that it must have an exact meaning, which everybody can know about. When a new Act is passed by Parliament, it is for the courts to say what it means and this can be difficult, since the words put into the Act by the members of Parliament may not be clear. The fact that the task is difficult, must not deter the court from doing its work, and deciding on a meaning. This meaning will be followed in future, and those who know of the decision will know the exact meaning of that Act. For this reason a layman who is not familiar with other aspects of the law should not assume that by reading an Act of Parliament, he necessarily comes to the correct conclusion about what the Act means. The same sort of position applies to the common law as laid down in cases. What has been laid down in one case is sometimes explained in a later case. This means that not only is it necessary to have all the Acts of Parliament, regulations, and cases available, but it is also necessary to know how the courts have interpreted the law, as well as the rules of interpretation that the courts have worked out over the centuries for deciding how to interpret statutes and cases correctly.

Chapter 2

The Growth of English Law

The law of England has been developing continuously for more than a thousand years, and many rules that were laid down centuries ago remain in force today. Because of this, some knowledge of legal history is essential for anybody who wishes to understand our modern law.

The Romans brought with them an efficient legal system but during the dark ages that followed their departure almost all traces of Roman law disappeared. On the other hand Roman civilisation continued to make itself felt after the fall of the Roman Empire through the Christian church; this was so because in early times most of those who could read and write were clergymen who could speak Latin and were familiar with the achievements of the Romans.

ORIGINS

Modern English law can be traced back to Saxon times. Before the arrival of William the Conqueror in 1066 there were courts in various parts of the country applying local customs and some written laws laid down by Saxon kings. The conquest opened a new era, but the changes it brought were very gradual. At first the Norman kings used the existing local courts to help them rule the country, but soon they began to send their own judges round the country to hear cases locally. This enabled them to control the country better, and also allowed them to compete with the local courts for the fees paid by litigants (those who take part in lawsuits). To attract litigants to the royal courts from the local courts, the royal courts began to offer better methods of trial. These measures were so successful that eventually all law courts came under royal control.

THE COMMON LAW

King Henry II (1154–1189) divided the country into routes, or "circuits" as they are called, and began regularly to send judges to the circuit towns. The early judges had no ready-made system of law to take with them, and so they had to do their best without one. At first they applied as law the customs that they discovered locally, but in the course of time they began to discuss among themselves the various customs, and eventually it was agreed that the best customs should be selected and applied everywhere. These customs were to be a law common to every part of the kingdom; it is from this origin that we get the name "the common law of England". Most of the law that we have today has been built up slowly since the twelfth century by judges who have been deciding cases continuously in the same careful way.

At the same time as the common law was developing and the judges were beginning to travel the circuits, there came into existence the courts of common law. The early Norman kings ruled with the help of an assembly of important men called the Curia Regis (king's court), and it was from the Curia Regis that the common law courts developed in the thirteenth century. They came into being to carry out certain duties of the Curia Regis more effectively. The first common law court to break away from the Curia Regis was the Court of Exchequer which was mainly concerned with taxation disputes; the second, the Court of Common Pleas was established at Westminster to carry out the same duties as the judges on circuit and the third, the Court of King's Bench, followed the King in his travels round the country.

The Court of King's Bench was the only one of the three to have criminal jurisdiction, and it became the most important. Just as the royal courts had competed with the local courts for business in earlier times, so the three common law courts competed among themselves, because the judges and officials were dependent for their incomes on the fees paid by litigants.

A person who commences an action (lawsuit) against another is called a plaintiff, while one who defends is known as a defendant. These are the usual modern names. In a common law court a plaintiff began an action by paying for a writ. This was a document that contained the complaint and ordered a jury to try the case. There were different sorts of action, each one with its own writ, and it was important to choose the right writ as if the wrong writ was chosen, the action would fail, whether the plaintiff ought to have won or not. A book called the Register of Writs was kept, and this showed the types of complaint for which a writ would be issued. If a man had any other type of complaint, the common law court would not help him. If a plaintiff won his action he was usually awarded damages. This meant that the defendant had to pay him a sum of money fixed by the court.

THE DEVELOPMENT OF EQUITY

In certain circumstances it was not possible for a wronged person to obtain help from the common law courts. This might happen because no suitable writ was available, or because the help offered by the common law court was inadequate, or for some other reason. In these circumstances it became the custom to ask the king for help, because he was looked on as the "fountain of justice", and people hoped that if he could not help them through his common law courts, he might be able to help them in some other way.

In many cases they were not disappointed. The King began to refer these requests for help to his most important official, the Chancellor. In early times the Chancellor was a bishop who had many duties. He was in charge of the office that issued writs, and one of his functions was to act as "keeper of the King's conscience". He regarded it as his duty, on behalf of the King to make sure that those who came before him had clear consciences.

So many people requested help that by the end of the fifteenth century the Chancellor had set up his own court, which was called the Court of Chancery. The Chancellor did not act like the common law judges, but instead developed his own type of law called "equity".

Trials in the Court of Chancery were quite different from trials in common law courts (where there were juries). There was no jury in the Court of Chancery. The Chancellor summoned the plaintiff and defendant before him and questioned them closely and at length with great skill in order to arrive at the truth. Then if he felt that one party was acting against his conscience, the Chancellor would order him to put matters right. If the party concerned refused, then he was sent to the Chancellor's prison until such time as he decided to clear his conscience and obey the Chancellor. There were difficulties of course in this, because successive Chancellors measured other people's consciences against their own, and consequently in early times equity changed with each new Chancellor. However eventually equity settled down to a known set of rules.

The Relationship of Common Law to Equity

Gradually, a number of Chancery courts were set up so that for several centuries two systems of law existed side by side in England; the common law which was administered in the common law courts, and equity which was administered in the chancery courts. At first the two sets of courts co-operated but eventually there arose a sharp conflict between them. This conflict developed because in certain matters common law and equity had different ideas as to how the question should be settled. An arrangement called the "Use" gives us an example of how a dispute could arise between a common law court and a court of equity.

The System of "Uses"

In some parts of the country the rule was that when a tenant of land died, the land passed to his eldest son, but the son had to give some money or a farm animal to the landlord. However, if the tenant gave away his rights over the land, nothing had to be handed to the landlord. Therefore some tenants, before they died gave away their rights over their land to a friend who promised to allow the son to use the land when the tenant was dead, so that the son would get the benefit of the land without having to give anything to the landlord. This arrangement was called a "Use". The common law courts refused to recognise the existence of uses, and as far as the common law was concerned, the friend had the rights over the land and the son had nothing. The Chancery courts, however, looked at the situation in a different way. They recognised the common law rights of the friend but simply said that these rights had to be used in accordance with his conscience. If, therefore, the friend refused to let the son benefit from the land, the Chancery court would send him to prison until he decided to clear his conscience by allowing the son his rights. Similarly if the friend won an action in a common law court, this would do him no good as a Chancery court would just imprison him if he took advantage of it. Therefore he had to carry out his promise. The friend was said to have the "legal interest", and the son the "equitable interest".

The difference between the legal interest and the equitable interest in land or goods remains important to this day, not only in connection with trusts which are mentioned below but also in connection with buying a house. The equitable interest in a house passes from vendor to purchaser when "contracts are exchanged" (see p. 220), but the legal interest passes only on "completion" (see p. 221). If the vendor refuses to pass the legal interest after exchange of contracts, the court using its equitable jurisdiction, will force him to do so because it is against his conscience to refuse.

Matters came to a head in the reign of King James I (1603–1625). The common law courts complained that they were suffering too much interference from the Chancery courts, and a personal dispute sprang up between the Chief Justice of the Court of Common Pleas, Sir Edward Coke and the Chancellor, Lord Ellesmere. The King decided that where equity and the common law were in conflict, equity was to prevail; after this the importance of equity increased. The courts of Chancery evolved other rules to assist people and co-operation between the two courts was strengthened.

The Trust

The King lost a great deal of money through the system of uses and in 1535 King Henry VIII asked Parliament to abolish most of them by passing the Statute of Uses. People realised that uses were a very convenient way of getting someone to look after property for others, such as children, and lawyers began to look for ways to avoid the Statute of Uses. After about a hundred years conditions changed and the Chancery courts developed a modern version of the use, which is called the "trust". Trusts are very common today. Each trust has three parties to it. First, there is a "settlor" who hands some of his property to a "trustee", the second party, who promises to look after it for the "beneficiary", who is the third party. Some trusts have more than one trustee or more than one beneficiary. Sometimes trustees are required to invest money and pay the interest to the beneficiary.

OTHER COURTS

As the population of England increased, as new discoveries were made and overseas trade became important, the need for new laws and specialised courts became apparent. Each branch of the law and each court made its contribution to our present system. Some of these courts are mentioned below.

The Courts Merchant

Merchants who travelled all round Europe trading at fairs developed rules of business law amongst themselves. These rules were called the "law merchant", and they were enforced in the Courts Merchant. In the course of time the common law courts took over the work of the courts merchant and incorporated the law merchant into the common law.

The High Court of Admiralty

This court dealt with matters concerning the sea and ships.

The Ecclesiastical Courts

Before the Reformation, the bishop of each diocese had a court administering the law of the church. When King Henry VIII became head of the Church of England the courts began to administer what developed into English ecclesiastical law. In addition to concerning themselves with church matters, these courts dealt also with two other important departments of the law, wills and intestacies (cases in which people have died without making any will), and matrimonial matters. Ecclesiastical courts continue to exist today but are now confined to church matters as a result of the foundation of the following two courts.

The Court of Probate

This court was set up in 1858 to take over responsibility from the ecclesiastical courts for wills and intestacies.

The Court for Divorce and Matrimonial Causes

At the same time that the Probate Court came into existence, this court was set up to assume responsibility for matrimonial matters from the ecclesiastical courts.

The Court of Exchequer Chamber

At different periods there existed four courts of this name. Their function was to give a limited right of appeal from the decisions of the common law courts. The last of these courts was set up in 1830. There could be a further appeal from the court to the House of Lords.

The Court of Appeal in Chancery

This court was set up in 1851 to hear appeals from Chancery courts. A further appeal could be made to the House of Lords.

The House of Lords

Besides being the upper house of Parliament, the House of Lords acted as a law court. Its jurisdiction varied from time to time but it eventually became the highest court in the land.

LAW REFORMS

The nineteenth century was the century of reform. There were many unsatisfactory features in the administration of the law at this time. The jurisdiction of various courts overlapped, the common law courts used an out of date procedure, and the Chancery courts were very slow in their work. Some improvements to the existing system were made by Act of Parliament, but these were only partly successful and so it was decided to sweep away the old system and set up a modern system of courts. This great reform was achieved by two Acts of Parliament, the Judicature Acts of 1873 and 1875.

The Effect of the Judicature Acts

The following courts were abolished:

(i) the three common law courts, *i.e.*, the Court of Queen's Bench, the Court of Common Pleas, and the Court of Exchequer, together with the Court of Exchequer Chamber;

(ii) the courts of Chancery together with the Court of Appeal in Chancery;

(iii) the High Court of Admiralty;

(iv) the Court of Probate;

(v) the Court for Divorce and Matrimonial Causes.

Secondly, in place of the old courts, the Judicature Acts set up a single new court called the Supreme Court of Judicature. This was divided into the High Court, which was to hear cases in the first instance, and the Court of Appeal, which was to hear appeals from the High Court. The High Court was divided into five divisions, namely, the Chancery Division, the Queen's Bench Division, the Common Pleas Division, the Exchequer Division, and the Probate, Divorce and Admiralty Division. The Court of Appeal took over the work of the Court of Exchequer Chamber and the Court of Appeal in Chancery.

The biggest change wrought by the Judicature Acts was that there was now only one High Court which in all its divisions, administered both law and equity. This meant that litigants who needed help from the common law and equity could henceforth get both kinds of help in one court. Every division was empowered to hear any kind of case, but for the sake of convenience each division dealt with the matters administered by the court or courts it had replaced. Another change was that the procedure of the courts was much simplified.

It was laid down that appeals from the High Court lie to the Court of Appeal, and that appeals from the Court of Appeal lie to the House of Lords, which has the final word. A decision of the House of Lords, can however be reversed by Act of Parliament although this is a rare occurrence.

In 1880 the Common Pleas Division and the Exchequer Division of the High Court were merged into the Queen's Bench Division, thus reducing the number of divisions to three.

Recent Changes

The Administration of Justice Act 1970 provided for the re-organisation of the High Court so as to consist of three divisions. These are the Queen's Bench Division, which includes an Admiralty Court and a Commercial Court, the Chancery Division, and the Family Division (see p. 42).

The Supreme Court of Judicature is slowly developing the common law and equity. The distinction between the two is becoming less important and some writers hold that the two have been, or are being merged into one, although others maintain the two remain distinct despite the fact that they have been administered side by side in the same courts since 1875.

WORLD LEGAL SYSTEMS

The two systems of law which have spread most widely in the modern world are the common law, which was taken overseas by British colonists, and the "Civil Law" system which is based on the laws of ancient Rome. (The expression "Civil Law" as used here must not be confused with the expression "civil law" used as a contrast with criminal law.) The Civil law was developed at the close of the middle ages from the code of laws prepared by the Roman Emperor Justinian in A.D. 533. This code was studied and adapted by nearly every country in Western Europe, except England. The Civil law was spread abroad by colonists, and adopted by some Eastern countries. The map of world legal systems (p. 46) shows some countries in which each system is dominant.

In Scotland, South Africa and Rhodesia a basically Civil law system has been much influenced by the common law. In many of the countries marked on the map local systems of law exist side by side with the civil or common law.

The United Kingdom and the European Community

A change took place in the constitution on the 1st January 1973 when the United Kingdom as well as Ireland and Denmark joined the European Community after a treaty called the Accession Treaty was signed and the European Communities Act 1972 was passed. The change meant that we had joined eight other countries and had agreed to work together with the aim of making Europe into a single prosperous area by, among other things, allowing all citizens of these countries to move freely to any of the other countries to take jobs, and by gradually abolishing customs duties between them in order to encourage trade. In 1975 our membership was confirmed by a Referendum.

The Accession Treaty had the effect of making the United Kingdom a party to three other treaties which already existed between the original six members of the European Community, These are the European Coal and Steel Community (E.C.S.C.) treaty which regulates coal and steel production and encourages efficiency, the Euratom treaty, which promotes co-operation between the member states on atomic energy matters, and the most important one, the European Economic Community (E.E.C.) treaty, which contains most of the rules on the encouragement of trade and competition as well as those dealing with company law and freedom to take employment in any of the nine member states.

Our partners in the European Community (which is often called the Common Market because customs duties are being abolished) are France, Germany, Italy, Belgium, Holland, Luxembourg, Denmark, Ireland, and Greece which joined on 1st January 1981.

The European Community has four institutions called (i) the Council of Ministers (who are the Foreign Ministers of each of the ten member states); (ii) the Commission, with 14 members (two from each the United Kingdom, France, Italy and Germany, which are the biggest member states, and one each from the rest); (iii) the European Parliament with 434 members of which 81 are British, and (iv) the European Court with 11 judges including at least one from each member state. The European institutions employ a number of civil servants as administrators, lawyers and translators, and they are often referred to as "Eurocrats".

Both the Council of Ministers and the Commission can make laws called Regulations and Directives which apply in all member states, about certain limited matters, see p. 32. Although the British members of the Council of Ministers and the Commission join in making these laws, they can come into force without anything being done by Parliament, which is a new situation.

The Commission and Council have their headquarters at Brussels in Belgium, whilst the European Parliament and the European Court are to be found in Luxembourg City in the Grand Duchy of Luxembourg.

The European Parliament is mainly an advisory body of members directly elected by the 260 million citizens of Europe.

The European Court has the task of making sure that the laws of the European Community are observed, and it gives rulings on the exact meaning of European rules of law to the courts of the member states. It ensures that European law is the same in all the ten member states.

Chapter 3

How English Law is Made

The law as it exists today is the result of contributions from several sources. Since the time of the Norman conquest the law has been developing slowly to meet the needs of changing conditions. In the earliest times the main source from which new rules of law came was custom. Later the decisions of the judges became an important source of law, and eventually statutes were extensively used to bring about changes in the law. These three sources remain the most important ones today, and we shall consider how each of them operates to bring into existence new rules of law.

CUSTOM

Customs are rules of behaviour that develop in a community without being deliberately invented. As we have seen, in early times the judges relied a good deal on customs to help them create the common law. There are two types of custom—general customs which apply all over the country, and local customs that apply in a particular locality. Most general customs have already been incorporated into the common law, and are not nowadays an important source of new law. Local customs, on the other hand, still give rise, very occasionally, to new rules of law.

A custom becomes a rule of the common law when it is recognised as valid by a court. Some customs are carried on without causing harm to anyone so that nobody bothers to test their validity in court. In practice only a person who is seriously inconvenienced by a custom or who stands to make a loss if the custom is ended will bring the custom to court, because a court action is an expensive business and the outcome is uncertain.

In order to establish that a custom is valid and fit to be incorporated into the common law, a number of facts must be proved. The more important of these are as follows:

1. The custom must have existed since 1189. This date, which is the year in which Richard the Lion-Hearted came to the throne was fixed a very long time ago and has never been changed. In the ordinary way it would be very difficult to prove what is required, but the law makes matters much easier by presuming that the custom goes back to 1189 provided that the oldest living witness gives evidence that the custom has gone on as long as he can remember and no-one can prove that it did not exist before then.
2. The custom must not be an unreasonable one.
3. The custom must be certain. This means that it must be quite clear who benefits from it, and what the benefit is.
4. The custom must be local. The exact locality such as a county or a city to which the custom applies must be shown. An example of a local custom that gave rise to a new rule of law is given by the case of *Mercer* v. *Denne* (1905) in which the fishermen of Walmer in Kent established their right to continue to exercise their custom of drying their nets on the beach.

DECISIONS OF THE JUDGES

Judicial Precedent

The duty of a judge is to listen to the evidence and legal arguments put forward by each side in a case. He must then state what the law is and decide which party has succeeded in proving his case. In doing this work the judge must follow a rule called the doctrine of judicial precedent. This rule says that if there has been a previous decision (a "precedent") of a higher court, in a similar case, he must follow it. A precedent that a judge must follow is called a "binding precedent". The rule goes on to state that if there is a precedent of a court of equal rank, the judge should consider it carefully, but he is not bound to follow it; this is called a "persuasive precedent". The consequence of this is that the barrister or solicitor appearing for each party will search his books for precedents favourable to his client before he comes to court, so that he may persuade the judge to decide in his client's favour.

The doctrine of judicial precedent is based on the fact that whenever a judge decides which party has won an action, he makes a speech in which he reviews the case. In this speech (or "judgment" as it is usually called), the judge will comment on the evidence and the points of law raised, and may also discuss matters of general interest arising from the case which are not directly related to it. From a legal point of view the most important part of the judgment is that in which the judge explains the legal principle on which he has based his decision. The words in which he expresses this legal principle are called the "*ratio decidendi*" (the reason for deciding). All the other words in the judgment are called "*obiter dicta*" (things said by the way). Only the *ratio decidendi* of the judgment forms a precedent, and it is this which will be quoted in subsequent cases. From time to time cases come before the courts where there has been no previous decision and the court, taking guidance from the closest possible previous cases will make a decision that constitutes a precedent for future cases and a new portion added to the common law. A great deal of law has been created in this way over a period of several hundred years in the common law courts, and over a somewhat shorter period in the courts of Chancery. The process is still continuing today. A good example of this is the modern case which is discussed and illustrated on pages 33–36, below.

The main advantages of this system are that it makes for certainty in the law and allows the law to grow when this is necessary. On the other hand it is said that the system is too rigid since it is difficult to avoid the consequences of a bad decision by a higher court, and it is a system that develops very slowly.

STATUTES

A statute is a law that has been passed by the House of Commons and the House of Lords and has received the assent of the Queen. In order to illustrate what a statute looks like the Gaming (Amendment) Act 1980 is discussed on pp. 36–38, below. If the common law differs from a statute, the statute will overrule the common law. Although in recent years the number of statutes issued annually has increased, the common law still constitutes the major part of our law, and statutes are enacted on the assumption that the common law will continue to apply to matters not mentioned in the statute. Statutes have the great advantage that they can alter the law quickly.

How Parliament Makes Law

First of all the Cabinet or a member of Parliament decides that a new piece of legislation is required, and instructs a lawyer who specialises in Parliamentary work, to draft the words of the legislation required in proper legal phraseology. This draft is called a bill and it is divided into paragraphs called "clauses". The bill is then introduced into Parliament. With the exception of money bills, which must be introduced first in the House of Commons, a bill may be introduced in either the House of Lords or the House of Commons. As soon as it has passed through one House, it must then go through the other. The procedure in the House of Commons is as follows:

First Reading.—A sheet of paper with only the title of the bill and the name of the Member introducing it, is read out by an official. Printing of the bill is then ordered.

Second Reading.—The broad principles of the bill are debated by those in favour of it, and those against. If nobody opposes it, or if a vote is taken on the bill and there is a majority in favour of it, it will go on to the next stage.

Committee Stage.—The bill is passed to a committee of members to be considered in detail. For some important bills the whole House sits as a committee.

Report Stage.—At this stage the committee reports back to the House on its discussions and proposed amendments.

Third Reading.—There is a final debate on the general principles, and a vote. If there is a majority in favour, the bill leaves the House of Commons and is passed to the House of Lords; the procedure there is similar to that in the Commons.

After passing through both Houses, the bill goes to the Queen for her assent but, since 1854, the Royal Assent has never been given by the Sovereign in person. By the Royal Assent Act 1967 it may be notified to each House separately by the Speaker of that House instead of being signified by Commissioners on behalf of the Queen in the presence of both Houses as previously. The bill is then an Act and so becomes law.

Delegated Legislation

In modern times it has been necessary for Parliament to make laws concerning many technical matters such as motoring and the construction of buildings. In the time available to them, members of Parliament could not possibly draw up all the detailed rules about every technical matter, and the difficulty is surmounted by passing a statute that makes it plain in general terms, what is required and then gives power to a local authority or a government department to make the detailed rules. The power to make laws is thus said to be "delegated", and the rules that are eventually made in this way are called "delegated legislation". Delegated legislation made by government departments is usually published in the form of regulations or "statutory instruments" as they are called (an "instrument" is a document). Delegated legislation is also issued in the form of an "Order in Council" by the Queen acting on the advice of members of the Privy Council which is an advisory body recognised by the common law. The most important members of the Privy Council, who take the responsibility of advising the Queen, are the members of the Government. Local authority delegated legislation appears in the form of by-laws. For an example of a statutory instrument, see pages 38–40, below. This one is an Order in Council as well as being a statutory instrument.

The duty of enforcing the law as declared in statutes and delegated legislation falls on the courts, and it is for the courts to say what the words used in statutes and other legislation mean. The courts cannot attach any meaning they like to the words of a statute, but most follow certain rules called rules of interpretation. One of the most important of these is the "golden rule" which requires the words of a statute to be given their ordinary, grammatical meaning whenever possible.

OTHER SOURCES OF LAW

Law Reports

For many years it has been the custom to record important decisions of the courts together with the reasons for the decisions as given in judgments. These records are called "law reports". The earliest law reports were called the Year Books and they covered the period from the thirteenth to the sixteenth centuries; they are seldom used today. In the sixteenth century what are called the "private" law reports began. Law reporters who had attended the trial, published under their own names details of arguments put forward by the advocates, as well as the judgment delivered by the judge. These private reports are still used today. They vary in accuracy, but the best of them are treated by lawyers with great respect. In the nineteenth century a special organisation was set up to produce law reports with the co-operation of the judges. This is the Incorporated Council for Law Reporting. Before the reports of this body are published, they are revised by the judges. These reports are called the *Law Reports*. There also exists another series of reports called the *All England Law Reports*, which began in 1936. These also are revised by the judges, and being issued in a convenient form, are the most widely used. The law report illustrated on page 34, below is taken from this series.

When an advocate is searching for a precedent he turns first to the *Law Reports* and the *All England Law Reports*, if he thinks that he can find a modern report. Failing these two he may look in the law reports published in *The Times* newspaper. He is entitled to bring to the notice of the court any law report that is signed by a barrister but he will prefer to use a full report instead of a newspaper report if he can, and the court will expect him to do this. If the advocate is looking for an older report, he will not look through all the hundreds of volumes that have been published down through the centuries, but he will consult the index of a work of reference, and this will lead him to the type of precedent he needs. Because the courts rely so much on law reports in developing the law, we call law reports a source of law.

Textbooks

In exceptional cases where no precedent can be found, advocates bring the opinions of textbook writers to the notice of a court, and on occasion judges accept statements in textbooks as representing the law. Textbooks written by Chief Justice Littleton who was a judge of the Court of Common Pleas in the fifteenth century and Chief Justice Coke (1552–1634) are particularly respected. Littleton wrote his book in French since at the time this was the language of the courts, and it was translated into English. In 1628 Coke wrote a commentary on the English version which is known as *Coke on Littleton.*

Sir William Blackstone (1723–1780) was a judge of the Court of Common Pleas and published his famous lectures, which he gave when he became a professor at Oxford under the name *Commentaries on the Laws of England.*

Apart from these "classics" the judges often rely on statements in modern legal textbooks.

European Law

Since this country joined the Common Market a new source of law has come into existence here. Under the E.E.C. Treaty the Council of Ministers and the Commission (see p. 24) can make laws which extend to all ten member states including our own. These laws, which are known as Regulations and Directives, are confined mostly to such matters as customs duties, competition in industry, agriculture and the free movement of workers.

The difference between a Regulation and a Directive is that usually Regulations are made and issued in Brussels, becoming law at once in all ten member states, whilst Directives are sent to each member state and are issued (in the case of the U.K.) in London by way of a British Statutory Instrument.

The decisions of the European Court are a source of law for all member states of the Community.

SOME SOURCES OF LAW ILLUSTRATED

A Law Report

Overleaf is reproduced the first page of the report in the *All England Law Reports* of a case decided by the Court of Appeal on 30th March, 1966. It occupies pages 508–512 of the second of the three volumes of reports for 1966. On the last page is the name of the law reporter who prepared it. He is stated to be a barrister-at-law, and it is important to know this, because the only reports that may be cited (quoted) in court are those signed by a judge or a barrister. Nowadays the words "-at-law" are omitted from a barrister's designation. It will be noticed that the letters A–I are printed vertically down the right-hand side of the page. These enable counsel in court to direct the attention of the judge quickly to any passage on the page, if, as is usual, both have copies of a report before them.

The case was brought by a Mr. E. F. Tucker (the "plaintiff") against a company called Farm and General Investment Trust, Ltd. (the "defendant") on the ground that the company had sold some lambs that belonged to him. The plaintiff alleged that what was done amounted to the tort of conversion (see page 177, below). Every case has a "reference", which is a series of words and figures that indicate where the report may be found in a law library. Legal books that mention a case always give its reference so that readers may find it easily and read all the details for themselves if they so wish. The reference of this case is composed of the names of the

TUCKER v. FARM AND GENERAL INVESTMENT TRUST, LTD.   A

[COURT OF APPEAL (Lord Denning, M.R., Harman and Diplock, L.JJ.), March 30, 1966.]

Hire-Purchase—Livestock—Ewes—Lambs born during hiring—Whether property of hirer or of finance company.

In August, 1963, P., a farmer, entered into an hire-purchase agreement with the defendant finance company relating to eighty-four ewes. The total hire-purchase price was £647, the initial payment was £120 and the balance was payable in two instalments of £263 10s. on June 28 and Aug. 28, 1964. The ewes were served and lambs were born. In April, 1964, P. sold the ewes and the lambs to the plaintiff, who was unaware of the hire-purchase agreement. The finance company seized the ewes and the lambs and sold them. In an action by the plaintiff against the finance company for conversion of the lambs,

Held: on a lease of livestock the progeny belonged to the lessee, unless the lease provided to the contrary, and the position was the same where the transaction was one of hire-purchase; accordingly the lambs belonged to the plaintiff and the plaintiff was entitled to damages for conversion of the lambs (see p. 510, letter A, to p. 511, letter B, p. 511, letters F and H, and p. 512, letter F, post).

Wood v. *Ash and Foster* ((1586), Owen 139) followed.

Appeal allowed.

[As to property in the young of domestic animals, see 1 HALSBURY'S LAWS (3rd Edn.) 655, 656, para. 1251, subject to the observation at p. 509, letter G, post; for the nature of hire-purchase agreements, see 19 HALSBURY'S LAWS (3rd Edn.) 510, 511, para. 823; and for cases on the leasing and right to increase of livestock, see 2 DIGEST (Repl.) 29, 30, *133-138*, 299, 300, *80-85*.]

Cases referred to:

Case of Swans, (1592), 7 Co. Rep. 15 b; 77 E.R. 435; 2 Digest (Repl.) 293, *18*.

Morkel v. *Malan*, (1933), C.P.D. 370. The series of reports is Cape Provincial Division Reports of South Africa.

Wood v. *Ash and Foster*, (1586), Owen 139; 74 E.R. 39; 2 Digest (Repl.) 29, *133*.

Appeal.

This was an appeal on notice dated Jan. 18, 1966, by Edwin Frank Tucker, the plaintiff, from a judgment of His Honour JUDGE PRATT given on Dec. 9, 1965, at Tiverton County Court, dismissing the plaintiff's action for damages for conversion of eighty-three lambs, alleged to be his property. The lambs were the progeny of ewes that were the subject of a hire-purchase agreement dated Aug. 28, 1963, and made between Mervin Thomas Petty (the lessee) and the defendant finance company, and the lambs had been born during the subsistence of the hire-purchase agreement. Under the agreement the ewes belonged to the defendant finance company, but there was no express provision therein regarding the property in the lambs. It was not in issue that the finance company was entitled to the ewes. The finance company had seized and sold both the ewes and the lambs. The plaintiff claimed damages for conversion of the lambs.

The case and the authorities noted below* were cited during the argument in addition to those referred to in the judgments.

H. E. L. McCreery, Q.C., and *M. Hutchison* for the plaintiff.

P. L. W. Owen, Q.C., and *S. B. Thomas* for the defendant finance company.

LORD DENNING, M.R.: In August, 1963, Mr. Perry, who was a farmer at Hockworthy near Wellington, Somerset, acquired eighty-four Kerry

---

* A. G. GUEST ON HIRE-PURCHASE: ACCESSION AND CONFUSION, MODERN LAW REVIEW, Vol. 27, pp. 506, 507; GOODE ON HIRE-PURCHASE LAW AND PRACTICE (2nd Edn.), p. 10; *Westropp* v. *Elligott*, (1884), 9 App. Cas. 815.

parties and the volume in which it is printed. In this case it is as
follows: "*Tucker* v. *Farm and General Investment Trust, Ltd.*, [1966] 2 All
E.R. 508, C.A.".

The report follows the usual form of modern law reports. Below
the name of the case is mentioned the court in which the case was
heard, and the names of the judges who composed the court. In
this instance the senior judge was Lord Denning, and the
abbreviation "M.R." after his name means "Master of the Rolls",
which is the position he holds as head of the Court of Appeal. The
other judges were both members of the Court of Appeal, and the
abbreviation "L.JJ." after the two names means "Lords Justices",
since Court of Appeal judges are called for example "Lord Justice
Smith", instead of "Mr. Justice Smith", which is the appellation of
High Court judges. Below the names of the judges there are set out
in italics the "catchwords", which show at a glance what the case
is about. Then, commencing with the words "In August ..."
comes the "headnote", prepared by the law reporter which
summarises the facts of the case and, following the word "Held",
the decision of the court. The next paragraph, in square brackets,
is a note by the law reporter who refers to statements of the
relevant law in *Halsbury's Laws of England* (see p. 12, above). Then
follows a list of decided cases referred to by the judges in their
judgments. Below this is a paragraph setting out the background
of the case, and the names of counsel appearing for the plaintiff
and the defendant. It will be observed that each side was
represented by a Queen's Counsel who appeared with a junior.
This is an indication of the importance attached to the case by the
parties. If they had considered it less important they, or either of
them, could have chosen to be represented only by junior counsel;
see pp. 74–76, below. Below the names of counsel are the first two
lines of the judgment of Lord Denning. The remaining pages set
out in full the judgments of each judge in which he explains the
reasons for his decision.

It will be seen that the case was originally heard in the County
Court at Tiverton, Devon, where the judge decided in favour of
the defendant. The plaintiff appealed and, as the report shows, the
Court of Appeal held that the decision of the county court judge
was wrong and "allowed" the plaintiff's appeal. So the defendant

was ordered to pay him £207 10s. od. damages for the loss of his lambs.

The case raised a point of law not covered by any Act of Parliament. It was therefore purely a question of common law on which there were, in fact, very few earlier decided cases and the Court of Appeal had to base its decision on a case decided as long ago as 1586. The only other cases referred to were one decided in 1592 and one decided in a court in South Africa in 1933 where a similar problem had arisen under the law of that country. From the footnote (below the line) it can be seen that counsel also supported their arguments by referring to an article published in a legal journal (the *Modern Law Review*) and to a passage in a leading textbook on the law of hire-purchase.

An Act of Parliament

On the next page is printed an Act of Parliament (statute). Like most statutes, it has two titles (names), a long one and a short one. The short title of this Act is printed at the top of the page: it is the Gaming (Amendment) Act 1980. The long title is "An Act to amend subsection (3) of section 20 of the Gaming Act 1968 to enable the Secretary of State, by order, to amend the limit of £1,000 therein", and it describes the purpose of the Act. Judges sometimes use the long title to help decide the Act's meaning. The Act is always referred to by its short title. At the top of the page is the name of the monarch reigning at the time of the passing of the Act, Elizabeth II. Below that again, is the royal coat of arms, which is also the coat of arms of our country, the United Kingdom. The shield combines, on the quarterings the arms of England, in the first and fourth quarters, the lion of Scotland in the second quarter and the Irish harp in the third quarter. It is a matter of regret that Wales, being a principality, instead of a kingdom is not symbolised. The arms reflect the current claims to sovereignty of the British Crown. In times past, when our monarchy laid claim to the throne of France, the fourth quarter was charged with the fleur-de-lys.

Below the coat of arms is a number that serves to identify the statute. The words "1980 Chapter 8" indicate that this Act was

Gaming (Amendment) Act 1980

1980 CHAPTER 8

An Act to amend subsection (3) of section 20 of the Gaming Act 1968 to enable the Secretary of State, by order, to amend the limit of £1,000 therein.

[20th March 1980]

BE IT ENACTED by the Queen's most Excellent Majesty, by and with the advice and consent of the Lords Spiritual and Temporal, and Commons, in this present Parliament assembled, and by the authority of the same, as follows:—

1.—(1) Subsection (3) of section 20 of the Gaming Act 1968 (which specifies the maximum permitted aggregate amount of the winnings in respect of games of bingo played in one week simultaneously on different bingo club premises) shall be amended in accordance with subsection (2) below.

Amendment of s. 20 of Gaming Act 1968.
1968 c. 65.

(2) At the end of subsection (3) there shall be added the following proviso:—

" Provided that the Secretary of State may by order provide that this subsection shall have effect with the substitution, for the reference to £1,000, of a reference to such other sum as may be specified in the order."

2. This Act may be cited as the Gaming (Amendment) Act 1980.

Short title.

passed in 1980, and the Act itself constitutes "Chapter 8. Each Act passed by Parliament is a separate chapter beginning each year at 1.

After the long title is the date 20th March 1980; this is the date on which the Queen's assent was given, and which changed the Bill, as passed by the House of Lords and House of Commons into an Act.

Below the long title are the words of enactment. These now follow the same short form in most statutes. They are the words that declare that a new law has been made by the three necessary parties acting together, the Queen, the House of Lords, and the House of Commons. In times past the words of enactment were often contained in a long "preamble" which set out in detail the reasons why the Act had been passed.

Below the words of enactment will be seen a bold figure 1. This is the beginning of "section 1". Every Act is divided into sections, and sometimes, into subsections as well. It should be remembered that *Bills* which are going through Parliament are divided into *clauses* and that when a Bill becomes an Act, its clauses become sections.

Statutes are printed under the direction of an official known as the Queen's Printer of Acts of Parliament. This Act, like any statute or statutory instrument, may be bought at Her Majesty's Stationery Office or from any bookseller. Prices will vary according to length.

Delegated Legislation—A Statutory Instrument

On the next page is printed a specimen statutory instrument. The number at the top of the page indicates that it is the 1057th statutory instrument to be numbered in 1978. Each year the numbers begin again at No. 1. Often statutory instruments are merely referred to by their number. This one would be "S.I. 1978 No. 1057" meaning "Statutory Instrument No. 1057 for the year 1978". Below the number, in heavy type, is the general subject matter, judges, and below that again, is the official title. After the title are to be seen firstly the date the statutory instrument was signed by the Clerk of the Privy Council.

1978 No. 1057

JUDGES

The Maximum Number of Judges Order 1978

Laid before Parliament in draft

Made -   -   -   25*th July* 1978

At the Court at Buckingham Palace, the 25th day of July 1978

Present,

The Queen's Most Excellent Majesty in Council

Whereas a draft of the following Order was laid before Parliament and approved by resolution of each House of Parliament:

Now, therefore, Her Majesty, in exercise of the powers conferred on Her by section 1(2) of the Administration of Justice Act 1968(**a**), is pleased, by and with the advice of Her Privy Council, to order, and it is hereby ordered, as follows:—

1.—(1) This Order may be cited as the Maximum Number of Judges Order 1978.

(2) The Interpretation Act 1889(**b**) shall apply to the interpretation of this Order as it applies to the interpretation of an Act of Parliament.

2. The maximum number of ordinary judges of the Court of Appeal which is prescribed by section 1(1)(*b*)(i) of the Administration of Justice Act 1968, as amended(**c**), shall be increased from 16 to 18.

N. E. Leigh,
Clerk of the Privy Council.

EXPLANATORY NOTE

(*This Note is not part of the Order.*)

This Order increases the maximum number of ordinary judges of the Court of Appeal from 16 to 18.

(**a**) 1968 c. 5.   (**b**) 1889 c. 63.
(**c**) The relevant amending instruments are S.I. 1970/1115, 1975/1215.

The next paragraph sets out the power under which the Queen in Council made this new law. It will be seen that this was section 1(2) of the Administration of Justice Act 1968. Footnote (a) tells us that this Act was Chapter 5 (c.5) of 1968.

The whole of the Statutory Instrument is printed here as it is unusually short, although it is accompanied by a short explanatory note which is not a part of the Order. Sometimes this note is very detailed and useful.

An interesting feature of this Statutory Instrument is that it is also an Order in Council made by the Queen at Buckingham Palace on the advice of the Privy Council.

Chapter 4

The Courts of Law

There are two main types of court, those which administer criminal law and those which administer civil law, although a few courts administer both. As we have seen in Chapter 1, criminal law is concerned with wrongful acts that harm the whole community, while civil law is concerned with disputes over private rights. From time to time the courts, being human institutions, make mistakes and so in many cases the law allows those who are dissatisfied with the outcome of the first trial to appeal to a higher court. Courts that try cases for the first time are called "courts of first instance" and those which rehear cases are called "appeal courts". An appeal court is free to decide whether the court of first instance was correct or mistaken in its decision. If the appeal court finds that the court of first instance was mistaken, it will usually set aside the decision and replace this by its own decision.

FIRST INSTANCE CIVIL COURTS

The County Courts

There are some four hundred county courts distributed all over the country. They were set up in 1846 to provide a speedy and inexpensive method of settling small disputes locally. In some parts of the country the courts have little work and one judge can travel round to attend to the work of several courts. Under the

THE PRINCIPAL CIVIL COURTS TODAY

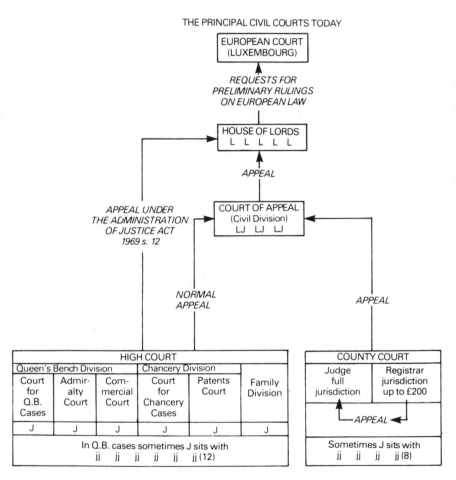

Note: The diagram takes account of the provisions of the Administration of Justice Act 1970, the Courts Act 1971, the European Communities Act 1972 and the Patents Act 1973.
The symbols indicate the approximate composition of the Court.
L=Lord of Appeal; LJ=Lord Justice; J=Judge; j=Juryman.

THE PRINCIPAL CIVIL COURTS PRIOR TO THE
COMING INTO FORCE OF THE ADMINISTRATION
OF JUSTICE ACT 1970

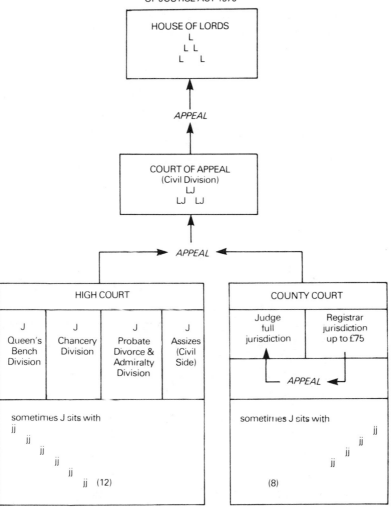

NOTE.–The "Supreme Court of Judicature" consists of the High Court and
the Court of Appeal.

Symbols: L= Lord of Appeal   LJ= Lord Justice
            J= Judge   j= Juryman

Courts Act 1971, county courts are staffed by certain Circuit Judges and Recorders, who are chosen to sit in county courts (see p. 65). Each court hears only cases connected with its own district. In addition to the judge each court has a registrar who acts as assistant judge and is in charge of the office staff. Nearly always the judge or registrar tries cases without a jury, but in very rare instances, as for example where an allegation of fraud is made, the judge will be assisted by a jury of eight persons. Appeals from county courts are made to (*i.e.*, lie to) the Court of Appeal (see p. 55). Many types of case are dealt with by the county courts; they are mostly small matters affecting ordinary people. The more important are as follows:

(i) actions in contract or in tort where the sum involved does not exceed £2,000;

(ii) cases concerned with equity, such as trusts and mortgages (see p. 19), as well as the ending of partnerships (see p. 95). Here the sum involved must not exceed £15,000;

(iii) actions concerning ownership of land where the rateable value of the land does not exceed £1,000;

(iv) actions concerning probate and letters of administration (see p. 242), where the value of the property left by the deceased is less than £15,000;

(v) adoption of children;

(vi) hire-purchase cases;

(vii) admiralty proceedings where the sum claimed does not exceed £5,000 but in salvage cases £15,000;

(viii) in certain cases the county court registrar may try cases involving an amount not exceeding £200.

Generally speaking, where the property or money in dispute exceeds the limits mentioned above, the case will have to be brought before some other court; this will usually be the High Court.

It is possible for a person to act on his own behalf in a county court. He can get from the court office a booklet of advice called

"Small claims in the County Court" which explains the procedure.

In most cases where the amount in issue is not more than £200 the case will be referred automatically to arbitration. Usually it is best to accept the registrar or judge as arbitrator since an outside arbitrator will require a fee.

In August 1980 the Lord Chancellor's office published a consultation document proposing to raise the county court limits as follows: general limit £5,000, Equity £50,000, registrar's cases £500.

The Supreme Court

As we saw in Chapter 2, the Supreme Court of Judicature was set up in 1875 when nearly all the old courts of common law and Chancery were abolished. The court consists of two separate parts, the High Court, which is a court of first instance, and the Court of Appeal, which is, of course, an appeal court. The functions of the Court of Appeal are mentioned below. The Courts Act 1971 provided that the Supreme Court is to consist of three parts, namely, the Court of Appeal, the High Court, and the Crown Court (see p. 65).

The High Court is able to deal with a very wide range of matters involving any sum of money. It is the court in which nearly all cases involving important points of law are commenced. There are three branches (or divisions) of the High Court which are all of equal importance, but which deal with different types of case. Two of these divisions are named after older courts which were abolished in 1875 (see p. 22). The names of the three divisions are the Queen's Bench Division, the Chancery Division, and the Family Division.

The Queen's Bench Division does the work of the old courts of Queen's Bench, Common Pleas, Exchequer and the High Court of Admiralty (mainly collisions at sea and salvage). It deals with the greatest number of cases and does any work not allocated to one of the other divisions. In particular it deals with contract and tort cases. Another important part of the work of the division is concerned with the Prerogative Orders (see p. 52). The

THE HIGH COURT CIRCUITS

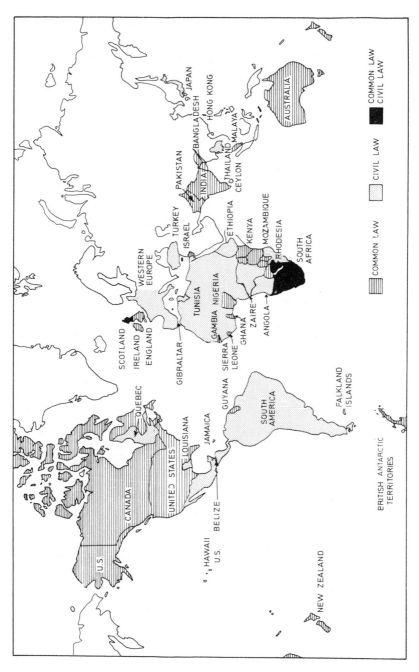

WORLD LEGAL SYSTEMS (See p. 23)

Commercial Court, which has a speedy procedure, is a part of the Queen's Bench Division. The Chancery Division carries on much of the work of the old courts of Chancery and Probate, and the more important topics that it deals with are trusts, mortgages, partnerships, actions to obtain specific performance of contracts (see pp. 71 and 220) and wills and intestacies including probate in solemn form which may involve contentious proceedings, (see Chapter 14). Since the Patents Act 1977 the Chancery Division has included a Patents Court. The Family Division continues the work of the Court for Divorce and Matrimonial Causes and is concerned with cases concerning minors, probate in common form and the granting of letters of administration (see Chapter 14).

The High Court in its present form came into being as a result of the passing of the Administration of Justice Act 1970. The diagram shows the divisions of the High Court before and after the Act came into force.

There are a number of courts associated with the High Court. These include the Court of Protection, which is charged with the duty of safeguarding the property of mental patients (see p. 91).

Judges of the High Court still travel round the country on circuit as they have done for centuries. They hear both civil and criminal cases locally, but the old system of Assizes under which the judges had to visit certain towns only has been abolished, and they may now sit anywhere in England and Wales to hear civil cases.

Administrative Tribunals

In twentieth century Britain there are many more laws regulating all aspects of present day life than there ever were in times past. New inventions, the growth in population, and the demand for higher standards of living have all contributed to the increasing number of laws. Among the subjects covered are some that affect almost everybody's way of life, such as rent control, national health insurance, and conditions of work. Many of these laws lead to disputes of a kind that are best settled in a common sense kind of way. To cope with this situation a large number of special courts called Administrative Tribunals have been set up,

FIG. 1—"THE FIRST DAY OF TERM"

This picture, taken from an eighteenth century engraving, shows the scene in Westminster Hall on the first day of the legal term. From the reign of Henry II (1154–1189), when the Court of Common Pleas emerged, cases were argued here before the various courts and so the law of England took shape within its walls, until in 1882 the courts were moved to their present building in the Strand.

In this picture can be seen

A the entrance to the House of Commons
B the Court of King's Bench
C the Court of Chancery
D the Court of Common Pleas

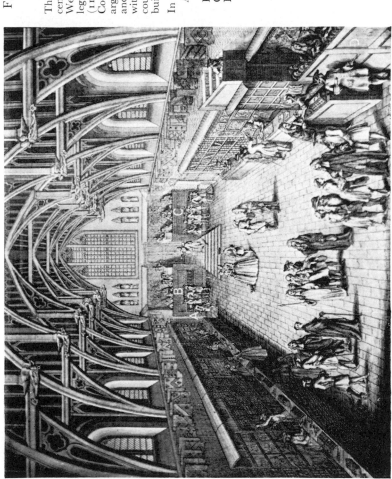

FIG. 2—A CRIMINAL TRIAL ON INDICTMENT

Judge's clerk

Witness

Court Officer

Instructing
solicitors for
prosecution
and defence

Judge

Clerk

Usher

Jury

Other barristers
not concerned
with case

Junior counsel
for the
prosecution

Junior counsel
for the defence

Prisoner in the
dock

FIG. 3—SOME FAMOUS JUDGES OF THE PAST

A SIR THOMAS LITTLETON (1422–1481), *a judge of the Court of Common Pleas, 1466–1481; author of* Tenures, *the first printed English Law book.*

B LORD ELLESMERE (1540–1617), *Lord Chancellor, 1603–1617.*

C SIR EDWARD COKE (1552–1634), *Chief Justice of the Common Pleas, 1606–1613; and of the King's Bench, 1613–1616; author of the* Institutes.

D LORD NOTTINGHAM (1621–1682), *Lord Chancellor, 1675–1682; "the father of modern equity".*

E LORD MANSFIELD (1705–1793), *Chief Justice of the King's Bench, 1756–1788.*

F SIR WILLIAM BLACKSTONE (1723–1780), *a judge of the Court of Common Pleas, 1770–1780; author of the famous* Commentaries.

A   B

C   D

FIG. 4—SOME MODERN JUDGES

A THE RT. HON. LORD GEOFFREY LANE, *Lord Chief Justice of England.*
B THE RT. HON. LORD DENNING, *Master of the Rolls.*
C THE RT. HON. SIR JOHN ARNOLD, *President of the Family Division.*
D SIR NICOLAS BROWNE-WILKINSON, *President of the Employment Appeal Tribunal.*

and numerous disputes go to these tribunals instead of to the ordinary courts. The tribunals differ from ordinary courts in two ways. Firstly, they each deal with only one kind of dispute (*e.g.*, about rents) and secondly in coming to a decision they are allowed to take into consideration points such as the housing situation and local conditions which would carry less weight in an ordinary court. In the past some administrative tribunals have been criticised for their methods and so the Council on Tribunals was set up to keep a watch on the working of a number of tribunals. The Tribunals and Inquiries Act 1971, provides for this to be extended in scope by statutory instruments. There is usually a possibility of appeal from the decision of a tribunal. Tribunals are subject to the control of the High Court by means of the prerogative orders (see p. 52, below).

Among the most important tribunals are the industrial tribunals which are, in the main, regulated by the Employment Protection (Consolidation) Act 1978. There are a number of these in various parts of the country and they hear cases concerning a number of matters of great importance to employees. These include unfair dismissal, equal pay for men and women, sex discrimination, racial discrimination in employment and redundancy payments.

An appeal lies from an industrial tribunal to the Employment Appeal Tribunal in London which is presided over by a High Court Judge, Sir Nicolas Browne-Wilkinson, and thence to the Court of Appeal.

A striking example of the important part now being played as regards employees' rights by both the system of industrial tribunals and the Court of Justice of the European Communities in Luxembourg is afforded by the case of *Macarthys Ltd* v. *Wendy Smith* (1980).

Wendy took a job in a pharmaceutical warehouse, sending goods to chemists' shops, at £50 a week. She discovered that her predecessor, a man who had left, had been getting £60 a week for the same job, and she began proceedings before an industrial tribunal under the Equal Pay Act 1970, which lays down that "for men and women employed on like work the terms and conditions of one sex" must not be "in any respect less favourable than those of the other". Her case went on appeal from the industrial tribunal to the Employment Appeal Tribunal and then to the Court of Appeal. The Court of Appeal held that Wendy was not entitled to £60 a week under the British Equal Pay Act because the wording of it applied only to men and women working *at the same time*.

This was not the end of the matter because it was pointed out to the Court of Appeal that Article 119 of the E.E.C. Treaty (see p. 56) lays down that:

> "Each Member State shall ... ensure and subsequently maintain the application of the principle that men and women should receive equal pay for equal work."

The Court of Appeal therefore adjourned the case and, in accordance with the procedure laid down by Article 177 of the E.E.C. Treaty sent a question to the European Court in Luxembourg asking for an interpretation of Article 119. When the answer came back Lord Denning, the Master of the Rolls, said:

> "We have now been provided with the decision of that Court. It is important now to declare—and it must be made plain—that the provisions of **Article 119** of the Treaty of Rome take priority over anything in our English statute on equal pay which is inconsistent with **Article 119**. That priority is given by our own law. It is given by the European Communities Act 1972 itself. Community law is now part of our law: and, whenever there is any inconsistency, Community law has priority. It is not supplanting English law. It is part of our law which overrides any other part which is inconsistent with it. I turn therefore to the decision given by the European Court. The answer they gave was that the man and the woman need not be employed at the same time. The woman is entitled to equal pay for equal work, even when the woman is employed after the man has left. That interpretation must now be given by all the courts in England. It will apply in this case and in any such case hereafter. Applying it in this case, Mrs. Wendy Smith was right."

Consequently Wendy was entitled to her £60 per week.

Arbitration

Whenever a dispute is brought before a court, the parties must accept two inconveniences. The first is that they must attend court at a time and place that suits the court and may not suit them, and the second is that the proceedings will be in public and so their private affairs may be published in the press. Many disputes arise out of contracts, particularly contracts of insurance and partnership contracts, and very often the parties to such contracts agree with one another that they will not take any dispute that may arise to court. They agree instead to arrange for somebody with the appropriate type of business experience to take the place of a court.

Instead of having a trial before a judge appointed by the Queen, the parties have an "arbitration" before an arbitrator that they have appointed themselves. In this way they can keep their business affairs private, and can arrange for the arbitration to take place at a convenient time and place, *e.g.*, in the evening after work, in an office building. The agreement to put a dispute to an arbitrator is called a "submission", and the decision of the arbitrator, after he has heard the case is called his "award". If two parties to a contract have agreed to send their disputes to an arbitrator, and then one of them begins an action in a court, the other can usually get the court proceedings stopped by informing the court of the fact that there was an arbitration agreement. At the end of the arbitration the parties are compelled to accept the award as if it were the decision of a judge. In cases where there are two umpires who disagree the matter is referred to an "umpire", chosen by them previously, who then gives a decision. Under the Arbitration Act 1979 an appeal lies to the High Court on any question of law arising out of an award. The main statute that regulates arbitration procedure is the Arbitration Act 1950. The Administration of Justice Act 1970 gives power to judges of the Commercial Court to act as arbitrators.

CIVIL COURTS OF APPEAL

The High Court

Not only is the High Court a court of first instance, but it is also an appeal court. When a case is heard at first instance in the High Court, it usually comes before a single judge, but when it is heard on appeal it normally comes before two or three judges sitting together. A court with two or three judges is called a "Divisional Court". There are Divisional Courts in all three divisions. For example a Divisional Court of the Family Division will hear appeals from magistrates' courts concerning some matrimonial matters. It is in the Queen's Bench Division, however that the Divisional Court is most used.

The Queen's Bench Division is unusual. Not only does it hear cases both at first instance and on appeal; it also hears both civil and criminal cases. Its duties in connection with criminal matters are mentioned below. The Divisional Court of the Queen's Bench Division plays a very important part in our legal system. It does this in two ways. Firstly it hears appeals from lower courts (such as Furnished Houses Rent Tribunals), in the same way as do the Divisional Courts of the other divisions, but secondly, and this is its most important function, it controls inferior courts and tribunals, and even public officials by means of its power to issue what are called the "Prerogative Orders". These are commands issued by the court in appropriate cases.

The Prerogative Orders

Among the various remedies open to people to protect their rights, the prerogative orders are very important. There are three prerogative orders, each designed for a different purpose. If somebody believes that his rights are being infringed, and that there is no other way of putting matters right, he can go to a solicitor and ask him to arrange for an application to the Queen's Bench Division for one or more of the prerogative orders to be made against the person or body responsible. The orders are as follows:

PROCEDURE FOR CIVIL CASES

	Type of Case	At First Instance		First Appeal	Second Appeal
I	Minor Civil Cases	County Court		Court of Appeal (Civil Division)	House of Lords
II	Major Civil Cases	High Court Ch. Div. _Either_ Q.B. Div. Family Div.	Ordinary Admiralty Commercial	Court of Appeal (Civil Division) or House of Lords (see p. 51)	House of Lords
III	Safeguarding of Mental Patients' Property	Court of Protection		Court of Appeal (Civil Division)	House of Lords
IV	Social Legislation	Administrative Tribunal (other than Industrial Tribunal)		This depends on which tribunal heard the case at first instance	Supervision by Queen's Bench Division through use of _Mandamus Prohibition_ or _Certiorari_
V	Employment Legislation	Industrial Tribunal		Employment Appeal Tribunal	Court of Appeal

(see p. 51)

Mandamus.—This is a Latin word meaning a command, and this prerogative order is used to compel a person or body of persons to carry out some duty placed on him or them by the law. If however a person is *allowed* by law to do something, but is not obliged to do it, then it will not be possible to get an order of *mandamus* against him.

Mandamus has been used, for example, to make a local authority produce its accounts and to make another local authority hold an election of aldermen. *Mandamus* can even, in some cases be used against a government department. A case of this kind will arise where the department refuses to carry out some duty to a citizen imposed on it by statute.

Prohibition.—This order prevents something from being done, unlike *mandamus* which orders something to be done. An order of prohibition can be issued to prevent an inferior court or tribunal from trying a case it has no right to try; as for example if a county court were about to try a case involving a sum of money above the county court limit an order of prohibition could issue. If a court refuses to try a case that it ought to try, *mandamus* may be used to make it hear the case.

Certiorari.—This order is used to transfer to the Queen's Bench Division cases that are in progress before inferior courts or tribunals or cases that have recently been dealt with, by them. *Certiorari* may be applied for by a person who believes that the inferior court has been guilty of either of the following: trying a case it was not authorised to try, or not complying with the principles of natural justice. The principles of natural justice which every court is bound to observe are rules recognised by the common law as being necessary to ensure a fair trial. The rules are as follows:

1. No man may be a judge in his own cause. This means that no one who may be affected by the outcome of a case is permitted to take part in deciding it. For example in 1852 the Lord Chancellor heard a case against a company in which he was a shareholder, and therefore his decision was set aside.

2. *Audi alteram partem.*—This is a Latin expression meaning

that both sides must be given the chance of being heard. If one side decide to say nothing, they cannot afterwards complain.

3. The court or tribunal must reach its decision in good faith.

In addition to administering the prerogative orders, the Queen's Bench Division hears applications for *habeas corpus*. This means that any person who is detained against his will, or somebody acting on his behalf, may apply to the Queen's Bench Division to decide whether or not the detention is lawful. This could happen, for example in the case of a person detained in a mental hospital. The court can issue a document called a "writ of *habeas corpus*" ordering the detained person to be brought before it and may then order his immediate release if it finds the detention to be unlawful (see also p. 105).

The Court of Appeal (Civil Division)

This court may have a maximum of nineteen judges, who are the Master of the Rolls and eighteen Lords Justices of Appeal. Three judges sit together to hear each appeal, so that the court can hear four cases at a time. It hears appeals from all divisions of the High Court, the Court of Protection, and the county courts, among others. When hearing an appeal the Court of Appeal has before it both the notes of the judge in the court below, and a shorthand record of what was said: it can confirm the decision of the court of first instance, reverse its decision, amend its decision, or order a new trial. By the Criminal Appeal Act 1966, the former Court of Criminal Appeal was abolished and its jurisdiction was transferred to the Court of Appeal which now has two divisions: (a) civil, and (b) criminal.

The House of Lords

Not only is the House of Lords part of Parliament and therefore concerned with making laws, it is also the highest appeal court in England and Wales for both civil and criminal cases and hears appeals from the Court of Appeal. Under the Administration of Justice Act 1969, some appeals may be made direct from the High Court, where the meaning of an Act of Parliament is involved. It also hears appeals from Northern Ireland and the civil courts in Scotland. The only members of the House of Lords who actually hear appeals are the Lord Chancellor, a maximum of eleven specially appointed Lords of Appeal in Ordinary, who are life Barons, and other members of the House who have held high judicial office. Appeals can be heard by three judges, but usually five sit together to hear each case.

The Judicial Committee of the Privy Council

This Court has the same membership as the House of Lords but it also includes a number of judges from Commonwealth countries. It sits in a courtroom at No. 1 Downing Street, London, to hear cases, instead of in the House. Its main duty is to act as the final court of appeal for cases from the Channel Islands, the Isle of Man, the colonies, and certain Commonwealth countries. It also hears appeals from certain English courts and tribunals, *e.g.* ecclesiastical courts (see p. 21).

THE COURT OF JUSTICE OF THE EUROPEAN COMMUNITIES

This court, which is often called simply the European Court, has been a part of the legal system of the whole United Kingdom including Scotland since we joined the Common Market under the European Communities Act 1972. The main treaty signed by this country on joining was called the European Economic Community (or E.E.C.) Treaty.

Article 177 of the E.E.C. Treaty lays down that when an undecided point of European law comes up in a court from which there is no appeal (i.e. the House of Lords or the Judicial Committee of the Privy Council), such court *must* suspend the case concerned and send the question to the European Court in Luxembourg for a decision called a preliminary ruling. Any lower court *may* send such a request, but is not bound to. This rule applies to all the ten member states of the Common Market, so that there is only one court making decisions on European law, which remains the same in each of the countries.

The European Court decides the point of European law and sends the answer back to the English or Welsh court, but is careful to say nothing about how this answer affects the case in this country. It is then the turn of the English court to put the answer into practice here, and to make its decision according to our system of justice, as between the parties, but following the preliminary ruling from Luxembourg.

The European Court is building up what may be called a European "common law" which is based to a great extent on the laws of the member states, and for this reason it is to be hoped that in the future many English cases will go to Luxembourg so that our law can exercise its proper influence. The eleven judges of the European Court include Lord Mackenzie Stuart. Before the court decides any case, in addition to listening to advocates for both sides, it also listens to an Opinion delivered by an independent member of the court called an Advocate-General of which there are five, including Sir Gordon Slynn from England. His impartial view assists the court.

PROCEDURE IN CIVIL COURTS

The rules of procedure are the rules that lay down how to go about bringing or defending an action in court. These rules say what must be done, when it must be done, and by whom. Appended to the rules are a number of forms that must be filled in correctly and filed in court in the course of an action. The rules are changed from time to time, and are published in annual volumes. The rules of Supreme Court procedure are published in the *Supreme Court Practice*, which is better known as the "White Book" from the colour of the binding. The rules of county court procedure are published in the *County Court Practice*, or "Green Book". Procedure varies from court to court, but an outline of Queen's Bench procedure is a typical example.

Queen's Bench Procedure

Proceedings are started by getting the court office to issue a writ. The plaintiff's solicitor (see p. 73) fills in a form and pays a fee. The form is then sealed and becomes a valid writ. A copy of the writ is served on the defendant; it tells him that he must either fill in and return the "Acknowledgement of Service" which accompanies it within fourteen days, or risk losing the case which may be heard in his absence. After this the plaintiff's solicitor will send to the defendant's solicitor a "statement of claim" which is a document that has probably been drawn up by the plaintiff's counsel (barrister) (see p. 74). It sets out in detail what the plaintiff is claiming from the defendant and why. The defendant's solicitor will send the statement of claim to the defendant's counsel, who will read it, consider the legal position, and draw up the "defence". This is an answer to the statement of claim and sets out the defendant's point of view. This goes via the two solicitors to the plaintiff's counsel. By this time, which may be a matter of weeks or months, depending on the difficulty of the case, everybody knows exactly the two points of view that must be laid before the court.

Preparations will then be made for the trial. One of the solicitors will enter the case in the list of cases awaiting trial. Both solicitors will prepare and send to their counsel the "brief". This is a bundle of papers that contains instructions to counsel to appear in court to conduct the case, together with statements made by witnesses and any other necessary material such as maps or photographs. In court the task of each counsel is to do two things. He must seek to convince the court that his version of the facts is the correct one, and then he must try to persuade the court that his version of the law to be applied to those facts is correct. He establishes his version of the facts by calling witnesses of his own and by cross-examining the witnesses of the other side. For example if Alice is suing Jack for having run her down with a car, Alice's counsel may call as witnesses Alice herself, and a passer-by who saw the accident. Jack's counsel may call Jack and a passenger in the car. Every witness promises to tell the truth and is first questioned by the counsel who called him. This first questioning is called "examination in chief". In examination in chief counsel will ask questions with the intention of producing answers favourable to his client.

After examination in chief comes "cross-examination". This means that the witness is then questioned by counsel for the other side. The opposing counsel will ask questions designed to produce answers unfavourable to the person on whose behalf the witness speaks. It may be that a witness is forgetful, or was even a liar. Cross-examination is the opposing counsel's opportunity to show up the witness in his true light, by asking carefully chosen questions. For example, Jack may say that Alice ran quickly into the road in front of the car. This sounds reasonably possible and the court may be inclined to believe it. Smith's counsel may know, however, that Alice had a broken leg and cannot run at all. He says nothing when he hears the examination-in-chief, but his first question in cross-examination is "Do you know that Alice had a broken leg?" Jack will say "no", and Alice's counsel will then say: "How do you reconcile the fact that Alice had a broken leg with your statement that she ran into the road?" The judge will watch Jack carefully to see how long he takes to answer, and what sort of a look comes over his face. His answer will be carefully recorded. It may become apparent to the judge that Jack was wrong, and equally apparent to both counsel. If this point is reached, Alice's counsel may put further questions to Jack to show that he was not being truthful. Meanwhile during the cross-examination Jack's counsel will be whispering to Jack's solicitor, asking for Jack's version of the facts, and it may seem to him that Jack made a genuine mistake. If this happens, then, when cross-examination is over, Jack's counsel can stand up and begin what is called "re-examination". This is his chance to put right the effect of what he considers to be any misleading answers made by his client in cross-examination. His questions will be directed at showing that Jack was genuinely mistaken when he said that Alice ran into the road. The judge will then make up his mind, taking into account everything that has been said, whether Jack was untruthful or mistaken. His decision about this will be one of the factors that will influence him in giving his judgment.

When the witnesses on both sides have been called, each counsel will address the court on the law, and may read quotations from statutes and law reports to support their contentions. Finally the judge will give judgment in a speech that consists partly of *ratio decidendi*, and partly of *obiter dicta*. In a civil case the two sides are on an equal footing, and the judge must decide in favour of one of them. If, therefore the arguments presented by one side are only slightly better than those of the other, this will be sufficient to secure success. This is not so in criminal trials.

At the end of the judgment counsel for the successful party will get up and ask the judge for "costs". This means that he asks the judge to direct that the loser pay most of the legal expenses of the successful party in addition to his own. The judge usually complies with this request, unless there are unusual circumstances. If a plaintiff is successful, the judgment ordinarily includes mention of a sum of money that the defendant must pay to the plaintiff. If the defendant does not pay, there are various courses open to the plaintiff; for example he may apply to the court to have the sheriff seize and sell sufficient of the defendant's goods to pay the requisite sum.

In courts of first instance a judge usually sits alone, but in some types of proceedings such as defamation he may sit with a jury. Under the Juries Act 1974, s. 17, a jury may give a unanimous verdict, but if it cannot reach one, it may give a majority verdict of 11–1 or 10–2.

FACTS AND FIGURES ABOUT CIVIL COURTS

Every year the Lord Chancellor's Department prepares detailed statistics on the various civil courts in England and Wales and a few of the more important figures relating to 1979 are set out below.

All Civil Courts

Total number of proceedings commenced in all
courts of first instance 2,076,335

County Courts

Total number of proceedings commenced........ 1,650,064
Total number of proceedings tried in court 41,282

This figure represents about 2 per cent of the proceedings commenced. The rest were ended in other ways, notably by debtors paying up.

Number of judgments entered by county court
judges 36,146
Number of judgments entered by county court
registrars................................. 100,441

The High Court

Chancery Division

Total number of proceedings commenced at first
instance................................... 13,848
Total number of proceedings disposed of after a trial
or hearing................................. 470

Contentious probate proceedings (in solemn form)
Total number of writs issued 119
Disputes relating to trust property........... 238

Queen's Bench Division

Total number of proceedings commenced at first
instance.................................... 149,244
Total number of actions determined after trial ... 2,008

Admiralty

Total number of writs issued 1,345
Total number of cases tried in court............. 16

Prerogative Proceedings

Number of orders granted:

    Mandamus 72
    Prohibition............................... 10
    Certiorari................................. 115
    Writ of *Habeas Corpus* 13

Number of appeals to the Queen's Bench Division:

    To a single judge 103
    To the Divisional Court.................... 110
    Criminal appeals from the Crown Court to a
    Divisional Court........................ 19
    Criminal appeals from courts of summary
    jurisdiction to a Divisional Court 72

Family Division

Probate.—Non-contentious proceedings

    Number of Probates and Letters of Ad-
    ministration with the will annexed granted
    by the Court in common form 175,777
    Number of Letters of Administration without a
    will granted by the Court in common form 82,234

Divorce

    The total number of matrimonial petitions
    filed.................................... 167,511

Decrees *nisi* granted:
  (i) For dissolution of marriage   139,503

The chief grounds on which decrees *nisi* for dissolution of marriage were granted number as follows:
    adultery.   40,702
    desertion.   4,127
    unreasonable behaviour   45,297
 (ii) For judicial separation.   3,650
(iii) For nullity   994
(iv) On separation for two years and mutual consent   38,714

Court of Appeal

Total number of appeals disposed of during year .   688
How High Court appeals were disposed of:
    Withdrawn or struck out without a hearing . .   181
    Affirmed   250
    Varied   5
    Reversed   133
    Otherwise disposed of.   119
Total county court appeals disposed of during year   327

The House of Lords

Total number of appeals disposed of during the year   71

The courts from which appeals came:
    Court of Appeal
      (Civil)   64
      (Criminal)   4
    Divisional Court of Queen's Bench Division . .   0
    Court of Session (Scotland).   5
    Court of Appeal (Northern Ireland).   1
    Court of Criminal Appeal (Northern Ireland) .   0

Judicial Committee of the Privy Council

Total number of appeals disposed of after a hearing
    in court.   54
Number of appeals from overseas courts   34

CRIMINAL COURTS OF FIRST INSTANCE

Magistrates' Courts

Magistrates, or justices of the peace, as they are also called have played a large part in our legal system for over six hundred years. They are usually well-known members of the community who act in their spare time, receiving expenses but no salary. Most magistrates are not lawyers, but they are expected to acquire some knowledge of the law and associated subjects. In court they have a legally qualified clerk to assist them. Although the great majority of magistrates are laymen (non-lawyers), there are some legally-qualified magistrates employed in certain towns. Because they are paid they are known as "stipendiary magistrates". In order that a case may be tried there must be at least one stipendiary or two lay magistrates. Much of the law relating to magistrates is contained in the Justices of the Peace Act 1979.

The law divides crimes into two main categories: indictable offences, which are the more serious, and summary offences, the less serious ones. The gravest indictable offences must be tried by a judge and jury, in the Crown Court (described below). The least serious summary offences must be tried by magistrates. All other indictable and summary offences may be tried either by judge and jury or by magistrates. The jurisdiction and procedure of magistrates is largely covered by the Magistrates' Courts Act 1980.

Magistrates have two main functions. They try minor cases for which they can impose a sentence of imprisonment of up to six months, and in connection with serious cases it is their duty to act as "examining magistrates". This means that before anyone can be brought before a judge and jury for trial in respect of an indictable offence, the details of the accusation must be given to the magistrates, who will decide whether or not there is a *prima facie* (reasonable) case against the accused. If they decide there is no *prima facie* case they will release him, but if they consider that a *prima facie* case exists, they will send him to be tried at the Crown Court. From magistrates' courts an appeal is possible to the Crown Court, where there is a re-hearing of the case, and thence to a Divisional Court of the Queen's Bench Division on a point of law only, or directly to the Divisional Court on a point of law.

Juvenile Courts

Children and young persons who are accused of crime are normally tried by juvenile courts, which are a type of magistrates' court. For the purposes of the criminal law a "child" is a person under fourteen years of age, while a "young person" is anybody who is aged 14 years or over, but under 17.

The Crown Court

This court was set up by the Courts Act 1971. It replaces both the old quarter sessions and the Assizes (criminal side). Prior to the Act, magistrates in counties and boroughs met quarterly in quarter sessions for two types of work. Firstly, a bench of magistrates and a jury heard cases involving indictable offences. The cases were sent to them by examining magistrates. Secondly, magistrates sitting at quarter sessions without a jury heard appeals from magistrates' courts by way of a re-hearing. At the Assizes (criminal side), before the Act came into force, a High Court Judge and a jury heard cases involving indictable offences. The Assizes were held only when a High Court Judge arrived on circuit in the Assize town, which was infrequent. There was some overlapping between the cases heard on indictment at quarter-sessions and Assizes, and the system, after several centuries, began to become very inefficient. This was why the Crown Court was set up.

The Crown Court is a part of the Supreme Court of Judicature and although it is a single court, it has court buildings in all parts of the country and it may sit anywhere in England and Wales. There may sit in the Crown Court, a High Court Judge, a Circuit Judge or a Recorder. A Circuit Judge is a full-time judge, whilst a Recorder is a part-time judge. When sitting in the City of London the Crown Court is known as the Central Criminal Court, or more popularly, as the Old Bailey. It tries crimes committed in Greater London and on the high seas.

Jurisdiction of the Crown Court

The Crown Court hears all trials on indictment by means of a judge and jury. High Court Judges hear only the most serious

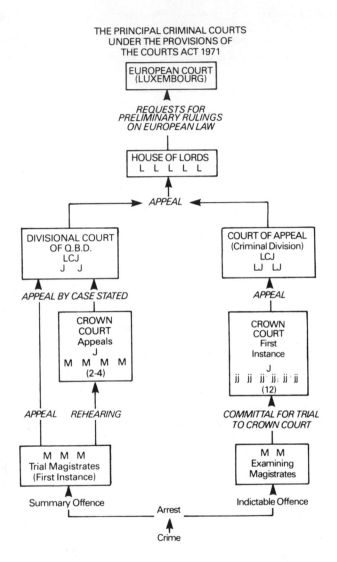

THE PRINCIPAL CRIMINAL COURTS
UNDER THE PROVISIONS OF
THE COURTS ACT 1971

EUROPEAN COURT
(LUXEMBOURG)

*REQUESTS FOR
PRELIMINARY RULINGS
ON EUROPEAN LAW*

HOUSE OF LORDS
L L L L L

APPEAL

DIVISIONAL COURT
OF Q.B.D.
LCJ
J   J

COURT OF APPEAL
(Criminal Division)
LCJ
LJ   LJ

APPEAL BY CASE STATED

APPEAL

CROWN
COURT
Appeals
J
M   M   M   M
(2-4)

CROWN
COURT
First
Instance
J
jj   jj   jj   jj   jj   jj
(12)

APPEAL   *REHEARING*

*COMMITTAL FOR TRIAL
TO CROWN COURT*

M   M   M
Trial Magistrates
(First Instance)

M   M
Examining
Magistrates

Summary Offence   Indictable Offence

Arrest

Crime

The symbols indicate the approximate composition of the Court.
Symbols: L=Lord of Appeal; LJ=Lord Justice; LCJ=Lord Chief Justice;
           J=Judge; M=Magistrate; j=Juryman.

THE PRINCIPAL CRIMINAL COURTS PRIOR TO THE
PASSING INTO LAW OF THE COURTS ACT 1971

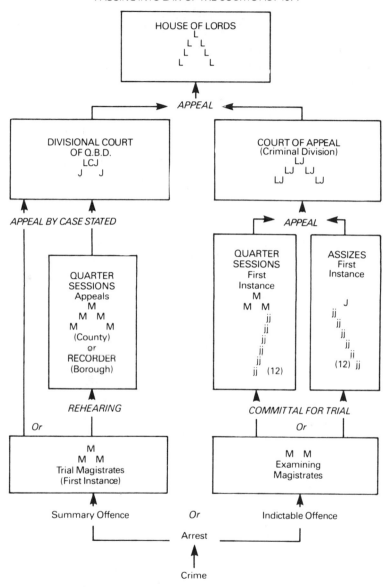

·The symbols indicate the approximate composition of the Courts:

L = Lord of Appeal   LCJ = Lord Chief Justice
LJ = Lord Justice   J = Judge
j = Juryman   M = Magistrate

cases, Circuit Judges and Recorders hearing the remainder. In addition the Crown Court hears appeals from magistrates' courts by way of a re-hearing, with all the witnesses giving their evidence all over again, when there is a judge or recorder and between two and four magistrates sitting with a jury.

All cases reaching the Crown Court come from a magistrates' court, either from justices of the peace sitting as examining magistrates, or by way of appeal from a decision of the magistrates.

The accompanying diagrams illustrate the systems in force before and after the Courts Act 1971 came into force.

Coroners' Courts

Coroners, who must be barristers, solicitors, or doctors, have the duty to enquire into violent and unusual deaths that occur in their areas. If a coroner believes that a death may be due to murder, running down by a car, or one of certain other causes he must summon a jury. If the jury decides that a death resulted from murder, manslaughter or infanticide it may return a verdict that the victim was "killed unlawfully", but it must not name any suspect.

In the case *R.* v. *Hammersmith Coroner, ex parte Peach* (1980) where the coroner refused to summon a jury to sit with him when a man died following a demonstration the Court of Appeal issued an order of certiorari to quash the coroner's decision and an order of mandamus requiring him to continue the inquest with a jury.

A coroner is allowed to accept a majority verdict if the minority consists of not more than two members of the jury.

CRIMINAL APPEAL COURTS

Crown Court

Appeals are heard from magistrates' courts by way of a rehearing.

Divisional Court of the Queen's Bench Division

In addition to its civil jurisdiction this court hears appeals from magistrates' courts and the Crown Court on points of law. These appeals are said to be by way of "case stated" which means that the party appealing asks the magistrates to prepare a document that sets out their findings. This document is forwarded to the Divisional Court, and forms the basis on which that court can decide whether the magistrates' decision was correct in law.

Court of Appeal (Criminal Division)

Appeals from the Crown Court acting as a court of first instance, lie to the Court of Appeal (Criminal Division). Usually three judges sit together to try cases. The jurisdiction of the assizes and quarter sessions is transferred by the Courts Act 1971 to the Crown Court (see p. 65).

House of Lords

The House hears appeals from the Court of Appeal (Criminal Division) and the divisional court of the Queen's Bench Division but no appeal can be taken to the House of Lords unless the court below certifies that a point of law of general public importance is involved and where leave to appeal has been given by either the House or the Court of Appeal. The court's membership is the same as for civil appeals.

It may be necessary to make a request for a preliminary ruling from the European Court in a criminal case just as in a civil case. This was done by the House of Lords in the case of *R*. v. *Henn* (1980) where an importer of pornographic articles was convicted under the Customs Consolidation Act 1876. On appeal he submitted that the 1876 Act had ceased to apply since this country had joined the Common Market because Article 30 of the E.E.C. Treaty says that restrictions on imports shall be prohibited. When the House of Lords put this point to the European Court in Luxembourg by way of a question under Article 177, the European Court replied that Article 36 of the E.E.C. Treaty, which allows imports to be forbidden on the ground of public morality, applied. On receiving this answer the House of Lords held that the 1876 Act was still valid and confirmed the conviction of Mr. Henn.

THE SANCTIONS IMPOSED BY THE COURTS

The meaning of "sanctions", as far as civil law is concerned, refers to the means by which the courts secure compliance with their decisions. As far as criminal law is concerned, the expression refers to the punishments that may be imposed.

Civil law

Civil courts are concerned mainly with restoring injured parties to their former positions and with compensating people who have suffered harm. The common law courts developed the remedy of damages for this purpose. It means that if a common law court decided that someone had caused unlawful loss to another the court would order the wrongdoer to pay the other a sum fixed by the court called "damages". They also developed prerogative orders and *Habeas Corpus* (see p. 55).

The Chancery courts developed the "equitable remedies", which existed alongside the common law remedies. These are:

(i) *Injunction.* This is a court order issued to a defendant. If an injunction is disobeyed the person concerned may be sent to prison. The main types of injunction are (a) "mandatory injunction" that orders something to be done; (b) "prohibitory injunction" that forbids something to be done.

(ii) *Specific performance.* This is an order of a court that commands a defendant to carry out the terms of a contract.

Since the Judicature Act 1875 both common law and equitable remedies may be granted in all civil courts.

Criminal law

The main punishments that may be imposed are: (i) death, for

PROCEDURE FOR CRIMINAL CASES

	Type of Offence	Before Trial	At First Instance	First Appeal	Second Appeal	Final Appeal
I	Minor summary offences		Magistrates' Court	*Either* Crown Court *or* Divisional Court of Q.B.D.	Divisional Court of Q.B.D.	House of Lords House of Lords
II	Major summary offences *and* minor indictable offences	These may be dealt with either as in I (above) or as in III (below)				
III	Indictable offences	Examining magistrates	Crown Court	Court of Appeal (Criminal Division)		House of Lords

treason (see p. 140), imprisonment, for most offences, and a fine (which may be imposed instead of, or in addition to imprisonment) for most offences. Children between the age of 10 and 17 who have been convicted of an offence punishable by imprisonment may be sent to live in a "Community Home", while those between 15 and 21 may be sent for borstal training. First offenders are often put on probation—under this system they must be of good behaviour and keep a probation officer informed of their activities. Under the Criminal Law Act 1977, a Court convicting anybody for an indictable offence, may award to any person aggrieved, on application by the latter, a sum not exceeding £1,000 to be paid by the person convicted. This power is to be used by the court to compensate for loss or damage to property but it does not extend to motor accident cases.

Where a person over 17 is convicted of an offence punishable by imprisonment, a court may instead make a community service order requiring him to perform unpaid work for a given number of hours. If he does not do the work properly without any good reason he may be arrested, the order may be revoked and he may be dealt with in the usual way.

Chapter 5

The Personnel of the Law

THE LEGAL PROFESSION

The two branches of the legal profession are "barristers-at-law" and "solicitors of the Supreme Court", who are usually known as barristers and solicitors. Each branch does its own type of work, though certain duties can be carried out by either a barrister or a solicitor. The word "lawyer" has no exact meaning and is applied to both barristers and solicitors; sometimes the word is used to include judges and legal writers as well.

Solicitors

There are about 38,000 solicitors and most of them work in partnerships (see p. 95). Although solicitors may represent their clients in certain courts such as county courts and magistrates' courts, they work mostly in their offices on such matters as: conveyancing (buying and selling houses and mortgaging them (see p. 217)); probate (settling the affairs of deceased persons (see p. 241)); forming companies for promoters (see p. 98), and preparing a variety of documents such as contracts and pleadings. If a layman (non-lawyer) requires legal advice he must go to a solicitor and not to a barrister because barristers take instruction only from solicitors. If the matter is one requiring the attention of a barrister, the solicitor will act as intermediary. The relationship between solicitors and barristers is similar to that between general medical practitioners and specialists. The solicitor will usually choose a barrister who specialises in the branch of law in question and either put the problem to him in a written form, or arrange to take the client to a conference at the barrister's chambers. It should be mentioned here that barristers are recognised as being of a higher rank than solicitors, and a rule of etiquette prevents them from ever visiting the solicitor's office. The solicitor and client must go to the barrister. There are strict rules laid down by the Law Society (which governs the solicitors' branch of the profession) to ensure as far as possible that solicitors are strictly honest. Their fees are regulated by statute, their accounts are examined annually, and they have to contribute several pounds a year each to a fund that has been set up to repay anybody who might lose money due to the dishonesty of a solicitor.

In order to become a solicitor it is necessary to serve an apprenticeship of between two and a half and five years as an "articled clerk", and to pass the qualifying examinations. The length of articles depends on whether or not the articled clerk has a university degree. When the articled clerk has served his articles and passed his examinations he is then "admitted" as a solicitor.

Legal Executives

Most solicitors employ office staff who are "unadmitted", and many of them do legal work of a high standard. After serving for a number of years these members of a solicitor's staff may attain professional status by becoming legal executives. In order to do this they must become members of the Institute of Legal Executives and pass certain examinations similar to those taken by solicitors. There are some 13,000 members of the Institute, including student members. Legal Executives who wish to become solicitors are given partial exemption from the Law Society's examination in certain instances.

Barristers

Barristers are collectively called "the bar" and are also known as "counsel". There are some 4,600 practising barristers. Each works on his own account, although he usually shares the services of a "barrister's clerk" and "chambers" (offices) with other counsel. The duty of a barrister's clerk is to act as business manager to the barristers who employ him. He arranges with solicitors for counsel to attend court and give written advice, and he is the one who fixes fees and arranges payment. Barristers' clerks are traditionally remunerated by taking a proportion of the fees paid to counsel but some now work for a salary. The duties of counsel consist partly of "paper work", and partly of advocacy. Paper work is the preparation of statements of claim, defences, and opinions on questions of law for solicitors, as well as other matters. Advocacy means putting a case verbally in court. Barristers have a right to appear in any court, and advocacy is their speciality. In some courts such as county courts a client can choose between being represented by a solicitor or a barrister. If he chooses to be represented by counsel it is likely to cost a little more, but he will nearly always be better served. This will be so partly because he will have two lawyers working for him instead of one, and partly because of counsel's expertise.

In order to become a barrister it is necessary to join an Inn of Court, of which there are four, the Inner Temple, the Middle Temple, Lincoln's Inn, and Gray's Inn. These are independent societies each governed by a body known as the "Masters of the Bench" who are judges and senior counsel. They have had their own premises in the heart of legal London for centuries, and here there are libraries, dining halls, offices and gardens. The student who is "reading for the bar" must dine in the hall of his Inn a specified number of times in each of the four legal terms for three years, as a condition of being "called to the Bar". This is to ensure that he meets and gets to know other students, barristers and judges. There are of course examinations to be passed. Courses of lectures are provided both at the official "Council of Legal Education" and at private law schools. After being called to the Bar a young barrister does a year "reading in chambers". This means that he becomes the pupil of a practising barrister and goes to court with him besides reading all his master's paper work and attending his master's conferences. Only then is he allowed to set up on his own. A committee under the chairmanship of Ormrod J. considered the whole system of legal education with a view to making suggestions for improvement and its report which was published in 1971 made a number of recommendations. The most important of these are that the normal method by which a person should become a barrister or a solicitor ought to be by obtaining a law degree, followed by a year's vocational training and some training "on the job".

There are two types of barrister, "juniors" who are ordinary barristers and bear this name whatever their age, and "Queen's Counsel", also called "silks", because they wear a silk gown in court instead of the stuff gown worn by juniors. After practising for a number of years a junior may apply to the Lord Chancellor to be made a silk, and if he is successful in this application for promotion, he will thenceforth appear in court accompanied by a junior and will charge higher fees. Many barristers hope one day to become judges, and a step on the road is taken by becoming a Recorder.

Judges

High Court and Circuit Court Judges are appointed from the members of the Bar by the Crown on the recommendation of the Lord Chancellor. Elevation to the Court of Appeal and to the House of Lords is usually from members of the Bench (*i.e.* the High Court judges) by the Crown on the recommendation of the Prime Minister, though on some occasions a barrister is appointed direct to the Court of Appeal. The qualifications for becoming a judge vary with the position, but, for example, to be appointed to the House of Lords the minimum qualification is two years as a Supreme Court judge or fifteen years at the Bar. The judges are independent of the government, which under our constitution must not interfere with their work. For example cases pending in court are not debated in Parliament, although debates are sometimes held on decided cases. Judges of the House of Lords and the Supreme Court hold office during good behaviour, and may be removed by the Crown on an address presented by both Houses of Parliament. This provision was first laid down in the Act of Settlement 1701, but is now contained in the Supreme Court of Judicature (Consolidation) Act 1925.

Magistrates

A document called a Commission of the Peace is used to appoint magistrates for every county and certain boroughs. Magistrates are appointed from among well known members of all sections of the community. No special qualification is required. The Lord Chancellor or, in Lancashire, the Chancellor of the Duchy of Lancaster, appoints county magistrates on the advice of the Lord Lieutenant of the county and a committee, while he appoints borough magistrates on the recommendations of an advisory committee of the borough. There is power vested in the Lord Chancellor to remove magistrates for incompetence. Much of the law concerning the appointment and organisation of magistrates is contained in the Justices of the Peace Act 1979.

Jurors

The Lord Chancellor is responsible for summoning jurors under the Juries Act 1974. In the High Court and in criminal cases there are twelve jurors, in county courts there are eight (on the rare occasions when a jury is required), while a coroner's jury must consist of seven, nine or eleven persons. The duty of members of the jury is to watch and listen to the proceedings carefully, and at the end to give a verdict on the question of fact that is put to them by the judge. The judge has the duty, after counsel on both sides have put their cases, to sum up the various arguments impartially, and to tell the jury the law. In this connection it is for the jury to take the law from the judge and to ignore the various suggestions of counsel on both sides. Sometimes there has to be a protracted argument on law between counsel to help the judge to come to a decision, and on such occasions the jury is temporarily sent out of court so that it is not influenced by the arguments.

MEMBERS OF THE JUDICIARY AND LEGAL OFFICIALS

The Lord Chancellor

This post is unique because it is both a political and a judicial appointment. The Lord Chancellor is appointed on the recommendation of the Prime Minister, and is a member of the government. He acts as Speaker of the House of Lords and is highest in rank among the judges. One of his functions is to preside over the House of Lords when it sits as a court of law. He changes with the government.

The Lord Chief Justice

This judge is the head of the Queen's Bench Division. He also presides over the Court of Appeal (Criminal Division) and the divisional court of the Queen's Bench Division.

The Master of the Rolls

This is an ancient office, and the name is derived from previous holders of the position who were concerned with the preservation of the court records. He is the head of the Court of Appeal (Civil Division). He is still the official head of the Record Office, which houses records of court cases going back for many generations.

The President of the Family Division

This judge is the head of the division.

The Vice-Chancellor

The office of Vice-Chancellor, which existed before 1875 was revived by the Administration of Justice Act 1970. The judge appointed to the post acts in practice as the head of the Chancery Division, in place of the nominal head, the Lord Chancellor.

Lords of Appeal in Ordinary

These are the judges of the House of Lords. There may be a maximum of eleven of these Law Lords as they are also called.

Lords Justices of Appeal

In addition to the Master of the Rolls there may be a maximum of eighteen Lords Justices of Appeal who sit in the Court of Appeal.

Puisne Judges

These are the judges of the High Court. Their maximum number is seventy-five. In the Queen's Bench Division there are forty-nine judges in addition to the Lord Chief Justice. In the Chancery Division there are eleven puisne judges; although the Lord Chancellor is the nominal head of the Chancery Division, he never takes cases at first instance. The Family Division has sixteen puisne judges in addition to the President.

Circuit Judges

These judges together with High Court Judges and Recorders staff the Crown Court and county court circuits. They are appointed from among barristers.

Recorders

These are part-time judges sitting in the Crown Court. They are appointed from among both barristers and solicitors.

The Attorney-General

The Attorney-General is the legal adviser to the government. He is a practising barrister and a Member of Parliament who supports the government party, and is appointed by the Prime Minister.

The Solicitor-General

He acts as deputy to the Attorney-General. He too is a practising barrister and a Member of Parliament who supports the government. The Attorney-General and the Solicitor-General are together called the "law officers" of the Crown.

The Director of Public Prosecutions

The D.P.P. as he is also called, is a civil servant who is the head of a department which advises the police on prosecutions in many serious cases. His department also conducts a small number of prosecutions, the greater number being conducted by local police forces. His appointment and duties are governed by the Prosecution of Offences Act 1979.

The Parliamentary Commissioner

The Parliamentary Commissioner Act 1967 created this new post. The Commissioner has a limited power to investigate certain grievances, particularly in connection with allegations of maladministration. He may act only at the request of a member of Parliament. His powers are less extensive than those of the "Ombudsman" in Scandinavia.

The Law Commissioners

These are full-time officials appointed under the Law Commissions Act 1965. Their work is to keep the law under review and to make recommendations for reform and modernisation of the law. They work in conjunction with two part-time bodies, the Law Reform Committee, which deals with civil law reform and the Criminal Law Revision Committee.

The Judges of the European Court of Justice

This court has eleven judges, including one from each member state, the first British judge being Lord Mackenzie Stuart, from Scotland.

A   B

C

FIG. 5—THE EUROPEAN COURT

A SIR GORDON SLYNN, *British Advocate-General at the European Court.*
B LORD MACKENZIE STUART, *British Judge at the European Court.*
C THE EUROPEAN COURT OF JUSTICE IN LUXEMBOURG.

CARBOLIC SMOKE BALL

WILL POSITIVELY CURE

COUGHS Cured in 1 week	**CATARRH** Cured in 1 to 3 months.	**HOARSENESS** Cured in 12 hours.	**THROAT DEAFNESS** Cured in 1 to 3 months.	**INFLUENZA** Cured in 24 hours.	**CROUP** Relieved in 5 minutes.
COLD IN THE HEAD Cured in 12 hours.	**ASTHMA** Relieved in 10 minutes.	**LOSS OF VOICE** Fully restored.	**SNORING** Cured in 1 week.	**HAY FEVER** Cured in every case.	**WHOOPING COUGH** Relieved the first application.
COLD ON THE CHEST Cured in 12 hours.	**BRONCHITIS** Cured in every case.	**SORE THROAT** Cured in 12 hours.	**SORE EYES** Cured in 2 weeks.	**HEADACHE** Cured in 10 minutes.	**NEURALGIA** Cured in 10 minutes.

As all the Diseases mentioned above proceed from one cause, they can be Cured by this Remedy

£100 REWARD

WILL BE PAID BY THE

CARBOLIC SMOKE BALL CO.

to any Person who contracts the Increasing Epidemic,

INFLUENZA,

Colds, or any Diseases caused by taking Cold, after having used the **CARBOLIC SMOKE BALL** according to the printed directions supplied with each Ball.

£1000 IS DEPOSITED

with the ALLIANCE BANK, Regent Street, showing our sincerity in the matter.

During the last epidemic of **INFLUENZA** many thousand **CARBOLIC SMOKE BALLS** were sold as preventives against this disease, and in no ascertained case was the disease contracted by those using the **CARBOLIC SMOKE BALL.**

THE CARBOLIC SMOKE BALL,

TESTIMONIALS.	AS PRESCRIBED BY	TESTIMONIALS.

AS PRESCRIBED BY

SIR MORELL MACKENZIE, M.D.,

HAS BEEN SUPPLIED TO

H.I.M. THE GERMAN EMPRESS.

H.R.H. The Duke of Edinburgh, K.G.
H.R.H. The Duke of Connaught, K.G.
The Duke of Fife, K.T.
The Marquis of Salisbury, K.G.
The Duke of Argyll, K.T.
The Duke of Westminster, K.G.
The Duke of Richmond and Gordon, K.G.
The Duke of Manchester.
The Duke of Newcastle.
The Duke of Norfolk.
The Duke of Rutland, K.G.
The Duke of Wellington.
The Marquis of Ripon, K.G.
The Earl of Derby, K.G.
Earl Spencer, K.G.
The Lord Chancellor.
The Lord Chief Justice.
Lord Tennyson.

TESTIMONIALS (left column):

The DUKE OF PORTLAND writes : "I am much obliged for the Carbolic Smoke Ball which you have sent me, and which I find most efficacious."

SIR FREDERICK MILNER, Bart. M.P., writes from Nice, March 7, 1890 : "Lady Milner and my children have derived much benefit from the Carbolic Smoke Ball."

Lady MOSTYN writes from Carshalton, Cary Crescent, Torquay, Jan. 10, 1890 : "Lady Mostyn believes the Carbolic Smoke Ball to be a certain check and a cure for a cold, and will have great pleasure in recommending it to her friends. Lady Mostyn hopes the Carbolic Smoke Ball will have all the success its merits deserve."

Lady ERSKINE writes from Spratton Hall, Northampton, Jan. 1, 1890 : "Lady Erskine is pleased to say that the Carbolic Smoke Ball has given every satisfaction ; she considers it a very good invention."

Mrs GLADSTONE writes : "She finds the Carbolic Smoke Ball has done her a great deal of good."

Madame ADELINA PATTI writes ; "Madame Patti has found the Carbolic Smoke Ball very beneficial, and the only thing that would enable her to rest well at night when having a severe cold."

TESTIMONIALS (right column):

The BISHOP OF LONDON writes : "The Carbolic Smoke Ball has benefited me greatly."

The MARCHIONESS DE SAIS writes from Padworth House, Reading, Jan. 13, 1890 : "The Marchioness de Sais has daily used the Smoke Ball since the commencement of the epidemic of Influenza, and has not taken the Influenza, although surrounded by those suffering from it."

Dr. J. RUSSELL HARRIS, M.D. writes from 6, Adam Street, Adelphi, Sept. 24, 1891 : "Many obstinate cases of post-nasal catarrh, which have resisted other treatment, have yielded to your Carbolic Smoke Ball."

A. GIBBONS, Esq., Editor of the Lady's Pictorial, writes from 172, Strand, W.C., Feb. 14, 1890 : "During a recent sharp attack of the prevailing epidemic I had none of the unpleasant and dangerous catarrh and bronchial symptoms. I attribute this entirely to the use of the Carbolic Smoke Ball."

The Rev. Dr. CHICHESTER A. W. READE, LL.D., D.C.L., writes from Banstead Downs, Surrey, May 1890 : "My duties in a large public institution have brought me daily, during the recent epidemic of influenza, in close contact with the disease. I have been perfectly free from any symptom by having the Smoke Ball always handy. It has also wonderfully improved my voice for speaking and singing."

The Originals of these Testimonials may be seen at our Consulting Rooms, with hundreds of others.

One **CARBOLIC SMOKE BALL** will last a family several months, making it the cheapest remedy in the world at the price—10s., post free.

The **CARBOLIC SMOKE BALL** can be refilled, when empty, at a cost of 5s., post free. Address :

CARBOLIC SMOKE BALL CO., 27, Princes St., Hanover Sq., London, W.

FIG. 6—THE CARBOLIC SMOKE BALL

The advertisement which led to the famous case of
Carlill v. Carbolic Smoke Ball Co. (see p. 179)

The Advocates-General

Five independent members of the European Court, one of whom delivers an opinion in open court as to how each case should, in his view, be decided, in order to help the Court come to a decision.

Chapter 6

How Justice is Paid For

The English legal system employs thousands of men and women directly or indirectly; some of them, such as solicitors, work full-time and others, like lay magistrates give up some of their spare time. In addition to judges, barristers, solicitors and legal executives, the legal system requires the services of clerical staff in court offices, law reporters, law lecturers, "O" level law examiners and many others. The services of all these people have to be paid for, if we are to maintain our judicial system at a high level of efficiency, and raise the standards of justice in the interest of the community. There are various sources from which payment for legal work is made. Judges and stipendiary magistrates are paid by the state, while lay magistrates receive certain expenses from the same source. Funds for these purposes and for the payment of the civil servants who man the court offices and carry out other duties are raised by general taxation. Transactions such as the formation of companies, preparation of wills and buying and selling houses are carried out by solicitors at the expense of their own clients.

If a person is going to buy a house, have a contract drawn up, or engage in some similar enterprise which requires assistance from those in the legal profession, he will ordinarily set aside a sum of money to pay for the services he uses. It is when we consider the question of litigation that we find more people in difficulty over making payment. The reason for this is fairly obvious. Many litigants, perhaps most litigants, find themselves engaged in court proceedings unwillingly and often at a time not of their own choosing. A man may be involved in litigation at a time when he has lost income through injury, or a woman when she has been deserted by her husband. At such times litigants often find themselves with reduced funds and extra expenses. A plaintiff is in a slightly better position than a defendant in that he has a wider choice of dates at which to commence litigation, but for example, a man who has suffered .personal injuries at the hands of some negligent individual who refuses to compensate him must start proceedings within three years or find that his right to claim has expired, or, to put it in legal language, has become statute-barred by the Limitation Act 1939, as amended by the Law Reform (Limitation of Actions, etc.) Act 1954. He is therefore compelled to start proceedings within three years; this may seem a long time, but every year a considerable number of people fail to obtain their rights through inaction or ignorance. A defendant with a good answer to a claim against him must spring to his own defence in a matter of days or find himself in the greatest difficulties. Because of circumstances like these, legislation has been introduced to shift some of the burden of payment for the expenses of litigation on to the taxpayer. The arrangements in force are described below and the question whether the successful or unsuccessful party shall pay for the legal costs of the successful party in litigation is discussed. There are different arrangements for both these matters in criminal cases and civil cases.

LEGAL AID IN CRIMINAL PROCEEDINGS

The greater part of the law relating to legal aid in criminal proceedings is to be found in the Legal Aid Act 1974. A person being tried or appealing before any of the following courts may apply under the 1967 Act, for legal aid if he claims he is unable to pay for a lawyer:—magistrates' court, Crown Court, Court of Appeal (Criminal Division), and the House of Lords. He may be able to have legal aid in respect of an appeal to the Divisional Court of the Queen's Bench Division, or from that court to the House of Lords. Application should be made to the court dealing with the case which will supply an application form. There are no strict financial limits. The court must not refuse legal aid in criminal proceedings if the accused is on supplementary benefit or if his immediately available resources are less than £75 or £120 if married. Each applicant's resources are considered by the Supplementary Benefits Officer of the Department of Health and Social Security and if he is found to qualify, he will be granted legal aid either free of charge or on payment of a contribution towards the cost. Legal aid pays for advice in the preparation of a case, the services of a solicitor, and where necessary those of counsel as well.

Section 75(5) of the 1967 Act provides that in case of doubt as to whether or not legal aid should be granted, the doubt shall be resolved in favour of the applicant.

Duty Solicitor

In many magistrates' courts local solicitors make an arrangement for one of them to be available to advise accused persons on the spot under the legal aid scheme.

Legal Advice

Under the Legal Aid Act 1974 legal advice and assistance free of charge or at a reduced fee may be obtained from a solicitor on matters of criminal law or civil law by a person who has limited means. Where advice or assistance is sought by someone under school-leaving age, the solicitor must be seen by his parent or somebody else on his behalf. The income of whoever maintains the child will be taken into account in deciding eligibility for legal aid. A person receiving supplementary benefit or family income supplement will be entitled to free advice. Under the Act a solicitor's work extends to anything that is regarded as part of what he normally does, except for steps in court proceedings. He can advise, write letters, draw up wills, negotiate, take statements and visit persons in police stations and prison until the costs reach a total of £25 (although this may in some cases be extended).

In order to get legal advice and assistance it is necessary to go to a solicitor. Citizens Advice Bureaux have a list of local firms. It is best to make an appointment by telephone before going.

On arrival at the solicitor's office the person needing advice or assistance will have to give an idea of his means and sign a "Green Form", although he will not have to fill it up. It is for the solicitor to work out from the information given, whether the person comes within the financial limits.

Although the scheme is not intended for matters involving over £25 of solicitors costs, it applies of course to smaller matters as well, which may cost only a few pounds, and for which many people may pay nothing at all.

LEGAL AID IN CIVIL PROCEEDINGS

Assistance of a financial nature for poor persons involved in civil proceedings has existed to some extent since the reign of King Henry VII by virtue of a statute passed in 1495, but the present comprehensive system dates from the Legal Aid and Advice Act 1949. A number of statutory instruments have been made to implement various provisions of the Act, and there have been a few statutory amendments to the original scheme. If a litigant is granted legal aid under the provisions of the legislation, he may choose a solicitor from a long list, and, where necessary, counsel, to carry out the various duties involved in representing him. Legal aid is available for proceedings in the House of Lords, the Court of Appeal, all divisions of the High Court, all county courts, and certain other courts such as the Mayor's and City of London Court (which does county court work in the City).

Financial Conditions for Granting Legal Aid

The object of the legal aid legislation is to assist persons of limited means, and with this in view certain regulations have been laid down to restrict legal aid to those in real need of it.

When a person applies for legal aid in a civil court he has to make a statement of his financial circumstances, which is examined by a supplementary benefits office of the Department of Health and Social Security to find out whether he qualifies for legal aid on financial grounds. The applicant's income and capital are taken into account, as well as certain of his outgoings, such as rent, maintenance of dependants, and income tax, in order to arrive at two figures, known as the disposable income, and the disposable capital of the applicant. These two figures are what is left of the applicant's actual income and capital after the authorised deductions have been made from it. A person is normally eligible for legal aid if his disposable capital is not more than £2,500 and his disposable income is not more than £85 a week. If a person's disposable income does not exceed £1,700 a year he can get free legal aid. He may get some legal aid if his income is not more than £4,075 a year. The legal aid fund pays the difference between the costs and what the recipient of legal aid pays himself.

Suitable Cause of Action

In order to qualify for legal aid an applicant must not only satisfy the financial requirements, but must also have reasonable grounds for instituting or defending proceedings. In order to establish these reasonable grounds the applicant must convince a body of lawyers known as the legal aid committee that he has a case which is worth putting before a court at the public expense. If the applicant is successful in satisfying both the Supplementary Benefits Officer and his local legal aid committee, he will be issued with a certificate entitling him to legal aid. He may then choose a solicitor and go on with the proceedings. In practice there are two ways in which people set about getting legal aid. One way is to go first to the local head post office and get the address of the local legal aid committee, there being committees for every part of the country, and then go to the committee's offices for the necessary forms and information. The other way is to go to a solicitor's office and to enquire whether legal aid work is accepted. Usually it is; in which case the solicitor will explain what is to be done and will give advice as well as providing the necessary forms. The usual procedure for obtaining a legal aid certificate may be lengthy, and there are arrangements for granting emergency certificates where this is necessary. Some solicitors will give half an hour's advice for £5.

COSTS

Costs in Civil Proceedings

Another aspect of the financial side of justice which must be considered, is the question of who is to pay for the services of the solicitors and barristers involved in legal proceedings. Each party engages a solicitor, and if counsel is involved, the solicitor pays, and eventually charges counsel's fees to his client. This means in practice, that only the fees of each solicitor need be considered. The court has a discretion to decide who shall pay the solicitors' costs. This discretion is exercised on well-known principles, and the usual rule is that the losing party must pay his own solicitor and also the solicitor of the successful party. Only in exceptional cases where the successful party has acted badly, as for example by bringing forward some false evidence, will he be deprived of his costs. In such a case the court may make no order as to costs and each pays his own. If a court believes that it was unnecessary for the action to be brought, it may even order a successful plaintiff to pay the costs of both parties. The Legal Aid Act 1974 provides for the payment out of legal aid funds of the costs of a successful unaided party who is awarded his costs against a legally aided party. Once it has been decided that one party is to pay the other's costs, the next question is how much shall be paid. The party who is awarded costs may have been extravagant in the amount spent on preparing the case, *e.g.*, by employing an unnecessarily expensive barrister and will not be allowed to make the other side pay for this extravagance. The party paying is liable only for a reasonable sum, and the excess over this will have to be borne by the party who incurred the extravagance. The reasonable sum is arrived at by a process known as taxation. Taxation is carried out in the High Court by both the solicitors (or their clerks) appearing before an official called the Taxing Master, and arguing the merits of each of the items in the bill of costs which is produced by the solicitor who is acting for the party who has been awarded his costs by the court. In county courts the same procedure is carried on in front of the Registrar.

Costs in Criminal Proceedings

These costs are governed mainly by the Costs in Criminal Cases Act 1973. Under the Act courts have a very wide discretion and are entitled to order a convicted person to pay the costs of the prosecution. They are also empowered to order the costs of an accused person who is acquitted to be paid for out of local funds, but the principle in force is that acquittal does not constitute by itself grounds for awarding costs. Only in exceptional cases are costs to be awarded in this way, *e.g.*, if there has been a quite unnecessary prosecution that has failed. One merit of this system is that a person who is morally guilty may escape conviction on some technicality and yet find himself out of pocket in having to pay the costs of his own defence, if the court sees no reason to add to his good fortune.

Chapter 7

Persons and the Law

HUMAN AND ARTIFICIAL PERSONS

There are two classes of persons recognised by the law, "natural persons" and "corporations". Natural persons are human beings, while corporations are institutions created by the law and given certain powers: these are described more fully below on p. 97.

The Status of Persons

"Status" means having an attribute common to all members of a particular category of person which results in particular legal relationships. Everybody has more than one status as they will belong to more than one group. For example if a person is British, this is a status; if he is a member of Parliament, this is another, and if he is married, this is a third status. Persons under 18 have a particular status as do mentally disordered persons and criminals.

The Capacity of Persons

A capacity is a power to do something. Often a capacity is given or taken away by a status. Thus if a British person attains the age of 18, this status will give him the capacity to vote, but if he is then created a viscount and becomes a member of the House of Lords, this new status will take away his right to vote, because peers have no vote since they can speak up for themselves in Parliament. Some rules about status and capacity apply to corporations; a corporation can be British, but it cannot, of course, get married.

Nationality

A person's nationality is his status as a citizen of a country. Some people have no nationality and are said to be "stateless" (state means country). This situation can arise in a number of ways. For example some countries deprive their citizens of nationality if they commit certain offences. Other people have more than one nationality; this could come about, for example where parents are of different nationalities. The British Nationality Act of 1948 contains most of the law relating to nationality, and under the Act, the nationality of ordinary people of this country is, for legal purposes, such as passport regulations, "citizen of the United Kingdom and colonies". It is possible in certain circumstances for a foreigner to acquire British nationality ("naturalisation") and for a citizen of the United Kingdom and colonies to lose his nationality. In 1980 the Home Office issued a white paper called "British Nationality Law", outlining the government's proposals which will be incorporated in an Act, probably in 1981. It is proposed that there should be three categories of British citizenship, British citizenship, citizenship of British dependent territories and British overseas citizenship. Each category would have different rights.

Infants (Minors)

The modern law relating to the age at which a person attains his or her majority, and is thus recognised to be an adult, depends on the Family Law Reform Act 1969. Before this Act came into operation the age of majority was twenty-one, and persons under that age were called infants. Under the Act, the age of majority is eighteen years, and infants may be described as "minors". There are special rules relating to minors, and some of them are as follows:

1. The law contract has particular rules in relation to minors (see p. 184).

2. A minor cannot take part directly in civil proceedings in court. If he is a plaintiff he must have a "next friend", and if he is a defendant he must have a "guardian *ad litem*". Usually his father

serves in the requisite capacity. A minor accused of crime, appears himself in court and may be defended like anybody else by a solicitor or barrister.

3. As a general rule a minor cannot make a will, but there are exceptions to this (see p. 238).

4. A minor below the age of ten years cannot be guilty of any crime. As far as children between ten and fourteen are concerned, the law presumes that they are not capable of forming the necessary intent to commit a crime but, if it is proved that in fact they did intend to do so, they can be punished. The Children and Young Persons Act 1969 makes provision for raising the age at which a child becomes capable of crime above 10, and in October 1970 the Government announced that it will, in due course, raise the age to 12, but not above this.

5. A legitimate infant takes the nationality of his father, while an illegitimate one takes the nationality of his mother (see p. 236).

6. A minor under the age of sixteen years cannot marry at all, while a minor between the ages of sixteen and eighteen requires the consent of his parents to enable him to marry (see p. 223).

7. A minor who has attained the age of sixteen years may choose his own National Health Service doctor and may give a valid consent to surgical, medical or dental treatment.

8. A minor cannot vote at Parliamentary or local government elections. Although the Representation of the People Act 1969 lowered the voting age to eighteen, it left the age at which a person becomes qualified to become a member of Parliament or a member of a local authority at twenty-one.

Persons Suffering from Mental Disorder

The Mental Health Act 1959 contains the greater part of the civil law relating to mental disorder. Rules are laid down in respect of both voluntary and compulsory admission to mental hospitals, and in order to prevent persons from being detained wrongfully or unnecessarily, a right of appeal to a Mental Health Review Tribunal is given to a person under detention. The Act covers the work of the Court of Protection which appoints a "receiver" (who is usually a close relative) to look after the property of the patient during his illness, and then supervises the receiver to make sure that the property is managed properly.

If a mentally disordered person does not realise what he is actually doing, he cannot enter into a valid marriage, make a valid will, or give any of his property away. There are particular rules in the law of contract and the law of tort relating to mentally disordered persons.

In criminal law it is a defence to any accusation to show that the accused was suffering from insanity at the time he committed the crime. Everybody is presumed to be sane unless the contrary is proved, and it is therefore for the accused to produce evidence of his insanity. The Crown Court has the power to send mentally disordered persons accused of crime to mental hospitals for long periods, and because of this mental disorder is raised as a defence less frequently than would otherwise be expected. It is most common as a defence in murder cases. If accused of murder a mentally disordered defendant may be able to rely on one of the two defences discussed below; which one is open to him will depend on the degree of his insanity.

If he wishes to show that he was completely insane at the time he committed the murder, he must prove to the court that his degree of insanity came within the scope of certain rules ("the M'Naghten rules"), laid down in 1843 by the judges following the case of *R*. v. *M'Naghten* (see p. 126). If his insanity was less serious he may be able to show nevertheless that his mental responsibility for what he did was reduced because his mind was abnormal at the time. In this type of case he will try to bring his case within the scope of the Criminal Procedure (Insanity) Act 1964, and will plead "diminished responsibility" (see p. 127).

The Crown

The Queen has two statuses; first, she has the ordinary status of a natural person; this is her private capacity. In her private capacity she can enter into a contract or make a will, although, by a rule of the common law, the Queen can do no wrong, and cannot be sued or prosecuted for anything she may have done. Her other status is that of a "corporation sole" (see p. 97). The

Queen is also referred to as "the Crown", and, depending on the context, this may mean the Queen in her private capacity, or in her public capacity or it may even mean the Government, because the government is carried on in the name of the Queen, under the constitution.

Chapter 8

Associations, Trade Unions and Corporations

People often join together to achieve some common aim. This aim may be concerned with trade, politics, wages or any of a hundred subjects. The law recognises joint action as a legitimate method of securing proper objectives, and lays down rules relating to various groups with differing aims. Some of the more important provisions of the law are considered below.

UNINCORPORATED ASSOCIATIONS

The least formal type of arrangement for joint action is the unincorporated association. It consists merely of a number of persons who have come together for a common purpose. Debating societies, social clubs, and sports clubs are all typical examples. The law has developed very few rules relating to unincorporated associations. The property of the association is usually regarded as belonging jointly to all the members. If a member enters into a contract on some business connected with the association, and then commits a breach of such contract (see (see p. 193), or if he commits a tort while doing something in connection with the association, he will usually be the only one who can be held responsible. On the other hand, if the affairs of the association are managed by a committee, which has authorised a tort, or agreed on a breach of contract, all the members of the committee may be held responsible. There are two important types of unincorporated association which are the subject of special rules, and which are dealt with below; these are partnerships and trade unions. In *Conservative Central Office* v. *Burrell (Inspector of Taxes)* (1980) it was held that because of the way the party was constituted, the party leader being the only link between all members, the party was not an unincorporated association and not liable to tax.

PARTNERSHIPS

Partnerships are also called "firms"; they are regulated by the Partnership Act 1890 which defines a partnership as "the relation which subsists between persons carrying on business in common with a view of profit". The firm consists just of those who have joined together in this way, and they are called the partners. A partnership has no separate existence apart from the members of the partnership, and in this it differs from a corporation, which is a type of organisation described below.

When a partnership is set up the members agree among themselves what each shall contribute. For example one may give a large sum of money, but may devote only one or two days a week to the partnership business, while another may work full time and put in no capital. Bearing in mind what each contributes, the partners will agree how the profits shall be shared out, and how any losses are to be met. All the partners get the benefit of any transaction made by one of their number on behalf of the partnership, and similarly all are liable when one partner acts wrongly in the course of partnership business. If the partnership is unable to pay its business debts the business creditors can sue each of the partners individually, and if they do not pay, can even, through court proceedings, have the lands and goods of the partners seized and sold, to raise money for the creditors. Under the Limited Partnerships Act 1907 it is possible for some of the partners to be "limited partners". This is an arrangement by which the limited partner's liability for the firm's business debts is limited to the amount of capital he has put in. Thus, if the firm fails financially the limited partner will lose his capital, but will avoid the fate of the other partners, of having his personal possessions sold. Under the Limited Partnership Act, however, there must always be at least one ordinary unlimited "general" partner.

The Act provides that a limited partner ought not to take part in the management of the firm, but that if he should, he will be liable for debts in the same way as a general partner.

The maximum permitted number of members in a partnership is twenty, except where legislation allows an unrestricted number. For example, under the Companies Act 1967 there may be any number in a partnership of solicitors or accountants. It will be obvious that to run some kinds of business by means of a partnership could be very risky, and for this reason many businesses are run as "limited companies", which are a type of corporation, as described below. There are certain professions which are not allowed to be conducted in the safety of a limited company. For example if solicitors or chartered accountants wish to work together, their respective professional associations require that they do so in partnerships.

TRADE UNIONS

A trade union is a body of workers who have combined together mainly to negotiate with their employers on wages and conditions of work, *i.e.* for the purpose of collective bargaining.

The status of trade unions is governed by the Trade Union and Labour Relations Act 1974, s. 2 of which provides that although a trade union shall not be a corporation, it shall be capable of making contracts, it can sue and be sued, and can be prosecuted in its own name for any offence alleged to have been committed by it. The Employment Act 1980 s. 4 gives a trade unionist a right to complain to an industrial tribunal in respect of unreasonable exclusion or expulsion from a trade union.

CORPORATIONS

Corporations are artificial persons created by the law, to fulfil certain useful functions.

They may usually enter into contracts, commit breaches of contract, and be made liable for both torts and crimes. A court can award damages against a corporation, or impose a fine on it. Corporations may hold land on the same terms as natural persons.

Although they are treated as being separate entities, they have no physical existence and must act through natural persons. These natural persons are called "members" of the corporation. For example the British Broadcasting Corporation is a corporation with a number of members, through whom it acts. If by some mischance all the members of the B.B.C. were killed together, the corporation would not be brought to an end. It would continue in existence, although it could not act in the usual way until new members were appointed to it. The fact that a corporation has an existence separate from its members is the most important single characteristic attributable to it. This characteristic was demonstrated in the well-known case of *Salomon* v. *Salomon & Co. Ltd.* (1897). Here a corporation had various debts and could not repay them all. A Mr. Salomon who owned the corporation almost entirely, *i.e.*, was the major shareholder, had a debt which gave him a right to be paid before anybody else. The other creditors argued that he and the corporation were one and the same person, but the court held that the corporation was a separate person, and that Mr. Salomon was not debarred from being repaid first.

Corporations Sole

Some corporations have only one member, while others have a number of members. The former are called "corporations sole", while the latter are termed "corporations aggregate". A corporation sole is an official post that is filled by a natural person who changes from time to time. The Crown is a corporation sole, and so are the bishops of the Church of England. The property that belongs to a corporation sole is not without an owner when the holder of the post dies, since property belongs to an artificial person which cannot die, and it will be available to the next occupant of the post. New corporations sole are created nowadays by Act of Parliament.

Corporations Aggregate

These are more numerous than corporations sole, and are of three types which vary according to the way in which they were created. First, chartered corporations (or common law corporations) as they are sometimes called are set up by a royal charter. The B.B.C. is an example of a chartered corporation. An important characteristic of such corporations is that they have almost the same powers as a natural person, and the doctrine of *ultra vires* (below) does not apply to them. Secondly, there are corporations created by statute, which are usually connected with the state in some way; their powers are defined and limited by the relevant statute. The National Coal Board is a statutory corporation. Thirdly, and most important of all we have corporations created by registration under the Companies Act 1948. This type of corporation is called a company and its powers are discussed below.

Establishment of a Company

The provisions of the Companies Act 1948 are administered by the Department of Trade and Industry. In order to bring a company into existence it is necessary to comply with the procedure that has been established by the Department under the Act. A number of documents must be prepared and handed in to the Department of Trade and Industry together with certain fees. The most important of these documents are the "memorandum of association", which lays down what the company is entitled to do, and the "articles of association" which lay down how the company is to be run. When the "promoters", as those forming a company are called, have completed all the necessary formalities, the Department of Trade and Industry issues a "certificate of incorporation", and the company comes into existence on the date mentioned on the certificate.

There are three main types of companies; these are "unlimited companies", where the members are liable for the debts of the company in much the same way as are the members of a partnership, "companies limited by guarantee", where the liability of members for the company's debts is limited to a small sum that each member promises to pay if the company is brought to an end, and "companies limited by shares". Companies limited by shares raise money by attracting investment from people who wish to share in the profits the company is likely to make.

The promoters decide how much money the company is going to need for its enterprise—this is called the capital. The capital is obtained by selling "shares" in the company to those who are willing to risk an immediate payment in the hope that the future profits of the company will make their investment worth while. Each share sold entitles the holder to a certain proportion of the profits, and the more shares a person buys, the greater will be his proportion of the profits. If a company is being formed to go into the retail ice cream business, for example the promoters may decide that they need £50,000 capital for ice-cream vans, a garage, and some ready money. They may divide the capital into, for example, 500 shares of £100 each, and if there are five promoters each may take 100 shares. This means that each must pay the company £10,000. When each has paid, his name will be entered on a list called the "register of shareholders", and he will receive a document called a "share certificate", that shows his name is on the register as owner of 100 shares. If he loses his certificate, he does not cease to be owner of the shares. The legal owner is the one whose name is on the register.

If one of the promoters finds that he needs his £10,000 back, he cannot recover it from the company, because if the company gave it back, this would be a "reduction of capital", which is normally forbidden by the provisions of the Act. Instead, he must sell his 100 shares. The purchaser will replace him on the register, and will take over his right to receive a share in the profits. If the company does well, and sells plenty of ice cream it will make a profit; some of this will be paid to the government as tax, some will be set aside for the future needs of the company, and the rest will be distributed to the shareholders as a "dividend". If the dividends keep increasing, the value of the shares will keep increasing, and one day the shares that were bought for £10,000 may be sold for £30,000. On the other hand, if the company does badly, no dividends will be paid, and the value of the shares may sink to £100. This is the risk that an investor takes.

Some companies have the right to offer their shares to the public, and to have these shares sold on the Stock Exchange; they are called public companies. The others, which must not have more than fifty members or sell shares to the public, are called private companies.

The advantage of trading by means of a limited company is that the liability of each member (in this case each person who holds shares) is limited to the amount he must pay for his shares. Even if the company incurs large debts, the creditors of the company cannot insist that the member pays more than the price of his shares. A company may, of course enter into a contract without sufficient money, and cause loss to innocent creditors. This possibility was realised when the system was first introduced in the nineteenth century, and so, to warn all possible creditors of the danger of entering into contracts with limited companies, the rule was laid down that every limited company must, as a warning to others put the word "limited", or some such abbreviation as "Ltd." after its name. The Companies Act 1980, s. 1 distinguishes between public companies which have a share capital and a memorandum of association stating that they are public companies on the one hand and private companies, which are those that do not come within the definition of a public company. The Act lays down that a "public limited company" must have a name ending with those words, or the abbreviation "p.l.c." Under s. 78 a public company may end its name in Welsh with the words "CWMNI CYFYNGEDIG CYHOEDDUS" or "C.C.C."

The Act is coming into operation in parts as laid down by statutory instruments.

If anybody is thinking of entering into a large contract with a company, and sees the word "limited", he at once realises that he should look at the company's papers held by the Department of Trade and Industry, so as to learn something of the financial background of the company. A company created by registration under the Companies Act can be brought to an end by various means. When its existence is terminated, it is said to have been "dissolved".

The day to day management of a company is put into the hands of directors, who are usually elected by the shareholders. Generally the more shares a person holds in a company, the greater degree of control he has over it, since many important decisions affecting companies are taken at meetings where shareholders each have a number of votes which are proportional to the number of shares they hold. However, holding shares in a company does not necessarily give one any control over its management.

Local Authority Corporations

Among the corporations which exercise the most influence over the lives of ordinary people are the local authority corporations. These perform a wide range of duties on behalf of those who live within their boundaries. County councils were brought into existence by the Local Government Act 1888 while urban district, rural district and parish councils were created by the Local Government Act 1894. The Greater London Council and the London boroughs were established by the London Government Act 1963. A large number of boroughs, on the other hand are chartered corporations. Changes are made from time to time in local authority organisation, and a Royal Commission (a body set up to hold an enquiry) published a report in 1969 which is usually called the Redcliffe-Maud Report after the chairman of the Royal Commission. This report recommended changes in local government boundaries and new types of local authorities. Following the Report, which was not followed in all respects, the Local Government Act 1972 was passed. This set up six new Metropolitan Counties organised on lines similar to those used in Greater London, and 39 ordinary non-metropolitan counties, some of which are new. Eight new Welsh counties were created at the same time.

The powers of local authority corporations are limited in different degrees, depending on whether they are chartered or statutory corporations. It is plain from the case of *Attorney-General v. Fulham Corporation* (1921) that the doctrine of *ultra vires* applies to statutory corporations. In this case the corporation which was empowered by statute to provide places where local inhabitants could wash their own clothes, started a laundry in which clothes were washed by corporation employees. This form of activity was held to be *ultra vires* the corporation, and illegal, since it could not be shown that running a laundry came within the powers conferred on the corporation by the statutes in question. In coming to a decision on a case of this kind, a court will take account of the facts and examine the relevant statutes in order to find out what acts of the corporation are: (i) expressly authorised, (ii) impliedly authorised, or (iii) reasonably incidental to something authorised. Only if what is done comes within one of these three categories, will it be *intra vires* and legal.

The position in regard to the powers of chartered corporations is less clear than that relating to statutory corporations. Although ordinarily, chartered corporations have powers almost as wide as those of a natural person, it seems that the effect of certain statutes has been to restrict these powers in the case of municipal chartered corporations, although the law is not entirely settled.

Local authorities have powers conferred by statute allowing them to pass by-laws, which are a form of delegated legislation, and which have effect only within the area of the local authority making them. Most by-laws are made under the procedure laid down by the Local Government Act 1972, sections 235–238, which provides that after the proposed by-law has been made under the seal of the local authority, it must then be sent to a "confirming authority", which will be one of several government departments, depending on the subject matter of the by-law. The confirming authority, after examining the proposed text either confirms the by-law, so that it can come into force, or else it rejects it. From time to time the courts have to decide upon the validity of a by-law, and they do this by applying four tests. If a by-law does not pass these tests, it will be invalid. The tests consist of asking in relation to the by-law: is it reasonable? is the meaning of it certain? is it consistent with the general law? and, was it within the powers of the local authority to pass it?

Chapter 9

Freedom Under the Law

In England if our right to do something is challenged we often say "it's a free country!" The phrase reflects a national feeling that there is a legal system which will prevent or rectify the more serious injustices that can be perpetrated against citizens. In modern England and Wales no law-abiding citizen need fear that a pounding on the front door at night presages arrest by the secret police, imprisonment without trial, torture and death. Such things, however, are happening today in a number of countries. This situation has existed in England in times past, and it could return if the people were not watchful of their liberties. It has been well said that the price of freedom is eternal vigilance, and freedom once lost to a determined government with the resources of modern science at its command is not easily or quickly regained. We must consider what are the freedoms of which we boast, and what is the power that restrains tyranny. The freedoms and the legal sanctions are examined below, but the reality underlying the law is a complex of many factors; the national character of the British people, their political maturity, their refusal to submit to unnecessary restriction; and their instinctive feeling for justice. Without the continued operation of these underlying factors, our parliamentary system, the common law, and all our freedoms would wither away and be replaced by a regime of repression.

PERSONAL FREEDOM

It is one of the principles of the common law that nobody may be deprived of his freedom of movement by imprisonment, without proper justification. One of the tests of whether a nation is really free, or whether the freedom proclaimed by the law of that nation is merely a sham, is the test of imprisonment by the government. If there is no means in actual practice of securing the release of a person arbitrarily imprisoned by the government contrary to the law within a short space of time, then the freedom of that nation is dead or is about to be extinguished.

Writ of Habeas Corpus

In England and Wales this freedom is safeguarded by the writ of *Habeas Corpus* which is a command issued by the Queen's Bench Division to the person detaining the prisoner ordering him to produce the prisoner before the court so that his release may be ordered if the detention is found to be unlawful. If a person is believed to be unlawfully detained as, for example by order of the House of Commons, by order of the Government, by any private individual, by the superintendent of a mental hospital, by the governor of a prison, or the officer in charge of a police station, then the usual procedure to obtain his release is as follows. An affidavit (a written statement about the imprisonment, made on oath) is filed with the Divisional Court of the Queen's Bench Division by the solicitor acting in the case on behalf of the prisoner, and counsel instructed by the solicitor makes an application in court for the writ to be issued. An application for *Habeas Corpus* takes priority over all other business of the court. Normally the court will fix a date shortly after the application, on which the person holding the prisoner must attend and, if possible, justify the imprisonment, provided that the affidavit and the proceedings reveal a possibility that the imprisonment is unlawful. If the court decides that there is a question of urgency, as for example where the prisoner is being held on a foreign ship in an English port, and the ship is preparing to sail, the court may issue the writ of *Habeas Corpus* forthwith and fix a later date for argument on the question whether it was a proper case for the writ to be issued. If the person to whom the writ is directed fails to obey it, this constitutes the offence known as contempt of court, and the wrongdoer may be fined or imprisoned, and in addition he will be liable to an action in tort by the prisoner for damages for false imprisonment.

In appropriate cases force will be used in order to release a prisoner where necessary. Only the main outlines of the procedure have been mentioned here. Much of the procedure is governed by the Administration of Justice Act 1960. There are certain differences between applications in criminal and civil matters, and some rights of appeal. The important thing about *Habeas Corpus* is that it really works, and works quickly, and the High Court is in fact able to protect people against unlawful imprisonment by the government or anyone else. A single judge may hear applications if the courts are in vacation.

In recent years the remedy of *Habeas Corpus* has proved less effective in practice than it used to be in times past. The matter was investigated during a special B.B.C. programme in 1980 by the well known writer, Hugo Young, who interviewed judges and lawyers on the programme, and came to the conclusion that all is not well. In the course of the broadcast it was said that where a person is unlawfully "detained for questioning" in a police cell without being arrested and accused, when his lawyers apply to the court for *Habeas Corpus*, the judges sometimes fail to order his immediate release and let the police continue their illegal detention; it was said that the judges began some time ago to allow this for a day, but that this has now been extended for two days.

It was pointed out further that those most in need of the protection of *Habeas Corpus* are members of unpopular classes of society such as those suspected of crime or of being illegal immigrants. The changed attitude of the courts was illustrated by two cases in the Court of Appeal; *R. v. Governor of Pentonville Prison, ex parte Azam* (1973) and *R. V. Secretary of State for the Home Department, ex parte Choudary* (1978). The question in both cases was whether detention of a suspected illegal immigrant under the Immigration

Act 1971 could be challenged by *Habeas Corpus*. In the 1973 case Lord Denning, M.R., said comparing the 1971 Act to Wartime Regulation No. 18(b): "Under regulation 18(b) the decision could hardly ever be challenged by *Habeas Corpus*. Here it can". But in the 1978 case he said "There is not a remedy by way of the writ of *Habeas Corpus*".

POWERS OF ARREST

Magna Carta 1215, the Great Charter of the Liberties of England, is still in force in large part, and our present law, which forbids the imprisonment or arrest of anybody in an arbitrary manner can be traced back to it. Chapter 29 of Magna Carta, as confirmed by King Edward I in 1297, reads as follows:

> "No freeman shall be taken or imprisoned, or be disseised of his freehold, or liberties, or free customs, or be outlawed, or exiled, or any other wise destroyed; nor will we not pass upon him, nor condemn him, but by lawful judgment of his peers, or by the law of the land. We will sell to no man, we will not deny or defer to any man either justice or right".

The meaning of "disseised" is dispossessed, and of "lawful judgment of his peers" is trial by jury.

By Warrant

An arrest may be made by warrant, or in some circumstances, without a warrant. A warrant is a written order to the police, which is usually issued by a magistrate directing them to arrest the person named in the warrant. In order that a warrant may be issued, it is necessary for a statement to be made on oath to the magistrate, describing the offence. About two hundred years ago there was a series of decisions which arose out of cases in which the government overstepped its powers through the issue of "general" warrants which are warrants in which the person to be arrested is not named. In *Leach* v. *Money* (1765) the general warrant was issued for the arrest of the publishers of the *North Briton*, a paper which criticised the government, and it was held that general warrants were illegal, while in *Wilkes* v. *Lord Halifax* (1769) John Wilkes, who had written in the *North Briton*, and had been arrested under a general warrant issued by the Secretary of State, Lord Halifax, was awarded a large sum of money as damages. Nowadays a policeman may arrest only a person named in the warrant. If the arrest is made in respect of a criminal matter, the constable need not have the warrant with him at the time of the arrest, but it is provided by the Magistrates' Courts Act 1952, s. 102(4), that the warrant shall, on the demand of the person arrested, be shown to him as soon as practicable. On the other hand, in the case of arrest on warrant for a civil matter such as non-payment of maintenance (see p. 233) the common law requires that the constable shall have the warrant in his possession at the time of making the arrest; it is not good enough, if the warrant is at the police station for example.

Arrest without Warrant

Prior to the passing of the Criminal Law Act 1967 certain serious offences were classified as "felonies", and the common law permitted any person to arrest another who was committing a felony in his presence. The Act abolished felonies and introduced a new category of crimes which are termed "arrestable offences". These are offences for which a person may be imprisoned for five years or more. Section 2 of the Criminal Law Act 1967 lays down a number of rules relating to arrest without warrant. Thus, where an arrestable offence *has actually been committed*, any person may arrest without warrant anyone whom he reasonably suspects to be guilty. He will be under no liability if he makes an honest mistake.

If, however someone is arrested as the result of an honest mistake where *no arrestable offence has actually been committed*, the situation is different. Here the Act draws a distinction between constables and others, and gives the former a measure of necessary protection. A constable, unlike other persons, will be under no liability if he makes an arrest reasonably but mistakenly believing the person arrested to be about to commit or to have committed an arrestable offence. An ordinary member of the public would in these circumstances render himself liable to an action in tort for false imprisonment.

Anyone may, at common law, arrest another who is committing a breach of the peace and hand him over to a constable. Similarly, any person who finds another one committing an indictable offence (see p. 122) at night may arrest him and take him to a constable by virtue of the Prevention of Offences Act 1851.

It was laid down by the House of Lords in *Christie* v. *Leachinsky* (1947) that anybody being arrested without a warrant whether by a constable or a private person is entitled to be told at the time of arrest of the true reason for it. It is necessary to tell him only in general terms of the reason. He need not be told if he must know from the circumstances why he is being arrested, or if he makes it impossible to tell him by running away. In Christie's case two policemen arrested Christie under the Liverpool Corporation Act 1921, which gave them power to arrest certain suspects whose names and addressed they did not know. In fact they were well aware of Christie's name and address, and although they thought he had committed a felony, they were ordered to pay him damages for false imprisonment because they did not tell him the reason they were arresting him.

A person arrested without a warrant must be taken before a court as soon as possible. If it is not possible to take the arrested person before a court within twenty-four hours, then unless the alleged offence is of a serious nature, he must be released on bail by a police officer. If the offence is a serious one he may be kept in custody, until he can be brought before a magistrates' court. Either a person is arrested or he is not. A policeman may invite somebody to accompany him to the police station to make a statement, and that person will often be very willing to go. He might wish to make a statement to clear himself of unnecessary suspicion and he might prefer to do this in the privacy of the police station to doing so at his own front door in the sight of curious neighbours. On the other hand, if a person who is unwilling to go to a police station is taken there, then he has been arrested, and the question may arise as to whether or not the arrest was justified in the circumstances.

The recent spate of bombings in this country led to the enactment of the Prevention of Terrorism (Temporary Provisions) Act 1974 under which it is an offence to belong to a "proscribed" organisation such as a terrorist group, which has been named by virtue of the Act.

Under section 7, a constable may arrest without warrant a person whom he reasonably suspects to belong to a proscribed organisation, and the latter may be detained for 48 hours in right of the arrest. This period may be extended for a further five days by order of the Home Secretary.

Bail

An arrested person may be granted bail by the police or a magistrate. This means that he undertakes to give himself up for trial, and promises to forfeit a named sum of money if he fails to return. He may be called upon to find one or two other persons to agree to forfeit a sum of his failure to return as well, if it seems possible that he may abscond. The magistrates have a discretion as to the sum of money they will fix. Under the Bill of Rights 1688, bail must not be excessive. There are certain cases where the magistrates have no discretion; for example they may not grant bail to a person charged with treason. There are various matters that magistrates take into account in deciding whether or not to grant bail. These include previous convictions, whether the prisoner is likely to threaten prosecution witnesses, and questions of personal hardship. If bail is refused an appeal may be made to a judge of the High Court. The rules as to the granting of bail are governed by the Bail Act 1976 which by s. 4 creates a presumption in favour of bail but there are exceptions when bail need not be granted, as for example where the court is satisfied that the defendant, if released, would fail to surrender to bail.

ENTRY ON LAND

Unless there is some lawful authority for the entry, it is the tort of trespass to land to enter the land or premises of another against the wishes of the occupier. A policeman may enter private premises without being invited, for various reasons, *e.g.*, to suppress a breach of the peace that is in progress or even, when a public meeting is being held on private premises, if he expects a breach of the peace. The Criminal Law Act 1967 empowers a constable without a warrant to enter any place (if need be, by force), to search for and arrest any person whom he reasonably suspects of having committed an arrestable offence. Policemen may also enter premises to search them, if they are armed with a search warrant issued by a magistrate. There are various statutes giving power to magistrates to issue search warrants and in addition there are a number of statutes giving authority to various inspectors and public officials, to enter premises for a number of purposes.

Sometimes landlords have tried to regain possession of rented premises from tenants by harassing the tenants in order to drive them away before the end of the lease, and by cutting off water and other supplies. This type of behaviour is now dealt with by the Rent Act 1965, s. 30. The section makes it a crime to interfere with the peace or comfort of residential occupiers or to withhold services such as water in order to gain possession of the premises. Prior to the Act, if tenants remained in premises after the expiration of the lease, the landlord could, in some cases enter and turn them out himself. Section 32 of the Act forbids this, and landlords must now apply to a court if they wish to regain possession in such circumstances.

OWNERSHIP OF LAND

There is today a strict control over the use to which a landowner can put his land. For example, it is necessary to obtain permission to build a house on one's own land. The local authority, to whom application must be made, for permission, may lay down such details as the numbers of storeys the house shall have, and whether a flat roof is to be permitted. Permission is also required to alter the use of a building. If, for example Jack wanted to turn the garage of his house in a quiet residential road, into a fish and chip shop, he would require permission, but he would be unlikely to obtain it, as the local authority would probably consider such a change of use detrimental to the neighbourhood.

Land is often required by the government in large or small parcels for various purposes of benefit to the community, and there are statutes which allow the land to be compulsorily purchased from the owner. Land must be acquired, for example, if a new radar-controlled automatic landing system for aircraft is being set up, since this will require the erection of a line of aerial masts spaced out at regular intervals over a mile or so adjoining the airport, and the little plot of land required for each aerial mast must be made the subject of negotiations with each landowner. Unfortunately for landowners, the price paid for land acquired under compulsory powers is often below that hoped for. The court dealing with the amount to be awarded is the Lands Tribunal, from which an appeal lies to the Court of Appeal. The Compulsory Purchase Act 1965 contains much of the law on this subject.

FREEDOM OF SPEECH

Freedom of speech, is the right to say or write anything even though it may be critical of the government or institutions of the State provided that it does not infringe the law. We shall consider the limits which have been set to this freedom by various means. The first set of rules regulating freedom of speech is the law relating to libel and slander (see p. 166 for defamation in civil law and p. 142 for criminal libel). The next aspect of the law concerns suppression of publications likely to be harmful to readers. The Obscene Publications Acts 1959 and 1964 relate to books and other publications. They entitle magistrates to order the destruction of a work if it is obscene, and the 1959 Act lays down that a work is obscene if taken as a whole it tends to deprave or corrupt persons who may read it. It is an offence to publish an obscene work, but it is a defence to prove that the publication was for the public good as furthering the interests of science or for some similar reason.

The Children and Young Persons (Harmful Publications) Act 1955 provides that such publications as magazines or comics which may fall into the hands of children or young people may not be published or sold if they contain mainly stories told in pictures showing crimes, violence or incidents that might tend to corrupt a child or young person. A child is anybody under fourteen years, while a young person is someone who is aged fourteen or over and under seventeen years. The Customs Consolidation Act 1876, together with subsequent enactments, entitles customs officers at airports and harbours to seize obscene works sought to be imported, while the Post Office Acts 1953 and 1969 entitle postal officials to seize and destroy obscene works sent through the post in defiance of the prohibition imposed by the Acts. The law concerning sedition and blasphemy is another restriction on freedom of expression and is dealt with under the classification of criminal libel on p. 142.

Theatre and Cinema Censorship

Prior to the passing of the Theatres Act 1968, stage plays were subject to censorship by the Lord Chamberlain: The Act abolished censorship but it makes the presentation of obscene performances a criminal offence.

Under the Cinematograph Acts 1909 and 1952 and the Local Government Act 1972 local authorities, or those to whom they delegate their powers (*e.g.*, magistrates) may license premises for the showing of films, and may refuse to allow the exhibition of films of which they disapprove on grounds of morality. There is no official censorship of films on a national basis, but the film industry maintains a voluntary organisation known as the British Board of Film Censors that carries out censorship and puts films into one of three categories viz: U for universal exhibition, A for exhibition to adults and children under sixteen accompanied by adults, AA for exhibition only to those over fourteen years, and X for exhibition only to those over eighteen years. In practice most licensing authorities follow what has been recommended by the Board, but they are under no obligation to do so. It is for this reason that occasionally cinemas in some areas show films which have no certificate from the Board, or that some cinemas cannot show films which have a certificate.

Radio and Television Censorship

The B.B.C., Capital Radio, The London Broadcasting Company and other commercial stations are allowed to broadcast by virtue of licences granted to them by the Minister of Posts and Telecommunications and one of the requirements of the licence is that nothing shall be broadcast which the Minister forbids. If the B.B.C. disobeyed the Minister he could withdraw the licence. The effect of these arrangements is that both sound and television broadcasts by the B.B.C. may be censored by the Minister if the need arises.

The Independent Broadcasting Authority owns certain equipment such as transmitters, but does not provide programmes. These are produced by independent companies under contract with the I.B.A. By the terms of these contracts the I.B.A. can call for the scripts of programmes, and can forbid particular broadcasts. The Minister may order the I.B.A. not to broadcast certain programmes. Although advertising is forbidden on B.B.C. sound broadcasts, it has been possible for British organisations to advertise their wares through advertisements broadcast by radio stations in foreign countries, *e.g.*, in the Grand Duchy of Luxembourg. Before the passing of the Marine & c. Broadcasting (Offences) Act 1967 a number of "pirate" radio stations broadcast advertisements from ships and abandoned sea forts. The Act makes such broadcasting an offence if carried on from a British ship, aircraft or fort and makes it an offence for British and certain Irish subjects to assist in such broadcasting. This may be regarded as a form of censorship.

FREEDOM OF MOVEMENT

There are certain roads and other places in areas of military activity where ordinary people are forbidden to loiter or to take photographs. With these exceptions, citizens and foreign visitors are allowed to move about to any part of the country. If a United Kingdom citizen wishes to go abroad he will usually apply to the Foreign Office for a passport or other travel document. The granting or withholding of a passport is a matter not regulated by statute but falling within the royal prerogative (the authority of the Crown), and the Foreign Office, acting on behalf of the Queen may refuse a passport without giving any reason for doing so. The law is that a United Kingdom citizen may enter and leave the country without any passport, but he needs some proof that he is British, and of his identity. It is on trying to enter other countries that the lack of a passport is felt: admission may well be refused, although this is partly a matter of chance, since many other states have a much more casual attitude to immigration than ourselves.

Immigration

Commonwealth citizens as well as aliens wishing to enter the United Kingdom are controlled by the Immigration Act 1971. Criminals, those in bad health, and those likely to undermine the security of the state are not admissible. The main categories of Commonwealth citizens entitled to enter are those who can support themselves without working, students, and workers who hold vouchers entitling them to take employment. The wives and children of those allowed in, may also enter. The Act enables certain Commonwealth citizens who have committed crimes to be deported.

Aliens wishing to enter the United Kingdom have to face an immigration officer employed by the Home Office. Those who appear to be sick may have to face a doctor as well. If it seems that an alien has only a single ticket, no money and no relatives in this country he will usually be refused admission in case he has to be supported out of public funds. Likewise if he has a serious illness and no money, he is liable to be sent back whence he came in case he adds to the difficulties of the National Health Service. Aliens who are allowed in are not permitted to take employment here without permission, although this does not apply to citizens of the other Common Market countries, all of which admit United Kingdom citizens as workers without restriction.

It need hardly be said that criminals and stowaways are not permitted to remain. If an alien is admitted he may have to register with the police in the neighbourhood where he lives, and he may be deported on the order of the Home Secretary. The Immigration Act 1971 set up an appeal system for Commonwealth citizens and aliens refused admission to the United Kingdom. The Immigration Act 1971 provides for United Kingdom citizens (of whom there are many living outside Europe, *e.g.* in Argentina) to be divided into two classes. Those in the first class are called "patrial" citizens and have a *right* of abode in the United Kingdom. The second class, popularly called "non-patrials", are subject to immigration control, and may be allowed in upon certain conditions made by the Home Secretary. A United Kingdom citizen will be "patrial", generally speaking, if he is connected with the United Kingdom by birth, adoption, or naturalisation, if he has a parent or a grandparent with such a connection, or if he has lived here for at least five years.

Most aliens come as tourists or to conduct business, and of course no real difficulties are placed in their way. The Home Office has power to, and does, admit aliens whose only claim to be allowed in is that they are fleeing persecution of a political, racial or similar kind. This country has a long tradition of hospitality to such refugees.

FREEDOM OF ASSOCIATION

Trade Unions

Until the nineteenth century, associations of workers aimed at improving conditions of work were illegal conspiracies. The picture has changed completely and modern legislation even gives preferential treatment to trade unions. A trade union cannot be sued in tort if the tort is committed "in contemplation or furtherance" of a trade dispute, under the Trade Union and Labour Relations Act 1974. Both workers and employers have the right to join with others for their mutual benefit. Strikes, which are occasions when workers join together to stop work for the purpose of forcing their employer to concede some advantage, are generally legal, even though they involve breaches of contract. On the other hand the effect of the Police Act 1964 is to prevent police officers from striking, while certain strikes by workers in the water, gas and electricity industries are criminal offences if the strikers know that they are putting human life or valuable property in danger.

In some industries the system of the "closed shop" is operated. This means that only members of the appropriate trade union will be given employment. If a trade union member is expelled, he can no longer earn his living, because nobody in the industry will give him a job. There have been some cases in which members have been wrongfully expelled as the result of decisions made by union officials. In circumstances of this type certain members have managed to obtain redress from the courts, for example by suing for breach of contract, but there is no general right allowing a member to appeal from a union decision to a court of law.

Public Meetings and Processions

There is no positive right in English law to hold a public meeting, but on the other hand there is no general rule against it. In practice nobody is much concerned, unless the meeting is likely to be the scene of disorder. In that case, the Public Order Act 1936 as amended by the Public Order Act 1963 may affect the situation. Under the Acts it is an offence for anybody in a public place or at a public meeting to use threatening, abusive, or insulting words or behaviour intending to provoke a breach of the peace.

There are various local Acts which make police permission necessary for public meetings in certain places. With regard to public processions, it appears that these are to be regarded normally as lawful, although there are circumstances in which they may become tinged with illegality. Public processions often make use of the highway, and it is lawful to make a reasonable use of the highway by passing along it. If, however, the use of the highway is unreasonable as, for example, where the highway is obstructed for a considerable time by the procession, the crime of public nuisance may be committed. Another circumstance in which a public meeting may become unlawful is where it is held contrary to that section of the Public Order Act 1936 which entitles a Chief Officer of Police to ban it from a certain area, or to lay down the route it must follow. A public meeting may turn into a rout or a riot. These offences are discussed on p. 141.

FREEDOM OF RELIGION

In former times there were numerous restrictions placed on those who practised religions other than that favoured by the state. Nearly all of these have been swept away. For example an Act of 1974 declared that the office of Lord Chancellor is tenable by an adherent of the Roman Catholic faith. Despite the fact that the state now refrains from interfering with those whose religion it does not accept, it is nevertheless bound to give special preference to the Church of England, since that is the church established by law, and of which the Queen must be a member. Schools owned by local authorities are legally bound to begin the day with divine worship, and must give religious instruction. This instruction is in essence Protestant, and is calculated not to offend Protestant bodies outside the Church of England. Parents who do not wish their children to attend the instruction offered may withdraw their children from these lessons.

RACE RELATIONS

Neither the common law nor any statute discriminates against anyone on account of his race, and unlike some countries we have no rules about miscegenation (*i.e.*, mixture of races in marriage or otherwise). Equally it is not a valid excuse in law to refrain from carrying out a duty owed to the public, because of the race of the particular individual involved. Thus by the Hotel Proprietors Act 1956, and prior legislation, it is not lawful for any hotel proprietor who comes within the ambit of the Act to withhold accommodation, food or drink from anybody except for a limited number of reasons, *e.g.*, if the person concerned has no money or is drunk.

In the case of *Constantine* v. *Imperial Hotels Ltd.* (1944) a famous Trinidadian cricketer, Sir Leary Constantine, was refused accommodation at the Imperial Hotel in central London because of his race, and since race was not mentioned in the appropriate legislation as a reason entitling the hotel keeper to refuse admission, Constantine was awarded damages.

The common law grew up mainly during the period after problems of race that caused friction between Saxons and Normans, had subsided, and before the modern problems came into view. This being so, no requirement was ever introduced into the law of contract requiring people to contract with others whom they disliked for reasons of race, politics, hairstyle or anything else. In modern times this situation has caused difficulties, and the Race Relations Acts 1965 and 1968 make it unlawful for persons to be discriminated against on the grounds of colour, race, or ethnic or national origins in respect of the provision of various goods, facilities and services. The Community Relations Commission which was set up by the 1968 Act has a duty to encourage harmonious community relations. It is a criminal offence to stir up hatred against any section of the public distinguished by colour, race, or ethnic or national origins by publishing written matter, or using words in a public place that are threatening, abusive or insulting.

THE RIGHT TO VOTE

The rule is that anybody who is on the register of Parliamentary electors may vote for a member of Parliament. To qualify for inclusion in the register one must be British, eighteen years of age or more, resident in a constituency on a qualifying date, and not subject to any disability such as being a peer, or serving a long sentence of imprisonment.

THE PROTECTION OF LIBERTIES BY THE COURTS

If personal freedom is in danger, or indeed, if it has actually been infringed, the citizen will turn to the courts. There is no court specially charged with the protection of freedom, but in practice the court best able to help is the High Court. It was the common law courts that developed the writ of *Habeas Corpus* and today the writ is administered by the High Court. If a person suffers false imprisonment or malicious prosecution, he may sue for damages in a civil court, while if a victim of an assault or battery, he may himself institute criminal proceedings.

In defence of property interests the courts have available such remedies as the injunction. Freedom of speech is not a right the courts are often called on to support by positive action, and most cases, such as actions for defamation are concerned with whether or not the limits of freedom of speech have been overstepped. Censorship of films and broadcasts comes within the purview of the courts hardly at all, but they are concerned to a considerable degree, from time to time with censorship of printed words and pictures. There is very little interference with freedom of religion, but the courts may convict for the crime of sacrilege, which consists of breaking, entering and committing an arrestable offence in any place of divine worship. As far as freedom of movement is concerned the courts are not able to interfere with the granting or withholding of passports, and the right to hold processions is usually a matter for litigation only after a march has been made.

As will be seen, the protection of liberties by the courts is not a special function, or the work of a particular tribunal, but is carried out as the necessity arises in the course of the courts' ordinary work. There is, however a specialised type of tribunal that should be noted. This is the Election Court. If there is a dispute about the outcome of an election, anybody entitled to vote or anybody who claims he was a candidate or was entitled to be elected may start proceedings by presenting an election petition. Election petitions are heard by an election court consisting of two judges of the Queen's Bench Division. They normally sit in the constituency of the disputed election, and have the powers of the High Court. According to the circumstances, they may hold the election to be valid, declare that the runner-up has been elected, or just declare the election to be void, in which case there will be a new election.

Chapter 10

Criminal Law

TYPES OF CRIME

A crime is an offence against the community. Since the Queen is regarded as representing the community all criminal proceedings are initiated in her name. The purpose behind a trial in a criminal court is to discover whether or not an accused person has committed a crime, and if he has, to inflict punishment. There are various reasons for the imposition of punishment; firstly to prevent crime by imprisoning the offender and deterring others; secondly to avenge the wrongful act of the criminal; and thirdly to reform the criminal.

Crimes may be divided into two main groups; indictable offences, and summary offences. Ordinarily, indictable offences are tried by a judge and jury after a written accusation of crime (called an indictment) has been read out to the accused, while summary offences are tried by magistrates sitting without a jury. Indictable offences consist of more serious crimes than summary offences, and they are tried by a judge and jury, because in this type of trial, more time is available and the court has power to award heavy punishment if necessary. Summary offences are committed more often than indictable offences, but are less grave. In most instances it is possible to deal with them quickly as the facts are usually straightforward and few points of law arise.

The maximum sentence that can be imposed by a magistrates' court for any one offence is six months imprisonment and a fine. The position as to which type of court shall try a particular offence is rather complicated, since there are some offences which may be tried either on indictment or by magistrates. For example a person accused of a summary offence carrying a maximum sentence exceeding three months can generally demand a trial on indictment if he prefers this, while there are some indictable offences which may be dealt with by magistrates if the accused agrees. The freedom of choice available in certain instances may have a bearing on the outcome of the trial.

Indictable Offences

Indictable offences were for centuries divided into three categories: treason, felony, and misdemeanour. Treason is the gravest of crimes, and involves disloyalty to the Queen.

Felony and misdemeanour in former days represented a division into more serious and less serious crimes, but in more recent times the classification became almost meaningless because many misdemeanours created were more serious than certain felonies. The distinction was abolished by the Criminal Law Act 1967, as a result of which both types of crime may now be called "offences".

Historical Development

The old law was extremely harsh and at one time imposed the death penalty for stealing unless the thing stolen was worth less than 40 shillings. This harshness was mitigated mainly by the existence of a strange innovation known as "benefit of clergy" which arose in the following way. After the Norman Conquest ecclesiastical courts were set up under the control of bishops to deal with religious affairs. One of the functions of ecclesiastical courts was to try clergymen accused of crimes, and the sentences meted out by ecclesiastical courts were less severe than those imposed by common law courts. It came about that if a person was found guilty in a common law court of a crime punishable by death, and could prove that he was a clergyman, he could claim exemption, and the common law court had power only to send him to prison for a year, besides having him branded on the thumb to prevent him from claiming the privilege more than once. A man proved he was a clergyman by showing that he could read, because in times past most educated men were priests or "clerks in holy orders" as they were also called. It became the custom to test a man who was claiming benefit of clergy by getting him to read out the first verse of the fifty-first psalm: "Have mercy upon me, O God, according to thy loving kindness; according unto the multitude of they tender mercies blot out my transgressions". This procedure was seized upon by the common law courts as a method of avoiding the necessity of sentencing men to death for comparatively minor offences, and any man who could read out the verse was saved from hanging. The verse became known as "the neck verse", and those who could not read, learnt it by heart since their lives depended on it.

It was not until the seventeenth century that benefit of clergy was made available to all women, but there was another rule of law that benefited wives until its abolition in 1925. If a wife committed any felony except murder, in the presence of her husband, it was presumed that she had done so because she had been coerced by him into committing the crime, and this would be a defence. The result was, in some cases that even if a couple were convicted of an offence carrying the death penalty, both might be able to escape with their lives; he by benefit of clergy, and she because the court presumed her husband had forced her into the crime. Benefit of clergy has been dealt with at some length, not only to show the background to modern criminal law, but also as an example of the "legal fiction", which is a primitive way of changing the law or avoiding its more severe provisions. Also, many lives were saved by juries who returned verdicts stating that valuable objects and large sums of money were worth only 39 shillings.

Under the Criminal Law Act 1967 crimes are now divided into "arrestable offences" and other offences, to which no special name is attached. An "arrestable offence" is one carrying a sentence of five years imprisonment or more and anybody may make an arrest without warrant in respect of an arrestable offence in the circumstances set out on p. 108.

The new situation, therefore is that crimes may be divided into indictable offences and summary offences, while indictable offences may further be divided into treason, arrestable offences, and other indictable offences.

LIABILITY FOR CRIMES

The ordinary rule of the common law is that a person accused of having committed a crime is presumed innocent until proved by the prosecution in a court of law to be guilty. The duty of proving something in a court of law is known as the "burden of proof", and in criminal cases the burden of proof placed on the prosecution is a particularly heavy one. The rule is that the guilt of the accused must be established to the satisfaction of the court "beyond a reasonable doubt". If all the prosecution can do is to make the court think that the defendant is possibly guilty, or even probably guilty, that is not enough.

In nearly all crimes two main facts must be proved regarding the behaviour of the accused. It must be shown that the accused was guilty of *actus reus* (a wrongful act) and that he had *mens rea* (a guilty mind). If only one of these elements is shown to have been present at the time of the incident in question, no crime will have been proved. In a few exceptional cases it is not necessary for the prosecution to establish the presence of *mens rea*: all that need be shown is the *actus reus*. For example the Licensing Act 1964, s. 172, forbids the sale of liquor by a publican to a drunken person, and a publican can be found guilty even if he has no *mens rea*, that is to say even if he believed the purchaser to be sober. The duty of deciding whether the customer is drunk or sober is put upon the publican. These are examples of what are called "crimes of strict liability".

Exemptions from Liability

Coercion

If a person can show that at the time he committed a crime he was acting under physical coercion, he will escape liability. Thus if Alice has a carving knife in her hand and Jack seizes her hand and forces her to stab somebody, Alice will not be liable. Under the

Criminal Justice Act 1925 s. 47 it is a defence for a wife to prove that she committed a crime in the presence of her husband and under his coercion; this rule replaces the old presumption of coercion by a husband mentioned above.

Necessity

This is a defence that is available in certain circumstances. For example if Jack is the captain of a ship which is sinking and there is only one seaworthy lifeboat, and he orders the women and children into it, the result may be that the men will drown. If he is prosecuted for what he has done, Jack will have the defence of necessity. The situation is different where a person inflicts harm on another person to save himself. Thus in *R. v. Dudley and Stephens* (1884) two shipwrecked sailors and a cabin boy were in a small boat for nearly three weeks with very little food. The sailors killed and ate the cabin boy, and were later picked up. Their defence of necessity was rejected and they were convicted of murder although they were not executed.

Mistake

A mistake of law is no defence, since everyone is presumed to know the law. Sometimes a mistake of fact will be a defence. For example it is a defence to a charge of stealing if the accused can show he believed in good faith that he had a right to what he took.

Accident

A person cannot be convicted of an offence as the result of something that happens which is either beyond his control or is the unexpected consequence of some lawful act, *e.g.*, if a footballer lawfully charges another in the course of a match and the other accidentally suffers serious injury.

Automatism

It is a defence to an accusation of crime to show that the accused's actions were not controlled by his mind, as for example where he was sleepwalking.

Infancy

The Children and Young Persons Act 1963, provides that a child under the age of ten years shall be incapable of committing any crime. There is, in addition, a common law rule that a child between the ages of ten and fourteen years is to be presumed incapable of committing a crime, but that evidence may be put forward to show that he knew the act he did was morally wrong. In such a case the presumption is rebutted and he can be convicted. The Children and Young Persons Act 1969, the provisions of which are being introduced gradually, empowers courts to make a "care order" or a "supervision order," under which a local authority is given responsibility for the child or young person.

Drunkenness

If a person is affected by drink only to such an extent that he is more ready than usual to commit a crime, then drunkenness will afford him no defence. There are, however two situations in which drunkenness will affect criminal liability. First, if the effect of drink has been to cause insanity, the M'Naghten rules (below) will be brought into play. Secondly, in crimes where it must be proved that the accused had some particular intention, it will be a defence if it can be shown that the accused was too drunk to form that intention.

Insanity

In 1843 Edward Drummond the private secretary to Sir Robert Peel was murdered by Daniel M'Naghten who mistook Drummond for the Prime Minister. Following the case the judges were asked for their advice on the law relating to insanity in criminal cases, and as a result they formulated what are usually called the M'Naghten Rules. The law at present may be stated briefly in these propositions. First, everyone is presumed to be sane unless proved to be insane, so that it is for defendant to show he was insane at the relevant moment. Secondly, to prove insanity under the M'Naghten Rules it must be shown that at the time of the crime the defendant had a diseased mind giving rise to a defect of reason so that either he did not know the nature and quality of his act, or he did not know that he was doing wrong. If a person is found to be insane under the provisions of the rules, the Criminal Procedure (Insanity) Act 1964 lays down that a special verdict of "not guilty by reason of insanity" is to be returned, and the court is to order the accused to be admitted to a hospital specified by the Secretary of State. It is possible to appeal against such a verdict. In practice insanity is pleaded only in murder cases because a successful plea results in the detention in hospital of the accused for an indefinite period.

Diminished Responsibility

This defence, which was introduced by the Homicide Act 1957, s. 2, is applicable only in murder cases and the effect of raising the defence successfully is to allow the court to convict of manslaughter (see p. 134) instead of murder, and thus impose a lighter sentence. To prove diminished responsibility is better for an accused person than to prove insanity, since a finding of insanity might result in the accused being confined in a mental hospital for life. The defendant must show that he is entitled to succeed by virtue of the defence of diminished responsibility. To do this he must show that at the time of killing another he was suffering from such an abnormality of the mind that his mental responsibility for the killing was substantially impaired. The abnormality of mind may arise from retarded development of the mind, disease, or injury. The fact that the defendant acted in great anger will not be enough. The defendant need not establish this defence beyond a reasonable doubt: it is enough if he establishes it upon a balance of probabilities.

Corporations

In general, corporations (which, as we have seen, are artificial persons) may be convicted for crimes in the same way as natural persons. There are nevertheless some crimes such as bigamy which a corporation could not commit. The present position was arrived at somewhat hesitatingly by the courts after a series of decisions. The main difficulty in the way of deciding that a corporation could be guilty of crime was the requirement that *mens rea* must usually be proved. How, it was asked, could an artificial person without any mind, be said to have *mens rea* (a guilty mind)? The difficulty was first overcome in cases of vicarious liability (situations where one person may be made responsible for the wrong of another) where it was not necessary to show that the person on whom responsibility is thrown, had any *mens rea*. After this the courts made corporations liable directly and successful prosecutions have been brought against corporations for conspiracy and purchase tax offences.

PARTICIPANTS IN A CRIME

Principals

A person who actually commits a crime is called a principal and he renders himself liable to prosecution. In addition to principals there are certain other categories of person who may become involved in a crime to such an extent so as to put themselves in danger of prosecution. The circumstances in which this may come about are discussed below.

Vicarious Liability

There are some cases in which a person may be held guilty of a crime as a result of authorising another to commit it. In addition there are certain offences, such as public nuisance, in respect of which a master will be held liable for the crime of his servant even if he actually forbade the commission of the crime. Liability is imposed on masters in these cases because they are often in a position to prevent their servants from committing the offence in question, and they should, in their own interests, see that the law is observed.

Conspiracy

The common law offence of conspiracy has in almost all instances been replaced by the statutory offence of conspiracy which was created by the Criminal Law Act 1977, ss. 1–5. Under the Act if two or more persons *agree* to pursue a course of conduct which will necessarily involve the commission of an offence by one or more of them, they are guilty of conspiracy to commit that offence. It does not matter whether the unlawful act is carried out, as the crime of conspiracy is committed as soon as the unlawful agreement is reached. The old common law rule that a husband and wife are to be regarded as one person operates in connection with this crime and prevents a married couple on their own from being capable of conspiracy. It would be possible on the other hand for a married couple and a third person to commit conspiracy together.

Incitement to Commit a Crime

It is an offence at common law to incite another to commit an offence, and a person may be convicted of incitement whether or not the suggested crime was actually committed. Incitement may be committed in various ways, *e.g.* by publishing an article, or by making a rabble-rousing speech.

ATTEMPTS TO COMMIT CRIMES

To attempt to commit a crime is in itself a crime. A distinction has to be drawn between the preparations for committing a crime and the attempt to commit it. It is not always easy to be sure whether what was done amounts to mere preparation or constitutes an actual attempt at crime, since circumstances vary so much from one case to another. To amount to an attempt the act must be a step towards the commission of the crime and must be closely connected with it. For example if a man buys a hammer intending to hit somebody with it, this is only a preparation for the crime, but if he raises it to strike the other and is prevented from delivering the blow, this is an attempt. An example of a case where the acts of the accused were held to amount only to preparations is *R.* v. *Robinson* (1915). A jeweller at Oldham insured his stock for £1,200 and faked a burglary. He opened the safe door and hid the jewellery in a recess at the back of the safe where the police found it on making a search that was instituted because they disbelieved his story. He was convicted at Manchester Assizes of having attempted to obtain money by false pretences, but the Court of Criminal Appeal held that since he never got as far as applying to the insurance company for the money, all he had done was to prepare for the crime, so that he was not guilty of an attempt. In *Director of Public Prosecution* v. *Stonehouse* (1977) an M.P. in financial trouble insured his life in favour of his wife, faked his death by drowning in Florida and set off under another name to start a new life with his mistress, but he was found in Australia, extradited and found guilty of an attempt to enable his wife to obtain £25,000 due on his death from his insurance company. His wife was innocent and believed him to be dead. Stonehouse was held guilty because what he had done would cause the media to inform his wife and the insurance company of his death and cause payment to be made.

OFFENCES AGAINST THE PERSON

Homicide

Homicide is the killing of one human being by another. It may be lawful or unlawful. The following are examples of lawful homicide.

(i) *The carrying out of a sentence of death.*—Judgment of death by hanging can be pronounced only for treason, certain types of piracy and setting fire to the Queen's ships or arsenals. No sentence of death may be passed upon a person who was under the age of eighteen at the time of the offence, or upon an expectant mother.

(ii) *Self-defence.*—If a person's life is in danger from attack by another, he may kill the other to save himself, but only in most exceptional cases. He must try to save himself by other means if he can, and must retreat as far as possible before killing his attacker. In the case of a man being attacked in his own house however, no retreat is necessary.

In *R.* v. *Hussey* (1924) Israel Hussey rented a room at Brixton in London from a Mrs. West and a month later she gave him an invalid notice to quit. He refused to go and Mrs. West accompanied by a Mrs. Gould, and a man named Crook tried to force open the door of the room in which Hussey had barricaded himself. They were using a hammer, a spanner, a poker and a chisel and managed to break a panel of the door. Hussey then fired a gun through the opening, wounding Mrs. Gould and Crook. He was convicted at the Old Bailey (another name for the Central Criminal Court) of unlawful wounding and sentenced to twelve months imprisonment. On appeal to the Court of Criminal Appeal the Lord Chief Justice, Lord Hewart delivered judgment quashing the conviction. He quoted with approval the following passage from *Archbold*, an authoritative work on criminal law.

> "In defence of a man's house, the owner or his family may kill a trespasser who would forcibly dispossess him of it, in the same manner as he might, by law, kill in self-defence a man who attacks him personally with this distinction, however, that in defending his home he need not retreat, as in other cases of self-defence, for that would be giving up his house to his adversary."

(iii) *A homicide committed to prevent a murder.*—This may be lawful. For example in *R. v. Rose* (1884) a man shot and killed his father who was threatening to murder his mother and who had forced her against the balusters of a staircase, saying that he would cut her throat. In fact, although the son could not see this, the father had no knife in his hand. It was held that the homicide was lawful since the prisoner acted without vindictive feeling towards his father and he believed his mother's life was in immediate danger.

(iv) *Unexpected death.*—If a death is caused unexpectedly in the course of a lawful game that is being played in a lawful manner, the homicide may not amount to a crime. If a player is killed during a rough game of football in such circumstances that nobody would foresee the death there will be no criminal liability, but if the death is caused by a player who knows that his actions may cause serious injury and who acts recklessly, this will be manslaughter.

Murder

The classical definition of murder is as follows: "unlawfully killing a reasonable creature, who is in being and under the Queen's peace, with malice aforethought either express or implied, the death following within a year and a day". It is necessary to explain what is meant by various phrases in the definition since the language is ancient and some expressions have changed in meaning over the centuries.

"*Unlawfully*".—This distinguishes murder from lawful homicide.

"*Killing*".—This may involve not only an immediate slaying but also an indirect killing, as in *R.* v. *Holland* (1841). In this case the prisoner (as those being tried for felony were called) attacked the deceased and injured his finger. The surgeon of the deceased urged him to have the finger amputated, but he refused and within a fortnight lockjaw set in and this led to his death. The prisoner was found guilty of murder since the wound he inflicted was in the end the cause of death. Some writers have cast doubt on whether this decision would be followed today.

"*A reasonable creature*".—This means any human being not merely a human being who is sane.

"*In being*".—This means that the person murdered must have been born. An unborn person cannot be the subject of a murder charge.

"*Under the Queen's peace*".—In Anglo-Saxon times the King's peace was at most times limited to certain places such as the King's highway and the royal residence, and it was not until after the Norman conquest that the King's peace extended permanently throughout the country. An offence against the King's peace was more serious than other offences, since it made the offender an enemy of the King. At the present day everybody in the country is under the Queen's peace. The only exception would be in the case of British rebels and foreign enemies actually conducting hostile operations.

"*Malice aforethought*".—This phrase has been so widely interpreted by the courts that in practice, we can now say it is murder to kill another even without any malice in the usual meaning of that word, and even without planning the murder beforehand. There is malice aforethought if the accused intends to kill, but there will be implied malice aforethought if the accused intends to do grievous bodily harm or some act likely to cause death or grievous bodily harm.

"*A year and a day*".—This phrase means that if a person is wounded and dies on the anniversary of the attack, the crime will still amount to murder, but that if death follows at any later date the offence will not be murder. The rule was settled in former days when medical science was less able to determine whether or not death was to be attributed to an old wound.

Defences

Among the defences that may be raised to a charge of murder are insanity (see p. 126), diminished responsibility (see p. 127), and provocation. If the defence of insanity is established, the defendant will be found not guilty by reason of insanity and sent to a mental hospital, while a successful defence of diminished responsibility will result in a conviction for manslaughter. The Homicide Act 1957, s. 3, provides that where provocation is pleaded as a defence to murder, the jury must take into account everything said and done at the time of the killing, in order to decide whether or not a reasonable man would have lost his self control and acted like the accused. Only if the jury feel the provocation was sufficient, will the defence succeed. The effect of a successful plea of provocation is to allow a conviction for manslaughter instead of murder.

Penalties

For some centuries prior to 1957 the only penalty prescribed by the law for murder was death. The Homicide Act 1957 replaced the sentence of death by a sentence of life imprisonment for all except a few types of murder, and the Murder (Abolition of Death Penalty) Act 1965 originally abolished the sentence of death for murder altogether for a period extending until 31st July, 1970. It was made a permanent statute by resolutions of both Houses of Parliament passed in accordance with the terms of the Act in December 1969. This Act abolishes the death penalty in England, Wales and Scotland, but in Northern Ireland it is still possible for a court to impose the death penalty for murder. The usual rule that an English court has jurisdiction only over crimes committed in this country does not apply to murder or manslaughter, and a United Kingdom citizen can be tried here if he is accused of committing either of these crimes on land anywhere in the world. It should be noted in passing, with reference to Chapter 14 that a person found guilty of murder or manslaughter will not be entitled to inherit property from the murdered person even when it is left to him under a will.

Manslaughter

Manslaughter is the unlawful killing of another person without malice aforethought. There are two types of manslaughter: voluntary and involuntary manslaughter. Voluntary manslaughter is committed when a person kills another in such circumstances that he would have been guilty of murder, but for some particular circumstances. The most important types of voluntary manslaughter are killings committed by an accused while either suffering from diminished responsibility or acting under provocation.

Involuntary manslaughter is not connected with murder and may be committed in the following circumstances: (i) by causing death through an unlawful act of a kind that is likely to cause harm, but not grievous bodily harm or death, as in *R.* v. *Wild* (1837) where a guest who refused to depart was given a kick that resulted in his death. This was held to be manslaughter; (ii) by failure to perform a duty recognised by the law, *e.g.* where a child dies because of the neglect of its parents; (iii) by criminal negligence. This is a degree of negligence that greatly exceeds what is sufficient to prove negligence in the law of tort, and is equivalent to recklessness; *e.g.*, causing death by reckless driving. The maximum penalty that can be imposed for manslaughter is life imprisonment, but because circumstances vary so much in practice, widely differing sentences including fines are imposed.

Suicide

At common law it was a crime to commit or to attempt to commit suicide, but since the Suicide Act 1961 neither suicide nor attempted suicide is an offence. The Act lays down that to advise or to help another to commit suicide is a crime punishable by up to fourteen years imprisonment.

Battery and Assault

A battery is the use of unlawful force against another person. An assault is committed when a person behaves in such a way as to cause another to expect that force is about to be used against him. In most instances an assault and a battery are committed in the course of the same incident, but in law the two are separate. To advance menacingly on another brandishing a sword is to commit an assault even though the sword misses its mark, while a blow from behind without warning is a battery though not an assault. Because the two varieties of offence are usually committed together it has become common for people to lump them together under the name of "assault". There are various defences which may be raised in answer to a prosecution for assault or battery. For instance it is a defence for an accused to show that he was using reasonable force to protect his family or his home, or that he was assisting the police in arresting a criminal and used only moderate force for that purpose. Parents and schoolteachers in answer to a charge of assault or battery may avail themselves of the defence that they were administering reasonable chastisement to a child.

Much of the law relating to physical violence is contained in the Offences Against the Person Act 1861, which sets out various types of offence and prescribes appropriate maximum penalties. Some of these offences are mentioned below.

Common Assault

An assault and battery of a trivial kind is called a "common assault". It is an offence at common law as well as being covered by the Act. If proceedings are instituted under s. 42 of the Act, the accused must be tried by a magistrates' court and the maximum penalty is two months imprisonment or a fine. If, on the other hand the proceedings are instituted for common assault the offence is triable on indictment and is punishable under s. 47 by twelve months imprisonment. Proceedings under s. 42 are the subject of an unusual rule. They may be commenced only by the person assaulted and not by the police. The reason is that anybody tried under s. 42 and found guilty or not guilty is entitled to ask the justices for a certificate of conviction or a certificate of dismissal. This certificate exempts the person tried from all future civil proceedings as well as from all future criminal proceedings for the same cause. The Act thus reserves to the person assaulted, the decision as to whether or not he should forgo his right to sue in tort for trespass to the person in order to recover a sum of money from the person accused. The correct decision to make will depend on the circumstances. If the victim commences proceedings for common assault because the accused knocked off his hat with a stick in the course of an argument, then he will have little to lose by letting his right to an action in tort be extinguished, but if he commences proceedings for a body blow and hastily institutes a prosecution under s. 42, he may regret this, since the blow may in a few months give rise to complications for which hundreds of pounds could be recovered in a tort action were it not for the justices' certificate.

Grievous Bodily Harm

Under s. 18 of the Offences Against the Person Act 1861 it is a crime punishable by imprisonment for life to wound or cause grievous bodily harm to anybody. To constitute a wound the skin must be broken—a bruise will not suffice. In order to secure a conviction the prosecution must show that the act was committed with an intent to maim, disfigure, disable, cause grievous bodily harm or resist lawful arrest. To maim means to injure a man's body so that he is less able to fight; to disfigure is to impair personal appearance; to disable is to cause a permanent disability and grievous bodily harm is an injury that interferes seriously with normal health or comfort, even temporarily.

A less serious offence carrying a maximum of five years imprisonment is proscribed by s. 20 which makes it a crime to wound or inflict grievous bodily harm unlawfully. It is easier to secure a conviction under s. 20 than under s. 18 because under s. 20 it is not necessary to prove that the harm was inflicted with any particular intent. Another difference between s. 18 and s. 20 is that offences not coming within the definition of an assault or a battery and which therefore do not come within s. 18, are caught by s. 20. For example in *R.* v. *Martin* (1881) the defendant obstructed the only exit to a theatre, turned out the lights and shouted "fire", thus causing a panic in the course of which a number of people were injured. He was convicted under s. 20, despite the fact that he had committed neither an assault nor a battery to any of the injured. There are also many other offences dealt with in the Act.

Bigamy

Bigamy is committed when a married person goes through a ceremony of marriage with a third party while the original marriage is still subsisting. The offence is punishable with a maximum of seven years imprisonment under the Offences Against the Person Act 1861 s. 57. The prosecution must show that the original marriage mentioned in the indictment was both validly contracted and subsisting at the date of the later ceremony. If the prosecution fails to establish either of these facts, the accused must be found not guilty. An illustration is afforded by *R.* v. *Willshire* (1881). The prisoner was indicted for bigamy in 1881, the charge being that he bigamously married Edith Miller in 1880 while his wife, Charlotte was still alive (there being no question of any divorce). By way of defence, Willshire produced a certificate proving that he had already been convicted of bigamy for marrying Ada Leslie during the lifetime of his wife Ellen. This certificate proved that the prisoner's real wife was Ellen. The previous conviction took place in 1868 and the Court for Crown Cases Reserved (which was a criminal appeal court that was abolished in 1907 and replaced by the Court of Appeal (Civil Division)) took the view that Ellen must be presumed to have been alive in 1879 at the date Willshire went through a marriage ceremony with Charlotte, since there was nothing to show that Ellen was dead by then. It followed from this that the "marriage" to Charlotte, on which the prosecution relied in the indictment was invalid, so that one of the facts mentioned above, that must be established by the prosecution, had not been established. Willshire had not "married Edith Miller while his wife Charlotte was still alive", because Charlotte had never been his wife. He was therefore found not guilty.

It is a defence to a charge of bigamy, under s. 57 for an accused person to show that at the date of the purported marriage his or her spouse had been continuously absent for seven years and had not been known by him or her to be living during that time. If the missing spouse comes back unexpectedly, then although the partner who has been through a ceremony of marriage, will be exempt from a prosecution for bigamy, the "marriage" will be a nullity. It was decided in *R.* v. *Tolson* (1889) that it is also a defence to a charge of bigamy for an accused person to prove that at the time of going through the ceremony in question he or she reasonably believed his or her spouse to be dead. The facts were that Martha Tolson was deserted by her husband in 1881 and that she was later told by her husband's elder brother that her husband had been lost on a ship bound for America which had gone down with all hands. She re-married in January 1887 (before the statutory period laid down in s. 57 was up) and in December 1887 Tolson came back. The Court for Crown Cases Reserved held that she was not guilty because she had not the *mens rea* requisite to constitute the crime.

Bigamy is another of the few crimes that may be the subject of a trial in England even if committed abroad by a United Kingdom citizen. It is frowned on by the law for various reasons; it upsets the social order, it undermines the sanctity of the marriage ceremony, and it may be a weapon of seduction. In connection with the last reason, a curious fact may be noted. If a convicted man has seduced the innocent party before going through the purported marriage ceremony, he may be rewarded with a lesser sentence, since it will be assumed that the lady concerned has suffered correspondingly less as a result of the fraudulent ceremony.

OFFENCES AGAINST PROPERTY

Theft

The law relating to theft is contained mainly in the Theft Act 1968 which was a reforming Act. It abolished a number of offences of dishonesty which had developed over the centuries in such a way as to make the law confusing and technical.

The Theft Act, s. 1, lays down that a person is guilty of *Theft* if he dishonestly appropriates property belonging to another with the intention of permanently depriving that other of it. The most important words are "dishonestly appropriates property". By s. 2 a person is not dishonest if he appropriates property, (i) in the belief that he has a right to it, or (ii) believing that he would have the owner's consent to take it if the owner knew, or (iii) if he believed the owner could not be found by taking reasonable steps.

By s. 3 any assumption of the rights of an owner amounts to an appropriation. By s. 4, property includes money and land. By s. 4(3), it is not theft to pick mushrooms, flowers, fruit or foliage growing wild upon another's land unless this is done for sale on a commercial purpose. Section 8 makes *Robbery* punishable by life imprisonment and lays down that a person is guilty of robbery if he steals, and immediately before or at the time of doing so, and in order to do so, he uses force on any person or puts or seeks to put any person in fear of being then and there subjected to force.

Section 9 of the Act refers to *Burglary*. It lays down that a person shall be guilty of burglary either if he (a) enters a building as a trespasser intending to inflict any grievous bodily harm, or to rape a woman or to damage the building, or (b) if having entered as a trespasser he steals or attempts to steal something, or inflicts or attempts to inflict any grievous bodily harm. Burglary can be committed at any time, and not, as under the old law, only at night.

Aggravated Burglary is, by s. 10, burglary committed by a burglar with a real or imitation firearm, any weapon of offence or explosive. Section 15 has a widely-drawn provision which makes it an offence to obtain property belonging to another with the intention of permanently depriving the other of it by any "deception", which may be by words or conduct.

Section 16 deals with cases where there has been a deception, not to obtain property, but dishonestly to obtain "pecuniary advantage". This includes evading debts, borrowing by overdraft or winning money by betting.

Section 21 makes Blackmail an offence. To constitute this crime there must be an "unwarranted demand with menaces" by a person who wishes to make a gain for himself or to cause loss to another.

Section 22 makes it an offence to handle stolen goods, which means dishonestly receiving them, or keeping, removing, or disposing of them, or realising them, knowing or believing them to have been stolen. Under s. 28 courts are given certain powers to order stolen goods to be restored to those entitled to them.

The maximum penalties laid down in the Act are as follows: theft, ten years; robbery, life imprisonment and burglary, fourteen years; aggravated burglary, life imprisonment; obtaining property by deception, ten years; obtaining pecuniary advantage by deception, five years; blackmail, fourteen years; and handling stolen goods, fourteen years.

CRIMES AGAINST THE PUBLIC INTEREST

Treason

This is an offence which consists of a breach of allegiance to the Crown, and by Statute of Treasons 1351, is committed by doing any of the following:

(a) compassing (plotting) the death of the King, the Queen, or their eldest son;
(b) violating the Queen, the King's eldest daughter unmarried, or the wife of his eldest son;
(c) levying war against the King in his realm;
(d) adhering to the King's enemies in his realm, giving them aid and comfort in the realm or elsewhere;
(e) slaying the Chancellor, Treasurer or the King's Justices being in their places doing their offices.

The only sentence that may be passed for treason is death. In modern times treason is committed usually only in time of war.

Unlawful Assembly

This is a common law offence punishable with a fine and imprisonment. It is committed when three or more people come together in a public or a private place to arrange for, or to commit a crime of violence, or to do something likely to lead to a breach of the peace.

Rout

This is another common law offence punishable by a fine and imprisonment. It is committed when the members of an unlawful assembly proceed together towards their unlawful objective.

Riot

As soon as an unlawful assembly begins to carry out its illegal purpose intending to use force if necessary, or actually using force, it becomes a riot, which is another common law offence punishable by a fine and imprisonment.

Affray

Affray is a common law offence which after a long period of disuse has been revived by the courts in recent years in the suppression of violence. To constitute an affray there must be (i) unlawful violence or an unlawful display of force (ii) in a public place or in a private place before at least one terrified innocent bystander and (iii) in such a way that a bystander of reasonably firm character might expect to be terrified. The House of Lords in *Button* v. *Director of Public Prosecution* (1966) rejected the argument that this offence need not be revived. It can be punished with a fine or a term of imprisonment in the court's discretion.

Public Mischief

In *R.* v. *Manley* (1933) a woman pretended to the police that she had been robbed, and thereby wasted their time. Adopting the wording of a previous case, the court held her guilty of public mischief, saying that "such acts or attempts as tend to the prejudice of the community, are indictable". This very wide proposition has been doubted by the Court of Criminal Appeal which suggested the creation of a new statutory offence to cover such cases as *Manley's*. This suggestion was taken up by the Criminal Law Revision Committee and the Criminal Law Act 1967, section 5(2) provides that where a person causes wasteful employment of the police by making a false report he shall be liable to a maximum of six months imprisonment and a fine of two hundred pounds.

Criminal Libel

There are two headings that fall within the description of criminal libel.

Private Libel

A private libel is committed when a publication is made in permanent form which tends to lower a person or class of people in the eyes of right thinking members of society. It is punishable by up to two years imprisonment. There are several differences between the tort of libel (see p.166) and the crime of private libel. For example, there cannot be an action in tort for a class libel, while there may be a prosecution. Publication to the victim alone is sufficient publication for the crime, but to constitute the tort, there must be publication to a third party. Although justification (see p. 169) is a complete defence in tort, it is only a defence to the crime if the publication of the truth was for the public benefit.

Public Libel

Public libels are of three kinds. These are first, sedition, which is using words to incite others to use unlawful means to bring about alterations to the constitution, the monarchy, or the government. It is a common law offence punishable with a fine and imprisonment. The second type of public libel is blasphemy, which is committed by denying Christianity in such a way as to provoke a breach of the peace. It is punishable with a fine or imprisonment. The third type is obscenity which is dealt with on p. 112.

Only a few crimes have been discussed in this chapter, but it should be borne in mind that there are a large number of other offences affecting all aspects of life. For example, it is an offence for a passenger to get drunk on an aircraft; a person can be convicted for broadcasting without a licence from the Post Office, for unlawful drilling, for making signals to smugglers, or for carrying off slaves. The list is endless and in practice everybody has to learn those aspects of the criminal law that affect his own way of life.

HOW A CRIMINAL CASE IS TRIED

In a Magistrates Court

There are two types of criminal proceedings that may take place before magistrates; first, the trial of a summary offence, and secondly preliminary proceedings that lead up to a trial in a higher court. We will consider first what happens at a summary trial.

Summary Trial

A trial is often preceded by a police investigation in the course of which a policeman may come to the conclusion that he has found evidence casting suspicion on somebody. If he then decides to question that person he must precede the questioning by a warning. This is laid down in certain rules drawn up by the judges in order to insure that suspected persons are fairly and justly treated. If these rules are not observed they may result in a judge or magistrate deciding that the evidence so obtained should not be used in court. The warning is called a caution and is as follows: "You are not obliged to say anything unless you wish to do so but what you say may be put into writing and given in evidence." After asking further questions the policeman may decide that the person being interrogated is guilty of the crime in question and that he should be prosecuted. At this stage the policeman must say that there may be a prosecution, and must give another caution thus: "Do you wish to say anything? You are not obliged to say anything unless you wish to do so but whatever you say will be taken down in writing and may be given in evidence". After this the police will start the case by the procedure of laying an information.

The information.—To lay an information means to go to a magistrate in court, or if necessary at the magistrate's home, and ask the magistrate to sign either a summons or a warrant. A summons orders the person named in it to attend court to be tried at the place and time named in the summons, and it is issued when there is no reason to fear that the person summoned will run away. A warrant is a direction to the police to arrest and bring before the magistrates a named person. A "general warrant" is illegal (see p. 108). Anybody can apply to a magistrate for a summons or a warrant. Private individuals sometimes apply in cases where the police refuse to take action on the ground that, in their opinion, there is insufficient evidence available against the person in question. Arrest and bail are dealt with in Chapter 9.

Court proceedings.—At the courthouse there may be two or three courts sitting simultaneously, and in most instances there is a list of cases showing the order in which they are to be heard and in which court. As each case is to be heard, an official (who may be a policeman) calls out the name of the accused who thereupon steps into the dock, which is a small railed-off area in the centre of the court with room to sit and stand, and with room for prison warders or policemen as well. Usually the accused will be in the dock alone, unless charged jointly with others. The accused is first asked whether he is the person named in the summons or warrant. The clerk to the magistrates then reads out the charge, that is to say the accusation of crime, and asks the accused if he pleads "guilty" or "not guilty". If the accused pleads not guilty, the prosecutor, who may be a member of the public or a policeman, or a solicitor or counsel, opens the case. This means that he outlines what his witnesses are going to say, and what this evidence will, if accepted, prove. He then calls the first witness. The witness enters the court and goes into the witness-box where he stands up (unless ill). He promises to tell the truth and is then asked questions by the prosecutor. The rules concerning the examination (questioning) of witnesses are similar to those in civil courts. When a person is answering questions put to him by the person who called him, this is termed "examination-in-chief". The advocate (person conducting a case) when examining in chief, only asks questions to which he knows (or thinks he knows) the answer. He usually has in front of him a "proof of evidence" or statement made previously by the witness, and from this he picks out those points which are important. It would waste too much time, and cause confusion, if all the witnesses were allowed to enter the witness box and ramble on as they wished. In examination-in-chief the advocate is not allowed to use "leading questions", that is, questions which suggest the answer. The advocate, who wishes the witness to tell the court for example, where he was, if this is important, must not say "were you in Red Lion Square on Friday?", since this suggests the answer. He must say instead, "Where were you on Friday?" He knows what the reply will be, but he should not prompt the witness.

After examination-in-chief has been concluded, "cross-examination" takes place. This is conducted by the opposing advocate, who has the right and duty to put further questions to the witness. If the opposing advocate does not cross-examine, he is taken to have admitted the truth of what was said. The idea of cross-examination is to test the truth of what has been said, to show up any inconsistencies, and to obtain evidence favourable to the other side. In cross-examination, leading questions may be put, and of course the advocate does not know what answer to expect, although, by experience he will often be able to make a shrewd guess. By careful cross-examination liars can be exposed, contradictions in a story made evident, hot-tempered persons made to display their true colours, and truths established. There is no fixed time limit, and witnesses do not have the option of keeping quiet. If in cross-examination, something is said by the witness that his own advocate considers must be cleared up, then re-examination may follow cross-examination, but this is unusual. When all prosecution witnesses have given evidence, the prosecution case closes.

If the advocate acting for the accused considers that the

prosecution evidence is very weak, he is entitled at once to suggest to the court (the magistrates) that there is no case against his client that need be answered. If the court agrees, the accused is found "not guilty" without having to defend himself. If the court does not agree, the case for the defence is opened and the defence witnesses are called and examined in the same way as the prosecution witnesses. The advocate acting for the accused may make a speech either before or after calling his witnesses. In the course of this speech each advocate will address the court on the law that he considers is applicable to the case. The magistrates, who in most cases are not lawyers will then consider whether or not to convict, and if a point of law has arisen, they will be guided by their clerk who is a lawyer. If the court decides to convict, then and only then, will any previous criminal record that the accused may have, be produced. The sentence will be influenced by the previous record. This is considered to be an aid to justice, whereas if a court knew of the previous bad record before deciding to convict it is thought that this would prejudice the court unfairly against the accused.

It should be mentioned that there is a set of strict rules, derived partly from the common law, and partly from statute, laying down what information may be put before a court and what may not. These are the rules of evidence and they are somewhat complicated, although all advocates must have them well in mind when conducting a case. For example, it is a rule that a witness may speak only of what he saw or heard himself, and not of what he has been told by other people: in other words "hearsay evidence" is not admissible. Another rule of evidence lays down that generally where an original document is available, the court must not look at a copy. The rules of evidence are intended to see that justice is done by excluding anything that might be misleading, or to prevent either side being unfairly treated due to prejudice arising from the use of unfair material not strictly relating to the case in hand. If an accused pleads "guilty", the court can proceed to sentence him.

Committal Proceedings

The second type of proceedings in a magistrates court called "committal proceedings" do not amount to a trial. The magistrates sit not as trial magistrates, but as "examining magistrates" and they have a special function to perform. Generally before anybody can be tried on indictment by the Crown Court he must be brought first before examining magistrates, so that they can hear the evidence against him and decide whether or not there exists a worthwhile case against him. If they decide that there is no reasonable case, then he is not tried at all, but if the magistrates decide there is such a case, the accused is sent for trial. The accused is not asked to plead guilty or not guilty, but apart from this the proceedings start off rather like those in a trial. All the witnesses for the prosecution give their evidence and are examined and cross-examined in the usual way. Their evidence is written down and signed by them. These signed records of evidence are called depositions. The accused is given the opportunity of giving evidence and calling witnesses, but he does not usually avail himself of it, preferring to wait until a possible trial before putting forward any defence. If the magistrates commit the accused for trial they send the depositions and other papers to the higher court where the clerk of indictments or other official draws up the indictment. A rarely-used alternative to committal proceedings is the voluntary bill of indictment, which is a procedure that allows a High Court judge to commit an accused person for trial after hearing in private the evidence which would normally be given to examining magistrates.

Trial in the Crown Court

In the case of a trial on indictment before the Crown Court the proceedings begin with the "arraignment" of the accused. He is put into the dock and called to the front of it (which is called the "bar"). The clerk reads out the indictment and asks "How say you, guilty or not guilty?". The accused then pleads. The accused is sometimes called "the prisoner at the bar". If the accused pleads not guilty a jury is sworn in, which means first, that twelve persons whose names are on a list of citizens liable for jury service are called forward one by one into the jury box. The accused has the right, seldom used, to "challenge" or object to any seven jurors he wishes without giving any reason. There are few woman jurors, and this right is sometimes used by an accused to secure an all male jury, if he feels that this will help him. If an accused wishes to challenge more than seven jurors, he must show a good cause. Any jurors successfully challenged are replaced by others. For this reason, there are always a number of persons standing by ready to take their places on a jury.

The case proceeds much as a trial before magistrates. In the Crown Court the advocates are usually counsel. Under the Criminal Procedure (Right of Reply) Act 1964, the defence advocate makes the last speech to the jury, which is considered to be an advantage. While in a magistrates' court the magistrates decide on the facts themselves and consult their clerk on the law, in a trial on indictment, the jury decide on the facts and the judge lays down the law.

After both sides have closed their cases the judge makes a speech to the jury, which is called the "summing up". In this speech he goes over the evidence that has been put forward by both sides, and tells the jury their duties. He will tell the jury the law, having made up his mind on this, with the help of the speeches by both advocates in which previous decisions and statutes may have been mentioned. He will stress that it is for the jury alone to decide who is to be believed, and will send them to the jury room to consider their verdict. When the jury have reached a verdict they return to the court and this verdict is announced. The rule was that a unanimous decision must be reached by the twelve jurors, and that there had to be a re-trial if the jury could not agree. In some recent cases it was thought that accused persons had been committing the crime of embracery—corrupting jurors, by getting one juror to refuse agreement. The Juries Act 1974, s. 17, makes it possible for a jury to return a verdict if only a majority agree. This Act permits a majority of 10–2 to suffice for a conviction or acquital, so that embracery has become more difficult. The judge discharges the accused if he is found not guilty, or decides on the sentence if he is guilty.

JUVENILE COURTS

In respect of children and young persons there are special arrangements for trial. Normally they must be tried by a juvenile court, which is a type of magistrates' court. Not more than three magistrates sit together, and ordinarily one of them should be a woman. The magistrates are chosen from a special list of those specially qualified. The court must be held in a separate building from the ordinary magistrates court, or at a different time, and entry to the court is restricted to those having business there. Newspaper reports of proceedings at juvenile courts have usually to omit the names of offenders.

COMPENSATION

Although generally it is the function of civil courts to award compensation to those who suffer injuries or damage, criminal courts have power in certain cases to order convicted persons to pay up to £1,000 compensation for losses they have caused.

The Criminal Injuries Board which was set up in 1964 without special legislation being passed, is a public body which awards sums of money to persons injured by crimes of violence, if upon application by the injured person, and investigation, it considers that a grant should be made. Awards have already been made in many cases, some of them running into thousands of pounds.

FACTS AND FIGURES ABOUT CRIME

Every year the Home Office prepares detailed statistics on many aspects of crime in England and Wales, and the following are a few of the more important facts that emerge. The figures are those for 1978.

The number of persons in England and Wales
    capable of committing a crime (*i.e.*, above the age
    of ten years). . . . . approx   40,000,000
The number of persons found guilty of offences of
    all kinds   2,464,000
The number who commited non-indictable offences
    (including non-indictable motoring offences) . . .   2,040,000
The number who committed non-indictable
    motoring offences.   1,112,492
The number who committed indictable offences . .   424,000

The most common types of non-motoring indictable offence

Theft and handling stolen goods 56%
Burglary 22%
Criminal Damage 12%

The number of cases heard in the various types of court

Magistrates courts

All the non-indictable cases   2,040,000
Indictable cases   367,096

Crown Courts

Indictable cases only.   56,966

Murder

Total number of persons found guilty of murder in
    1978   110
Murder by persons who committed suicide or died
    before they could be arrested or found insane.
    Total number   22

Chapter 11

The Law of Tort

The law of tort like the law of contract dealt with in the following chapter is a branch of the civil law. The purpose of the civil law is to protect the rights of every member of the community, and enforce the duties that correspond to those rights. An infringement of a right laid down by the civil law is called a civil wrong. There are two main classes of civil wrongs, those which arise solely from a breach of contract or from a breach of trust, which are not torts, and those which arise from the breach of some other civil law rule, which are torts. The duties laid down by the law of contract and the law of trusts may be stated very simply; they forbid any breach of contract or of trust. The duties laid down by the law of tort, on the other hand are much more numerous, because the law of tort protects people from a much greater variety of wrongful acts or omissions than either of the other two branches of the civil law. For example, the law of tort forbids others to trespass on a man's land, to take away his good name, to conspire against him or to lock him up without lawful authority. If any of these things happen, the person whose rights are infringed can obtain redress by invoking the law of torts.

THE TORT ACTION

Nature of a Tort

Although it is possible to describe the purpose for which the law of tort exists, it is less easy to define a tort. This difficulty arises because there is more than one way of looking at a given situation. For example, if I deliberately walk off with somebody else's hat, is this a tort or a crime? It is in fact both, being the tort of trespass to goods, and the offence of theft. If it is both, what, then is the difference between a tort and a crime? The difference obviously does not depend on what I did, because I did only one thing. The answer is that it depends on the point of view from which my act is regarded. Looking at my act from the point of view of the law of tort we ask: was this an infringement on my part of the rights of the hat owner?—it was and so this is a tort in respect of which I must make amends to the owner.

Looking at my act from the point of view of the criminal law, the question we ask is whether such behaviour is against the interests of the community at large—it is and so I have committed a crime for which the community has provided a punishment. A tort, then is wrongful behaviour looked at from the point of view of the individual affected by it, as distinguished from the point of view of the community.

As we have seen, some wrongful acts are both torts and crimes. Others, which are usually less serious, such as slander, are only torts, and there is a category of wrongful acts such as espionage that do not affect individuals and which are therefore crimes only. This is not quite the end of the matter, however, since there are numerous wrongful ways of behaving of which the law takes no notice. Such things as bigotry, meanness and avarice are left to be dealt with by religion, conscience and public opinion.

Proof of Damage

If a plaintiff is to succeed in a tort action he must prove three things; first, that the defendant has done something he should not have done, or has failed to do something that he should have done; secondly, that the defendant intended the act or omission, or was negligent (in the sense of not thinking about what he was doing), or was breaking some strict rule of law, and thirdly, in most cases that he suffered some loss. The details of what must be proved vary from tort to tort, and these details are considered below. If the plaintiff in a tort action is successful in convincing the court of the justice of his claim, the court will order the defendant either to pay the plaintiff a sum of money, or to refrain from interfering with the plaintiff. In most cases a plaintiff can obtain judgment for a sum of money (in legal terms "damages") that the defendant must pay him and him only if he has actually lost some money, or something worth money as a result of the wrong.

Some rights, on the other hand, are considered so important that the law will make a defendant pay for infringing them whether or not any loss has been caused to the plaintiff. The most important of these rights are those protected by the law of tort relating to trespass, and libel. In a case of this type the defendant will have to pay the plaintiff a small sum of money known as "nominal damages"—often the amount awarded is around two pounds. Torts in this category are said to be actionable without proof of damage, or "actionable *per se*" (by their very nature).

Court Proceedings

Actions in tort are of course civil actions, and will usually be commenced in a county court if a small sum is claimed or in the Queen's Bench Division of the High Court if a large sum is claimed. The plaintiff, who has suffered at the hands of the defendant must decide in respect of which tort to bring the action, and he must try to convince the court that the essential elements of this tort were present among the facts of the case. The essential elements of each tort are considered below. The defendant will answer the arguments of the plaintiff in two ways; first, he will try to show that the essentials of the tort were not present. He may fail in this, but he still has another card to play as he can then try to show that although all the essentials of the tort are present, he is exempted by the law from having to pay for the damage. He will do this by putting forward one or more of the recognised "defences", which are grounds of exemption recognised by the law. There are "general defences" which are available in respect of a number of torts and there are what may be called "particular defences", each of which relates to one tort only.

From what has been said above, it will be apparent that in considering whether or not a successful tort action can be brought, the following matters must be taken into account: (i) what are the essential elements of the tort; (ii) were these essential elements present among the facts of the particular case; (iii) are there any general defences that apply here; (iv) are there any particular defences that apply here. An example will illustrate how the system works. Let us suppose that Jack has on his land a machine that makes a noise, and that Alice who lives next door decides to sue Jack for the tort of private nuisance. She (or those acting on her behalf) must prove that the three essentials of the tort are present among the facts of the case. These are: (i) an indirect interference with the use of land; (ii) damage; (iii) unlawfulness. She will tell the court all the circumstances, and will argue that the three essentials have been proved, so that she is entitled to be awarded damages.

Jack (or those acting for him) will play his first card by arguing that the circumstances do not show that the essentials of the tort of private nuisance are present. He may say for example that the noise was small and that a small noise is not unlawful, so that the third essential is missing. He will then play his other card by setting up his defences. He may first set up the general defence of "consent" by proving that Alice had agreed to let him make the noise; then he may set up the particular defence that the nuisance has been going on without interruption for more than twenty years which the law presumes to create a right which might not otherwise exist. The court will have to decide whether or not the essentials of the tort were present, and then whether or not the defences prevail. The judge will deliver his judgment setting out exactly what he has decided are the facts and the law applying to the case. He will say whether or not there was any tort, and if there was one, whether or not the defendant is exempted by his defences from having to pay. Bearing in mind how defences are used, we will now consider the general defences.

1. *Consent*

This defence is also known as "assumption of risk", as well as having the latin name "*volenti non fit injuria*". If a person suffers harm after having consented to run the risk of this harm, he cannot subsequently succeed in a tort action for such harm; his consent will be raised against him as a general defence. In order that a defendant may succeed with a defence of consent, he must prove two things: (i) that the plaintiff knew there was a risk; (ii) that he agreed to run this risk at his own expense. In the case of *Smith* v. *Baker* (1891) a quarryman was injured when a heavy stone was dropped on him, and he sued his employers. They set up the general defence of consent, but although they were able to prove he knew of the risk, they could not prove that he agreed to run the risk at his own expense; therefore their defence failed, and they had to pay him damages (a sum of money). Similarly if I let my horse dash towards an old lady, and you are injured in rescuing her, I will not be able to raise a successful defence of consent, if you sue me for the tort of negligence (see p. 173). Although you knew of the risk, you acted under a moral duty, and not because you were willing to take the risk at your own expense. The famous rescue case where this was laid down was *Haynes* v. *Harwood* (1935) where a policeman was injured rescuing an old lady from the defendant's runaway horses and cart.

2. Inevitable Accident

An inevitable accident is one that is brought about by very unusual circumstances. There have been very few cases. The best known is *Stanley* v. *Powell* (1891) where the defendant accidentally shot the plaintiff. A pellet from the defendant's shotgun most unexpectedly bounced off a tree and hit the plaintiff.

3. Self-Defence

A person is allowed to use reasonable force to defend himself or another against attack. If an attacker sues for an injury received from the person he is attacking, the defence of self-defence will defeat his action. It is also permissible to use reasonable force to defend one's goods or land.

4. Necessity

This defence can be used where the defendant has inflicted a small harm on somebody in order to prevent some greater harm

from happening. For example in *Cope* v. *Sharp* (1912) a gamekeeper
went on to adjoining land and set fire to some heather to make a
firebreak and protect his master's nesting pheasants from an
approaching fire. The occupier of the adjoining land sued for
trespass to land but the defence of necessity prevailed. Here the
defendant was injuring another to save himself, but in *Leigh* v.
Gladstone (1909) the defence of necessity was successfully raised
when warders forcibly fed a suffragette prisoner who had gone on
hunger-strike, in order to prevent her from dying of starvation.

5. *Statutory Authority*

A statute may authorise something to be done which would
ordinarily be a tort. In this event the defence of statutory authority
will be available for use against any plaintiff who sues because he
has suffered damage from the act authorised by the statute.

6. *Remoteness of Damage*

If the damage suffered by the plaintiff is not sufficiently closely
connected with the behaviour of the defendant, the defendant will
not be liable to pay damages to the plaintiff. In such a case the
damage is said to be "too remote" a consequence of the
defendant's behaviour. Remoteness of damage is not regarded as
a defence, but if a defendant can establish its existence, he will
escape liability. An example of remoteness of damage is the case
of *Hobbs* v. *London and South Western Railway* (1875). Late one night a
porter put the plaintiff and his family on the wrong train so that
they had to walk home four miles in the rain. The wife of the
plaintiff caught cold and required medical attention. In an action
against the railway company it was held that although the walk
home was closely enough connected with the porter's negligence
to merit an award of damages, the wife's medical expenses were
too remote a consequence of the porter's act, and the railway
company was not liable to pay them. A defendant is liable only for
such consequences of his acts as a reasonable man would have
foreseen.

7. *Limitation of Actions*

There is a limited time within which a plaintiff must start his action. If he delays beyond this time he will not be able to sue at all. There are different lengths of time laid down by statute in respect of various circumstances. After the time has expired the claim is said to be "statute-barred". The Limitation Act 1939, as amended by the Limitation Act 1975, s. 1 lays down that actions in tort must be brought within six years from the date of the injury, except in cases of personal injury, where the action must be commenced within three years, although subsequent Acts allow exceptions to this. The Limitation Amendment Act 1980 s. 2 deprives a thief of his former protection from an action in conversion (see p. 177) after he has had the stolen goods for six years.

VICARIOUS LIABILITY

In certain instances the law makes one person liable for torts committed by another. This type of liability is called vicarious liability. The two most important examples of vicarious liability arise in connection with partners and servants. Partners (see p. 95) are vicariously liable for one another's torts if these are committed in the course of the partnership business, and masters are vicariously liable for torts committed by servants in the course of their employment. The position in relation to partners is easy to understand, but the law in regard to servants needs a little more explanation.

The law divides those who are in employment into two categories, that is to say, servants, and independent contractors. The general rule is that an employer is liable for torts committed by his servants in the course of their employment, but is not liable for torts committed by the independent contractors he employs. Not everybody agrees on how to distinguish a servant from an independent contractor, and there is no authoritative ruling on the point. The best test, however is whether or not the employer controls the actual carrying out of the work. If he does, then the employee will probably be a servant, but if he does not the employee is likely to be an independent contractor. The employer of a factory worker will very likely explain in detail to his employee what is to be done, and how to do it, so that the employee is to be regarded as a servant. On the other hand the factory owner who calls in a firm of accountants to audit his books will not tell them how to do their work, and they will be independent contractors. There are one or two exceptional cases where an employer will be liable for the torts of his independent contractor; *e.g.* where the latter creates a danger in the highway.

TRESPASS

Trespass to the Person

There are three types of trespass to the person, all of which are actionable *per se*. These are battery, assault, and false imprisonment.

Battery

A battery is the unlawful application of force to another person. It includes punching, hitting with a stick, shooting, squirting water, and pulling off clothing. An act will not be a battery unless its effect is immediately felt by the person attacked. For example, it would be a battery to throw a log at somebody, but it would not be a battery to put it on the path so that he falls over it.

A defendant to an action for battery can plead any of the following defences: (i) consent (as for example where the parties to the action had been taking part in a boxing match); (ii) inevitable accident as in *Stanley* v. *Powell* (see p. 155); (iii) self-defence; (iv) necessity. In addition he may plead any of the following particular defences, if the circumstances warrant it: (i) lawful chastisement of a child by a parent or teacher; (ii) that the battery was committed to uphold the criminal law, as for example where a citizen assists a policeman. The remedy granted by a court to a successful plaintiff in an action for battery is an award of damages against the defendant.

Assault

An assault does not involve bodily force. It is an act that leads a person to expect that he is going to suffer a battery. To constitute an assault there must be some movement. Words alone cannot make an assault, although they can unmake one. For example in *Tubervell* v. *Savage* (1669) a man reached for his sword saying "If it were not assize time, I'd run you through the body." As it was assize time there was no assault for the words took away the effect of the gesture. An assault and a battery often take place together, as where the victim sees a blow coming and then feels it. On the other hand an expected blow may not come so that there is an assault alone, while a blow from behind will be a battery alone. The defences to an action for assault are consent, self defence, and necessity. The remedy for assault is an action for damages.

False Imprisonment

False imprisonment means wrongful imprisonment and it is committed when a person is wrongly prevented from going wherever he wishes. This tort may be committed in a variety of ways. Some examples are: locking a person in a house; compelling him to remain in an open space by pointing a pistol at him; or forcing him by threats to walk along a road. If anybody is unlawfully arrested, this amounts to false imprisonment. Unless a person is completely prevented in all ways from leaving the place where he is, he will not be falsely imprisoned. If there is some way out, and he prefers not to take that way, he cannot be said to be imprisoned. The law on the point is not certain, but it seems that a man may be falsely imprisoned without knowing it; *e.g.*, if he is asleep, or drunk. The defences to an action for false imprisonment are: (i) consent; this could apply, for example, where a prisoner's solicitor agrees to be locked in a cell with his client; (ii) statutory authority. The remedies for false imprisonment are: (a) an application for a writ of *habeas corpus* (see p. 105); (b) an action for damages.

Trespass to Goods

This tort consists of an unlawful interference with goods that are in the possession of somebody else. The term "goods" includes among other things books, animals and ships. Trespass to goods is actionable *per se*, *i.e.*, without proof of damage. There are three sorts of conduct that amount to trespass to goods; they are: (i) taking goods away from the person in possession of them; (ii) damaging the goods without taking them away (*e.g.*, by throwing a stone), or (iii) meddling with the goods, as for example by moving them around.

The general rule is that the damage must be an immediate result of the act of the defendant. The defences to an action for trespass to goods are: (i) consent, which applies where the plaintiff agreed to having his goods used or moved; (ii) self-defence, which would apply if a person were being sued for having injured an animal that was attacking him; (iii) inevitable accident. This defence succeeded in *National Coal Board* v. *Evans* (1951) where the defendant's mechanical excavator damaged an underground cable that had been laid without permission, and of which the defendants knew nothing. The remedy for this tort is an action for damages.

Trespass to Land

Trespass to land is a direct interference with another person's possession of land (which includes houses, shops, gardens and paths). It is actionable *per se*. The three types of conduct that constitute this tort are: (i) entering on land without permission; (ii) remaining on land after permission to stay has expired; (iii) placing things on land without permission. It is necessary to examine each of these more closely.

Trespass by entry on land can be committed even if the defendant goes on land that he believes to be his own. The question that matters in law is: on whose land did he go, *not* on whose land did he think he was going? Of course if somebody walks on to another's land by mistake the occupier will normally do nothing about it. The fact remains that in law the occupier is entitled to nominal damages even if the trespasser was unaware that he was doing wrong, and even though no harm was done to the land. If anyone decides to go on land that he may or may not be entitled to use, the risk is put on him. One type of trespass to land is called trespass by abuse of right of entry. For example where students are admitted to college premises, they will become trespassers if they start a fire, or go down to the boiler room, because there are express or implied restrictions placed on the use of the premises by those entitled to enter. These restrictions define the use the students may make of the building, and the parts of the building to which they may have access.

A well-known case on trespass by abuse of right of entry is *Harrison* v. *Duke of Rutland* (1893). The Duke owned an area of moorland (which he used for grouse shooting) and a road leading across the moor. He permitted members of the public to use the road. One day when the Duke and a party were about to begin shooting, Mr. Harrison came along the road and, in order to annoy the Duke, frightened away the grouse by opening and closing his umbrella. Because the plaintiff would not stop interfering, some servants of the Duke held him down on the ground for a while. Harrison sued the Duke for trespass to the person, but the Duke successfully raised the defence that members of the public, including the plaintiff were allowed on the private road to use it for travel only. In the circumstances the plaintiff had become a trespasser by abuse of right of entry, and the servants of the Duke were justified in what they did.

Trespass by remaining on land would be committed for example if the students at a college remained in their lecture room all night, since their permission to enter the college is subject to an implied condition that they must leave when the college closes for the night. Trespass by placing things on land can be committed in various ways. Tipping rubbish on to the ground, and firing arrows into the soil would both amount to this tort.

Trespass Above and Below the Surface of the Land

The occupier of land is regarded in law as being in occupation of the subsoil beneath the land and the airspace above it. It therefore constitutes trespass to land to tunnel under another's land without permission, or, to put up an advertising sign that overhangs an adjoining garden. Owners of "cattle" (which term in law includes various farm animals) are responsible for any trespass by their beasts. It has been held, therefore that if a horse puts its head over a fence surrounding the field of an adjoining owner, this intrusion by its head constitutes trespass to the airspace of the neighbour. The Civil Aviation Act 1949 lays down that neither the tort of -trespass nor the tort of nuisance is committed by an aircraft flying over land at a reasonable height. In *Lord Bernstein* v. *Skyviews Ltd* (1977) the plaintiff was unsuccessful in an action for trespass when an aircraft flew some hundreds of feet over his house to photograph it and later to sell copies of the photograph. The judge commented that one of the plaintiff's companies had itself sent helicopters to film private land without permission.

Remedies for Trespass to Land

There are a number of different remedies for trespass to land in order to cope adequately with the various ways in which this tort can be committed. These include: (i) an action for damages; (ii) an application for an injunction (see p. 70) to restrain further trespasses; (iii) an action for the recovery of land. This is used where the trespasser has forced out the occupier, or where the defendant becomes a trespasser by remaining on land; (iv) self-defence by throwing the trespasser out, without however using any excessive force; (v) distress damage feasant. This means seizing (distress) anything that is doing damage (damage feasant) on the land. The law provides that if any goods including animals come on land without the permission of the owner, and there do damage to that land, the occupier can seize and keep them until their owner pays for the damage.

Defences to an Action for Trespass to Land

The general defences of consent, self-defence, necessity, and statutory authority apply. In addition the particular defence of licence applies. A licence is. a permission to do something. A licence to enter on land is permission given by the occupier to another person to enter on his land for a limited purpose. The party granting the licence is called the licensor, and the party receiving it is known as the licensee. A licence does not give a licensee any rights over the land; it merely prevents him from being regarded as a trespasser. The following come within the category of licensees: hotel guests, cinema audiences, students in a college lecture room, customers in a shop, and visitors to a house. As soon as a licence is terminated the licensee must leave the land, and if he does not, he becomes a trespasser. The position, then in respect of licence as a defence to trespass to land is that as long as anybody can show he has a licence to be on land, he has a defence to an action for this tort, but as soon as his licence ends his defence ends with it.

NUISANCE

There are two types of nuisance which differ greatly from one another, public nuisance and private nuisance.

Public Nuisance

A public nuisance is an act or an omission that causes discomfort or inconvenience to a class of Her Majesty's subjects. If only a few people are affected, they will not constitute a class and in consequence, there can be no public nuisance. No exact figure has ever been laid down as to how many persons are required to form a class, as this will depend partly on the circumstances of the particular case. A hundred people would certainly form a class, and a much smaller number would suffice in appropriate circumstances. Every public nuisance is a crime and the perpetrator is liable to prosecution. The reason why public nuisance is considered here is that if anybody is more affected by a public nuisance than the other members of the public, he has a right to sue in tort for damages. Examples of public nuisance are selling impure provisions, carrying on an offensive trade, and obstructing a highway. In *Campbell* v. *Paddington Corporation* (1911) the defendants wrongfully obstructed the highway by erecting a stand from which spectators could view the funeral procession of King Edward VII. In addition to causing inconvenience to a class of His Majesty King George V's subjects, the stand blocked the view from the plaintiff's window so that she was not able to make a profit by letting spectators view the procession from her premises. The corporation was held liable in tort to the plaintiff.

Usually a public nuisance continues for some time, but this is not always so, and it has been held that a sudden explosion can constitute this tort. If a local authority fails to maintain a road properly it may be held liable in public nuisance, and the same would apply to a landowner whose tree fell across the road and injured someone or damaged some property, provided that he knew that it was in a dangerous condition and likely to cause harm.

Private Nuisance

This tort differs from public nuisance in three ways: it is not a crime; it may be committed against a single individual or a class; and it must be committed against land. Private nuisance consists of an unlawful interference with an occupier's use of his land. There are three essentials of nuisance, which a plaintiff must prove are present among the facts of the case. These are: (i) an indirect interference with the use of the land. The defendant may commit this interference by letting any of the following enter the land of the plaintiff: smoke, smells, gas, noise, heat, vibrations, water and the branches or roots of trees; (ii) damage; there must be either injury to the soil or an interference with the use of the land that causes discomfort or inconvenience. In one case it was held to be the tort of nuisance when fumes from a copper-smelting works damaged plants growing on adjoining land, and in another case the vapours and stenches from a candle maker's factory which caused inconvenience to neighbours were held to be an interference giving rise to actionable damage; (iii) unlawfulness; the existence or otherwise of this essential depends on a number of factors, and before bringing his action a plaintiff must consider each of them in turn in order to decide to what extent they will affect his case. Not all of these factors come into every case. These factors are: (a) reasonableness; (b) malice; (c) duration; (d) locality; (e) sensitiveness. Reasonableness is the most important of the factors, since it is difficult to prove that a man who is acting reasonably is at the same time acting unlawfully. The factors of malice, duration and locality all affect the question of whether the defendant was acting reasonably or not. For instance a noise made deliberately for a long time close to a house will probably be regarded as unreasonable. On the other hand occasional fumes emitted from a factory in an industrial area without malice on the part of the defendant will probably be regarded as emitted reasonably. If a plaintiff is suing because he or his property has suffered as a result of being unusually sensitive, he is unlikely to be able to prove unlawfulness on the part of the defendant. For example in *Robinson* v. *Kilvert* (1889) a plaintiff stored some sensitive brown paper in premises above a cellar that was heated by the defendant. The paper was damaged, but the action failed since the defendant had not done anything out the ordinary, and the reason for the loss was the unusual sensitiveness of the plaintiff's goods. In *Leakey* v. *National Trust* (1979) the defendants were held liable in private nuisance when earth and tree stumps fell next door from a mound on their land.

Only a person in occupation of land may sue in nuisance, but there are three possible defendants who may be sued:

(i) the creator of the nuisance can be sued;

(ii) the occupier of the land from which the nuisance came may be sued. In addition to being liable for nuisances he caused, he will be held vicariously responsible (see p. 157) for nuisances created by his licensees, his servants, and even for nuisances created by trespassers on his land, if he ought to have known of them. Thus in *Sedleigh-Denfield* v. *O'Callaghan* (1940) a trespasser entered the defendants' land and put a pipe in a ditch. Three years later the pipe became blocked and caused a nuisance by flooding adjoining land. The occupiers knew the pipe was on their land and ought to have realised that it might lead to the flooding. They were therefore held liable for the act of the trespasser in putting the pipe in position and causing the nuisance;

(iii) the landlord of the person in possession.

Defences to Private Nuisance

The general defences are consent and statutory authority. The particular defences are: (i) that the nuisance was caused by the act of a stranger who came on to the land of the defendant, and that the defendant did not know about this; (ii) that the nuisance was caused by an unsuspected process of nature such as a landslip; (iii) that the nuisance had been in existence continuously for twenty years.

The usual remedy for nuisance is an application for an

injunction to restrain the defendant from continuing the nuisance. Usually, where a plaintiff seeks an injunction he seeks to recover any damages he may have suffered in the same action. Instead of going to court the victim of the nuisance is sometimes able to use the remedy of abatement. This means that he puts an end to the nuisance himself. If trees overhang a garden the occupier will usually find it more convenient to cut the overhanging branches himself than to take the matter to court. Any branches or fruit that falls from trees on neighbouring land belongs to the owner of the tree and must be returned on demand.

DEFAMATION

Defamation is the tort of making a false statement about somebody. It was best defined by Professor Winfield, a well-known writer on the law of tort who described it in the following terms:

> "Defamation is the publication of a statement which tends to lower a person in the estimation of right-thinking members of society generally; or which tends to make them shun or avoid that person."

The word "statement" used by Professor Winfield has a wide meaning and covers words, pictures, statues, and gestures.

Libel and Slander, Actionable per se

There are two types of defamation, libel and slander. Libel is defamation in a permanent form while slander is defamation in a temporary form. Other differences between the two are that libel may be a crime, while slander cannot be a crime, and that all libels, but only some slanders are actionable *per se*.

If anybody repeats a defamatory statement that he has heard, he does so at his peril. If it turns out that the statement was false he will be under the same liability as the original author of the statement; it will be no defence that he thought the statement to be true.

Libels are actionable *per se* because of the great damage that can be done to a man's reputation by a defamatory statement which circulates over a prolonged period. There are certain particularly damaging types of slander that are made actionable *per se* as well. These are:

(i) an imputation that the plaintiff has committed a criminal offence for which he could be sent to prison;

(ii) an imputation that the plaintiff has an infectious or contagious disease, so that people would keep away from him;

(iii) an imputation that a woman or girl is unchaste;

(iv) any words that suggest that the plaintiff is unfit to carry on his business, trade, or occupation.

The Proof of Defamation

The three essential elements of the tort of defamation that must be proved by a plaintiff are: (a) that the statement was defamatory; (b) that it referred to him; (c) that the statement was published by the defendant; (d) that he suffered some damage (this does not apply, of course, to libel or the four types of slander mentioned above, which are actionable *per se*). These essentials are examined below.

Most defamation cases are tried by a judge and jury. It is for the judge to decide in the first place whether the statement could possibly be defamatory or not. If he decides that it could not reasonably be regarded as defamatory at all, he must not let the case go on to the jury; instead he must give judgment for the defendant. If, on the other hand, the judge considers that the statement might be defamatory he must put the matter to the jury who will decide whether or not it was defamatory. There are two ways in which a statement may be defamatory. Either it is defamatory on the plain meaning of the words, or it is defamatory because the words have a hidden meaning that those who heard or read them understood. A hidden meaning of this kind is known as an innuendo. For example in *Tolley* v. *Fry* (1931) chocolate manufacturers published an advertisement of their chocolate showing a caricature of Mr. Tolley who was an amateur golfer, and therefore not allowed to accept money for letting his name be used in advertisements. Mr. Tolley did not know that his name was to be used, and received no money, but some of those who knew him believed he had betrayed his principles by taking payment. The advertisement did not say that he had taken money, but since payment is usually made to well-known people whose names are used in advertisements, some of those who saw the advertisement read between the lines and Mr. Tolley's reputation was lowered in their estimation quite unjustifiably. This was defamation by innuendo. In *Foot* v. *Associated Newspapers Group* (1978) an M.P. was awarded damages against the *Daily Mail* for publishing an article alleging that he had received private treatment as a National Health Service patient, implying he was insincere in his advocacy of egalitarianism.

If a plaintiff is named, it is quite obvious that the statement refers to him; sometimes it may be a more difficult matter to decide. If somebody is described accurately although not named, he will be able to show that the statement referred to him. On the other hand if he is a member of a large class, such as politicians or bakers, which is the subject of adverse comment, this will not be enough—no baker could sue me if I said that all bakers are villains. On the other hand if the class were small, my defamatory statement about it might be held to refer to one or more individuals. This would be the case for example, if I said that "every assistant" in a certain shop gave short weight, when there were only two or three assistants working there.

In order to make the defendant liable the plaintiff must prove not only that there was a publication, but also that it was a publication for which the defendant was responsible. Publishing a defamatory statement means making it known to somebody other than the person defamed. The reason for this is that a man's reputation may go down in the estimation of other people who hear something defamatory about him, but his reputation will not go down in his own estimation; that is to say he will not think less of himself if he hears a falsehood about himself. If somebody shouts out a defamatory statement at a public meeting, or prints a defamatory statement in a newspaper, this will obviously be a publication for which he is responsible. There are, however some circumstances where the responsibility is less obvious. In *Theaker* v. *Richardson* (1962) for example, the defendants addressed a defamatory letter to the woman it defamed, but her husband opened and read it. It was held that the defendant was responsible for this publication, because in the circumstances of that case he ought to have expected that the husband would open his wife's letters.

Defences to Defamation

Justification.—The best defence to an action for defamation, if it can be established, is that the statement was true. The technical name for this defence is "justification". It is sufficient to show that the statement is accurate taken as a whole, and there is no need to prove the accuracy of each detail of it. If the statement contains an innuendo, the defendant is at liberty to prove that the innuendo was true.

Fair comment.—It is a defence to show that a statement was a fair comment on a matter of public interest. This defence protects the freedom of individuals to air their opinions on questions that affect everybody. There are various elements in this defence all of which should be present if the defence is to be accepted by the court. First, the subject matter of the statement must be something of interest to the general public. There are many such matters which would include the behaviour of the government, taxation, local politics, and the conduct of people in public life. The category includes matters deliberately brought to the notice of the public by advertisements or otherwise, such as musical performances and television broadcasts. Secondly, the comment must be made about some fact. For instance if Alice said "Jack came tumbling down the hill; he is clumsy", the words "he is clumsy" would be a comment, while the rest of the sentence would be a statement of fact. Thirdly the comment must be fair. This means that the comment must not be so outrageous that no honest man would have made it. A comment may be fair even though expressed in fairly strong language. The important thing to remember is that the question of fairness or unfairness is not to be judged by the opinions of others, but mainly by the honesty of the person expressing the opinion.

Absolute privilege.—There are certain circumstances when the interests of the community are best served by allowing people to say exactly what they like without fear of legal proceedings. These circumstances are called occasions of absolute privilege. If anybody speaks on an occasion when he is afforded absolute privilege, then he will have an absolute defence, even if he tells deliberate lies with some malicious intention. This would of course be very unusual, and would probably lead to some sort of trouble for the person guilty of such an abuse of his position. The defence of absolute privilege may be raised if the statement complained of comes within any of the following categories:

(i) any statement made in Parliament by a member of the House of Lords or the House of Commons;

(ii) Parliamentary papers published by order of the House of Lords or the House of Commons;

(iii) a statement made by one important government official (usually called "officers of state"), to another;

(iv) a statement made by a husband to a wife or vice versa;

(v) a statement made in the course of a trial in a law court, by the judge, or by a barrister, solicitor, witness or juryman. Of course a statement that had nothing to do with the case would not be privileged;

(vi) a newspaper report of a public trial. Here, however the report must fulfil the requirements of being fair, accurate and contemporaneous. If, for example, a newspaper printed an account of a trial giving what was said by one side only, this might be accurate, but it would not be fair. The requirement that the report be contemporaneous limits the time within which a newspaper may print a defamatory statement made in court and yet retain its absolute privilege.

(vii) words spoken or written by officials of the European Communities in their official capacity in accordance with a protocol to the Merger Treaty of 1965.

Qualified privilege.—This defence is less extensive than that of absolute privilege and it is afforded by the law to those who make statements on certain occasions when the public interest demands a certain degree of protection for those making statements, but not complete immunity. Immunity is lost if a statement in this category is made with malice or published more widely than necessary.

The occasions on which the law confers qualified privilege are discussed below.

1. Where a statement is made in the course of a legal or moral duty, the person making the statement will be able to raise the defence of qualified privilege, provided that the person receiving the statement has a corresponding legal or moral duty, or an interest in receiving it.

In *Watt* v. *Longsdon* (1930), a letter was sent to the defendant alleging that the plaintiff was, among other things, a thief and a liar. The defendant was a director of a company, and the plaintiff was abroad on the company's business. On receiving the letter the defendant told both the managing director and the plaintiff's wife of the allegations, which turned out to be false. It was held in an action for defamation that the defendant could use the defence of qualified privilege in respect of what he told the managing director, but not in respect of what he said to the wife. The reason for this was that the director had a duty to tell the managing director about the allegation and the managing director had a duty to listen to it, as the information affected their company. On the other hand the director had neither a duty nor an interest in telling the wife: the fact that the wife had an interest in listening to the allegation did not alone make the conversation an occasion of qualified privilege.

2. Where the statement is made in the protection of an interest, the same requirement as for statements made under a duty applies. This means that both the person making the statement and the person receiving it must have an interest or a duty in doing so. There are three interests that may be protected in reliance on the defence of qualified privilege. These are the interest of the person making the statement, the public interest, and the interest of the person receiving it.

3. Where the statement is made by a client to his solicitor or vice versa in the course of a professional communication.

4. Reports of proceedings in Parliament, whether the report appears in a newspaper, a private letter or elsewhere. For example if Alice went to the public gallery of the House of Commons and heard Jack who is a Member of Parliament slandering Michael, and repeated the slanders in letters or in conversation, Alice could raise the defence of qualified privilege if sued by Michael. Jack could of course raise the defence of absolute privilege since he uttered the slander in the House of Commons.

5. Fair and accurate reports of public trials published otherwise than in newspapers; *e.g.*, in books, advertisements, speeches, letters, or conversations. It will be remembered that newspapers have absolute privilege for fair, accurate and contemporaneous reports of public trials. If a newspaper publishes a fair and accurate report of a trial a long time after it has been held, then, because the report lacks the ingredient of being contemporaneous, it will be the subject of qualified privilege only.

6. Reports of public meetings: this category of qualified privilege stems from the Defamation Act 1952, s. 7. It covers reports in newspapers and also news broadcasts by radio and television stations in the United Kingdom. At the end of the Defamation Act 1952 there is an appendix, or "Schedule" as it is called, which sets out two lists of public meetings; those in Part I of the Schedule are the more important type of meeting, while those in Part II are the less important type of meeting. Those to whom the privilege is extended may use it without restriction in respect of reports about meetings listed in Part I. In respect of meetings listed in Part II the privilege will not be available if a plaintiff requests the publication of a contradiction or explanation and this is refused. Part I includes for example fair and accurate reports of the public proceedings of international organisations such as the United Nations at which the United Kingdom is represented, while Part II includes fair and accurate reports of the meetings of local authorities and of magistrates who are deciding whether or not to grant licences for public houses.

If a defendant sets up the defence of qualified privilege, this will be ineffective if he has been motivated by malice (which includes personal spite) in making the statement. The plaintiff must counter a defence of qualified privilege by proving, if such was the case, that the defendant abused the qualified privilege he enjoyed by exercising it maliciously. If a defendant apologises promptly and sincerely for a defamation, he may nevertheless have to pay damages, but his apology may have the effect of reducing what he must pay.

NEGLIGENCE

There are three essential elements in this tort, and if a plaintiff is to succeed in an action in negligence he must prove that all of them were present in the facts of the case. They are, first, a legal duty of care owed by the defendant to the plaintiff, secondly, breach of that duty by the defendant, and thirdly, damage to the plaintiff suffered as a result of the breach of duty. It is necessary to examine each of these essentials separately.

Duty of Care

It is important to know in what circumstances one person owes a duty of care to another. The law does not lay down any single rule that covers all situations, but there is one that is applicable in most circumstances. This rule was laid down in the House of Lords in 1932 by Lord Atkin while delivering judgment in the case of *Donoghue* v. *Stevenson*. This was a Scottish case involving an appeal from the Court of Session in Edinburgh, and it is an example of a situation in which the laws of Scotland and England are the same.

The facts of the case were that a young man went to a café with a girl and bought her some ginger beer. The ginger beer was in an opaque glass bottle which also contained a snail that had got in before the bottle had left the factory. The girl drank some of the ginger beer and when the rest was being poured out the snail appeared from the bottle. In an action for damages against the manufacturer she alleged that she became ill through seeing and drinking the contents of the bottle, and the question arose as to whether or not the manufacturer owed her any duty of care. Lord

Atkin first referred to the biblical rule that you should love your neighbour as yourself and then went on to say that in law this command was turned into a rule that you must not hurt your neighbour.

Pursuing this theme his lordship asked who in law is my neighbour and answered the query by saying that my neighbour is anybody who I can *reasonably foresee* as likely to be affected injuriously by my act or omission. In his own words, my neighbours are:

> "persons who are so closely and directly affected by my act that I ought reasonably to have them in contemplation as being so affected when I am directing my mind to the acts or omissions which are called in question".

Looking at the facts of the case in this way, it was apparent to Lord Atkin that the manufacturer of ginger beer could reasonably have foreseen injury to the ultimate consumer of ginger beer if he sent it out in an opaque bottle containing a snail. Therefore the girl was a neighbour to the manufacturer, who in consequence owed her a duty of care. He had failed in his duty and the result of his breach of the duty of care was damage to her. It is to be borne in mind that the outcome of the case might have been different if the snail and ginger beer had been put into a clear glass bottle. In such a case the ultimate consumer could have seen the snail and refused to drink the mixture. Because she was not able to protect herself in this way the duty of care was laid on the manufacturer.

The "Neighbour Test"

Since 1932 the "neighbour test" of duty has been applied in many sets of circumstances. For example in *Sharp* v. *Avery* (1938) a motor cyclist offered to show another motor cyclist the way, but drove off the road so that the pillion passenger on the following motor cycle was injured. It was held that the leading motor cyclist owed a duty of care to the pillion rider. In *King* v. *Phillips* (1952), a taxicab driver backed his vehicle carelessly into a tricycle ridden by a small boy. It was held that the driver owed no duty of care to the boy's mother who suffered a nervous shock while watching the incident from an upstairs window seventy yards away. The reason for the decision was that the mother was not a neighbour to the driver as he could not reasonably have foreseen the injury she suffered.

It has been mentioned that the neighbour test is not universally applicable; two examples will suffice to illustrate this. One example is that although the law requires a man not to injure his neighbour, it does not compel him to assist his neighbour. There is, consequently no duty of care in law that requires anybody to go to the aid of a person in difficulties; morally, of course, the position is otherwise. Another example is that it is evident that a shopkeeper's action in lowering prices will affect other traders, but here again the law recognises no duty of care towards neighbours.

The Congenital Disabilities (Civil Liability) Act 1976 laid down that if a child is born disabled due to the wrongful act of some person other than the mother before the child is born, then the child when born is entitled to sue for damages.

Reasonable Care

A plaintiff who has established that the defendant owed him a duty of care must show that the duty has not been carried out. He can do this by showing that in all the circumstances of the case the defendant did not act reasonably towards him. For example in *Paris* v. *Stepney Borough Council* (1951) the employers of a workman who had (as they knew) only one good eye were held to be in breach of their duty of care in not supplying him with goggles, with the result that his eye was injured while he was at work.

The plaintiff in order to succeed in this action must show that he suffered some damage as a result of the breach of duty. Negligence is not actionable *per se*. The damage must not be too remote a consequence of the defendant's action (see p. 156).

Res Ipsa Loquitur

Usually the plaintiff has to prove that the defendant has been negligent, but there are some exceptional cases in which the law will assume that the defendant was negligent, and leave it to him to prove the opposite if he can. This situation arises where it seems obvious that the accident would not have occurred without carelessness on the part of somebody. A set of circumstances of this type is called a "*res ipsa loquitur*" situation. *Res ipsa loquitur* means "the facts speak for themselves". For example in *Byrne* v. *Boadle* (1863) a barrel rolled out of an opening in an upper floor of the defendant's warehouse, and fell on the plaintiff who was walking along the street, injuring him. This was held to be a *res ipsa loquitur* situation, since accidents of such a nature do not usually occur without carelessness. The plaintiff was in no position to show that there had been some carelessness inside the warehouse and was not called upon to do so. It was left to the occupiers of the warehouse to show that they had taken all reasonable care to prevent such accidents; they were unable to do so and were held to have been negligent.

Defences to Negligence

The general defences of *volenti non fit injuria* (see p. 154), and inevitable accident, are available. In addition there is the particular defence of contributory negligence. This defence is regulated by the Law Reform (Contributory Negligence) Act 1945 which lays down that if a plaintiff's injury was due partly to the negligence of the defendant and partly to the negligence of the plaintiff himself, then the amount of damages recoverable by the plaintiff must be reduced. The reduction will be proportional to the fault of the plaintiff. Let us suppose that Jack on his motor cycle collides with Alice in her car, so that the motor cycle worth £300 is wrecked and the car is undamaged. If Jack sues Alice in negligence, and the court holds that Alice was two thirds to blame for the accident, while Jack was one third to blame, then Alice will have to pay £200 towards the cost of the motor cycle. She will be able to get the £200 from her insurance company, if she is properly insured. The remedy for negligence is, of course an action for damages.

OTHER TORTS

The torts detailed above represent only a part of the protection afforded by the law of tort. There are a number of other less common torts which may provide a remedy for someone who has suffered an injury. For example if someone has goods which belong to you in his possession and refuses to let you have them you may sue him under the Torts (Interference with Goods) Act 1977, s. 3(1) in order to recover them. Alternatively you may be able to sue him for "conversion", under s. 3(2) and obtain damages for their loss, especially if he has destroyed or consumed them, or sold them to someone else so that they cannot be recovered. The tort of conversion consists in dealing with another's property in such a way as to deny the true owners rights. (Reference may be made to the case illustrated and discussed on pages 33–36 above, which concerned an action for the tort of conversion.) The law of tort will also provide a remedy if someone induces another person to break his contract with you or invents injurious falsehoods that damage your business. There are other torts as well which are not within the scope of this book.

Chapter 12

The Law of Contract

WHAT IS A CONTRACT?

A contract is an agreement. It is an agreement of a special sort because it carries with it a right to claim help from a law court if it is not carried out. The agreement in a contract always takes the form of: (i) an offer from one party who is called the offeror followed by (ii) acceptance by the other party who is called the offeree. There are various types of contract but the most important is the simple contract.

Simple contracts

If an agreement is to amount to a simple contract it must contain all the following elements which are dealt with in detail below. There must be:

    (i) an offer and an acceptance;
    (ii) consideration;
    (iii) intention to create legal relations;
    (iv) capacity to contract;
    (v) validity of contract;
    (vi) lawfulness of object.

(i) *Offer and Acceptance*

Offer.—The first thing to be decided in considering the validity of a contract is whether or not there has been a valid offer. If there has been no valid offer there can be no acceptance and hence no contract. A valid offer must comply with the following requirements:

(a) The words must be intended as an offer. The courts have held that when a shopkeeper puts an article in his window marked with a price, this does not constitute an offer, but only an invitation to passers-by to come in and offer to buy at the price mentioned. The customer makes the offer and the shopkeeper accepts or rejects the offer.

(b) The offer must be certain, *e.g.*, an offer to employ an actor at £1,000 a week will be certain as far as salary is concerned, but an offer to employ him "at a West End salary to be arranged" will not be certain.

(c) An offer may be made to one person, to several persons or to the whole world. In *Carlill* v. *Carbolic Smoke Ball Co. Ltd.*, (1892) the company published an advertisement claiming that anybody using their smoke balls would avoid catching influenza. The advertisement promised £100 to anybody who used the smoke balls for fourteen days but caught influenza. Mrs. Carlill used a smoke ball in accordance with the terms of the advertisement, but nevertheless was stricken with 'flu. When the company refused to pay, she brought an action in contract claiming £100, and it was held that they had made an offer to the whole world, which she had accepted by acting on it. The court held also that in the circumstances of the case, it was not necessary for her to tell the company of her acceptance. Merely acting on the offer constituted a sufficient acceptance.

(d) In order that there shall be a valid contract, the offer must continue to be in existence when it is accepted. An offer ceases to exist as soon as any of the following occur:

(i) if the offer is accepted; as soon as this happens there is a contract;

(ii) if the offer is rejected. Rejection by the offeree destroys the offer. This means that an offeree who rejects an offer cannot change his mind afterwards and accept it, for there is nothing left to accept;

(iii) if the offer is revoked (cancelled) by the offeror; an offer can be revoked at any time before acceptance;

(iv) if the offer lapses (comes to an end automatically). If an offer is made, and the offeree is told that it will be kept open for a definite time, then it will lapse as soon as that time is up, and can no longer be accepted. If no definite time is stated during which the offer is to be kept open, it will lapse after a reasonable time. What is a reasonable time will depend on the circumstances of the case. An offer of fresh vegetables would obviously lapse before an offer of a house, because the vegetables would soon become worthless, while a house would normally retain its value for a considerable time.

Acceptance.—In order to be effective an acceptance must be an agreement to *all* the terms of the offer. Therefore if Alice offers Jack her car for £500 and Jack replies by saying "I will take your car, but I will pay only £400 for it", then there is no acceptance and no contract. In fact the reply amounts to a rejection of the offer which thereupon ceases to exist. A contract comes into being as soon as the offer is accepted so that acceptance is a very important matter in the law of contract. The ordinary rule is that there is no acceptance until notification of acceptance is made to the offeror. If the offer states expressly, or, as in *Carlill* v. *Carbolic Smoke Ball Co. Ltd.*, impliedly, that carrying out the terms of the offer shall be sufficient, then no notification will be necessary.

It is open to the offeror to lay down how the offer shall be accepted, and quite often an offeror makes it clear that the offer must be accepted by post. The question then arises, when is the contract made? Is it made when the letter is posted, or when it arrives in the hands of the offeror? In *Henthorn* v. *Fraser* (1892) it was held that the contract is made as soon as the letter is posted. Another question immediately arises however, when is an offer revoked? Is it revoked when the letter of revocation is posted, or when the letter is delivered? The rule is that there is no revocation until knowledge of this comes to the offeree. With this information we are able to answer the problem posed by a classical situation. The problem is this: what is the legal position if Alice, who has offered her car for £500 to Jack, posts a revocation at precisely the same moment as Jack is posting an acceptance? It is clear from *Henthorn* v. *Fraser* that there is a valid contract, since Jack's letter is effective as soon as he posts it, and when Alice's letter arrives it will be ineffective, for it is too late to revoke an offer once it has been accepted.

(ii) *Consideration*

The element of consideration is essential in any valid simple contract. It is this that turns a mere promise into a contract that the law will enforce. Every contract contains at least one promise and consideration is something given, done, or suffered in return for a promise; in come cases consideration may comprise all three of these elements. For example in Mrs. Carlill's case she had to give the price of the smoke balls, she had to sniff them for a fortnight, and she had to suffer from influenza in order to furnish the requisite consideration for the company's promise of £100. This was a contract with a promise on one side only, but some contracts consist of promises on both sides. For example if Jack agrees to buy Alice's car for £500, there is a contract consisting of Alice's promise to hand over the car, and Jack's promise to hand over the £500. The consideration for Alice's promise is the promise Jack gave her, and vice versa. The essential thing about consideration is that it means giving, doing or suffering on the part of the person furnishing consideration; it is not essential that the other party shall benefit from this. Obviously Alice will benefit from Jack's £500. Equally the Carbolic Smoke Ball Company benefited when Mrs. Carlill gave them the price of the smoke balls, but they were in no way better off because she sniffed them or because she caught influenza.

There are said to be two sorts of consideration, "executory consideration" and "executed consideration". Executory consideration is merely another name for consideration that consists of a promise. Executed consideration is the completed act of giving, doing or suffering something. In Mrs. Carlill's case the company furnished executory consideration by their promise, while she furnished executed consideration by what she did. Consideration to be recognised by law, must be "real". This means that it must have some value. Thus in one case it was held that a promise by a son to his father to stop complaining that he had been unfairly treated did not amount to consideration. On the other hand if Alice agreed to sell Jack her car for a penny, this consideration would be real, since it is of some actual value. The fact that a penny is a low price for a car makes no difference. It is necessary that consideration should be something given, done or suffered at the time of, or after the making of the contract if it is to be recognised by the law. This rule is expressed by saying that consideration must not be "past". For example in *Roscorla* v. *Thomas* (1842) *after* a horse had been sold by a contract under which the buyer gave consideration, the seller promised that the horse was in good condition. It turned out that the animal was not in good condition, and the buyer sued in contract relying on the consideration he had given. It was held that there was no consideration to support the promise, since the consideration given under the contract was already past at the time of the promise.

(iii) *Intention to Create Legal Relations*

If an agreement is to be treated as a contract, it is essential that the parties to it should have intended to enter into a legally binding realtionship. When coming to an agreement most people do not stop to think about what they intend, but if asked, most people would say that an arrangement to meet a friend socially would not be intended by them to have any legal consequences. In such a case, therefore, even if there were offer and acceptance and consideration, no action in contract could be brought if one of the parties did not meet as arranged. It is possible to have an agreement drawn up in such a way as to avoid legal liability, by putting in it a provision that it shall be "binding in honour only". Agreements between football pool companies and their customers are made by filling in a coupon, and the companies always put in a clause to the effect that the agreement shall be binding in honour only. This means that if the participant in the pool does not pay his stake, he cannot be sued for it, while if the company does not pay the participant the hundred thousand pounds he has won, it cannot be sued either. In business relationships courts assume an intention to create legal relations.

(iv) *Capacity to Contract*

The law applies special rules to certain persons in respect of their ability to enter into contracts. Some of these rules are designed to protect the persons to whom they relate. The categories we shall consider are minors, persons suffering from mental disorder, drunken persons, and corporations.

Minors.—Persons under eighteen years of age are called "infants" or "minors" in law. The rules relating to minors' contracts are designed to protect minors and the basic rule at common law is that if a minor makes a contract he or she can choose between going on with the contract or abandoning it. The contract will be enforceable by the minor but not against the minor. Only if the minor attains the age of eighteen years and then declares that he wants to go on with it will the contract be enforceable against him. This rule could lead to injustice in some cases, and the law has allowed various departures from it. However, first it is necessary to consider a number of cases in which minors can be sued.

Necessaries.—The Sale of Goods Act 1979, s. 3(2) lays down that a minor must pay a reasonable price for necessaries that are sold and delivered to him. Necessaries are defined by the Act as goods suitable to the condition in life of such minor, and to his actual requirements at the time of the sale and delivery. Whether the goods in any particular contract are necessaries or not will depend on the circumstances of the case. Food and clothes are necessaries to a minor without sufficient of either, but would not be necessaries if he had plenty. In *Nash* v. *Inman* (1908) an infant undergraduate with an adequate wardrobe contracted for the purchase of certain clothes inlcuding some fancy waistcoats, and it was held that the clothes were not necessaries, so that the court decided the supplier of the clothes had no right in law to payment. It should be noted that nothing need be paid for necessaries that are ordered but not delivered; thus the minor who makes a contract for the supply of necessaries, but later cancels the order and does not take delivery cannot be sued. The Act lays down that a reasonable price must be paid for the necessaries; this may be different from the contract price so that, for example, a minor who needs shoes and orders a pair by post at an exorbitant price, can be forced to pay for them, but if the case comes to court, will have to pay only what the court decides is a reasonable sum.

Beneficial contracts.—There are certain contracts which, when looked at as a whole are regarded as being for the benefit of the minor, and are therefore made enforceable against him as well as by him. These include contracts of apprenticeship and contracts to work for others. Contracts of this type are not one-sided, and the fact that the minor has some duties to perform, will not alone prevent the contract from being beneficial to him. If a court decides that a contract is, on the whole beneficial to the minor, it wll not exempt him from any disadvantages in the contract. Thus in *Doyle* v. *White City Stadium Ltd.* (1935) there was a contract to fight made by an infant boxer. It was held to be a valid contract even though there was a clause in it that deprived the boxer of his fee if disqualified. Contracts by minors for the purchase or sale of articles in the course of trade do not come within these rules.

Voidable contracts.—There are some contracts of a continuing type that are concerned with long-lasting property such as leases or shares in companies. The position of a minor in connection with a contract of this sort is that he is free to put an end to it at any time before he becomes eighteen, or within a reasonable time after attaining that age. The important characteristic of these contracts is that if the minor makes the contract and then does nothing, the contract will automatically become enforceable against him a reasonable time after he has attained his majority. What amounts to a reasonable time will depend on the circumstances of the case. In one instance it was held that a contract could not be avoided (ended) after a year had passed. If a minor makes one of these contracts and then avoids it, he is liable to pay whatever was agreed up to the date on which he avoided it. He will not be able to get back any money paid under such a contract, unless he can show that he received nothing at all.

The Infants Relief Act 1874, s. 1, makes the following contracts void in relation to minors: (i) contracts for the repayment of money lent; (ii) contracts for the supply of goods that are not necessaries, and (iii) accounts stated. Accounts stated are documents containing an admission that the person signing the account owes money. Under s. 2 of the same Act it is not possible for an infant debtor to make himself liable after the age of eighteen by a promise to pay the debt from which he was exempted through his infancy. If a minor obtains goods by fraudulently persuading another to enter into a contract with him, an application may be made to the court for the equitable remedy of restitution, which is an order to the defendant to return something to the original owner.

Persons suffering from mental disorder.—A person whose property is being controlled by the Court of Protection cannot make a valid contract. Other persons suffering from mental disorder can make a valid contract, but will be able to avoid it if they can show that the other party to the contract knew they did not know what they were doing. Even if not liable on a contract, a person suffering from mental disorder will be liable to pay for necessaries on the same basis as an infant.

Drunken persons.—If a party to a contract can show that he was so drunk at the time of contracting that he did not know what he was doing, and that the other party was aware of this, he can avoid the contract. He is in a similar position to an infant as regards necessaries.

Corporations.—There is no restriction on the contracts of chartered corporations. Statutory corporations can enter into any contract authorised by the statute creating them, and companies registered under the companies acts may make only contracts authorised by their memorandum of association.

(v) *Validity of Contract*

Sometimes there is a contract that appears valid on the face of it, but which is actually invalid because of the presence of one or more factors that undermine it. We shall consider each of these factors in turn.

Mistake.—A mistake as to the subject matter of a contract may mean that although the parties appear to be in agreement, this is not really the case. There is said to be no "*consensus ad idem*" (agreement to the same thing). For example in *Raffles* v. *Wichelhaus* (1864) a contract was made concerning a ship called the "Peerless". There were two ships of this name, and each of the parties to the contract was thinking of a different "Peerless", so that there was no *consensus ad idem*, and hence no valid contract. A mistake as to whether or not the subject matter of the contract exists may invalidate a contract. Thus in *Couturier* v. *Hastie* (1856) a contract was made for the sale of a cargo of corn which the parties both thought to be on a ship. Actually the corn had already been disposed of because it was deteriorating, and there was held to be no contract. If one party has made a mistake as to the identity of the person he is contracting with, this may or may not be of significance according to the circumstances. If a tobacconist makes a mistake as to the name of the customer to whom he sells a packet of cigarettes for cash, this error will not worry anybody and the contract will not be affected. If identity is important however, the situation is different. In *Cundy* v. *Lindsay* (1878) a manufacturer sent goods on credit to a swindler believing he was a certain regular customer. It was held that there was no contract, as the manufacturer had never heard of this swindler, and would have refused to enter into a contract with him if he had known who he was. The identity of the other party to the contract was a matter of great importance here. In another case a supplier sold goods to a man with whom he had already dealt, believing him to own a substantial business. He owned no business, in fact, but the contract was held valid. If one party makes an offer by mistake, as for example by putting in too low a price, and the other knows this when he accepts, there will be no contract. If a person's signature is obtained by fraud on a document, then any contract founded on this document will be void. Sometimes there is a mistake that does not affect the validity of the contract at all. The rule at common law is "*caveat emptor*" (let the purchaser beware). The effect of the rule is that a purchaser who buys something thinking that it is something else has only himself to blame if he does not make his requirement a part of the contract.

Misrepresentation.—A misrepresentation is a false statement made by one party to the other to induce him to enter into a contract. If the party conveying this impression knows that what he is saying is false, or if he says something without caring whether it is true or false, then the misrepresentation is said to be fraudulent. If the person making the statement is acting honestly, the misrepresentation is known as an innocent misrepresentation. In *Derry* v. *Peek* (1889) the directors of a company were sued for fraud because they had stated in a document issued to attract investors to buy shares in the company, that the company was allowed to run steam trams. The directors thought the company would be allowed to do this, but it was in fact forbidden to do so, after the document had been issued. It was held that the misrepresentation had not been fraudulent, since the directors honestly believed what they had said.

The victim of a misrepresentation may, if he wishes, carry on with the contract. On the other hand he may ask the court for rescission which means that the parties are put back by the court as far as possible into the situations they occupied before the contract. Where there has been misrepresentation, the injured party may claim damages. Formerly damages could be obtained only in the case of fraudulent misrepresentation, but under the Misrepresentation Act 1967 damages may be obtained for innocent misrepresentation, unless up to the time of the contract the person making the representation proves that he believed reasonably what he represented was true. Furthermore, under the 1967 Act, a party may rescind a contract where the other party has made a misrepresentation even though it has become a term of the contract or the contract has been performed. In cases where the misrepresentation was innocent, the court may award damages instead of rescinding the contract, if in the circumstances, it feels that it would be equitable to do so.

Duress.—Violence, actual or threatened which induces a person to enter into a contract is known as duress. The victim of duress may avoid the contract if he wishes to do so.

Undue influence.—Where one person exercises dominion over another so that the other is not able to exercise his free will and judgment, there is said to be undue influence. Should this undue influence be used to force a person into a contract, the victim may avoid the contract at his option. Ordinarily the party seeking to avoid a contract must prove that he was subjected to undue influence, but there are certain relationships where the law will presume undue influence to have been exercised; if the question comes before the court the stronger party in any of these relationships will have to prove that he or she did not exercise undue influence. Examples of these relationships are parent and child, doctor and patient, and solicitor and client. For example, if a patient sells a horse to his doctor at a very low price and then seeks to avoid the transaction, it is for the doctor to show that the patient acted quite voluntarily.

Contracts of the utmost good faith.—The law requires disclosure of all material facts in certain cases where the information on which the contract is based is available only to one of the parties, or where the parties are in a relationship where one puts his confidence in the other. The best known example of a contract of the utmost good faith which is also called by the latin name, a contract "*uberrimae fidei*" is a contract of insurance. Anybody wishing to contract with an insurance company must disclose to the company all the facts which the company requires to know in fixing the premium or in deciding whether to make the contract. Otherwise the company may avoid it. The Unfair Contract Terms Act 1977 limits the extent to which a business can avoid its liability for breach of contract or negligence. It cannot exclude its liability for death or personal injury. It can exclude its liability for negligence only in so far as the term or notice in the contract is reasonable.

(vi) *Lawfulness of Object*

There are some categories of contract that are not enforceable because they do not fulfil the requirement that they should be lawful. The following are considered below: contracts that are illegal at common law; contracts that are illegal by statute; and contracts that are void by statute. All illegal contracts are without effect in law, and the same applies to void contracts. The difference between the two is that an illegal contract will invalidate any other contract that depends on it, while this does not happen with a void contract. For instance in one case a person buying land for an illegal purpose had made a separate contract to pay money owed in respect of the land. It was held that the illegal contract made the other one void also.

Contracts illegal at common law.—The common law prohibits contracts to commit crimes or torts, contracts to commit sexually immoral acts, and contracts in contravention of public policy. Public policy means the public interest as seen by the judges. There are a number of contracts that have been held to contravene public policy; the following are a few examples: (a) marriage-brokage contracts; these are contracts made by marriage bureaux and private individuals to introduce two people with a view to marriage. If the client of a marriage bureau pays a fee to be introduced to others with a view to marriage, and the bureau makes various introductions unsuccessfully, then the client may sue and recover back the whole payment. This was decided in *Herman* v. *Charlesworth* (1905); (b) contracts tending to promote corruption in public life, and (c) contracts in restraint of trade. The last named is the most common type of contract contravening public policy. Sometimes an employer enters into a contract with his employee under which the employee agrees to accept a restraint on the employment he takes after leaving the service of the employer. Unless a restraint protects an employer against disclosure of trade secrets or against loss of customers, it is void. Even if the restraint does protect one of these interests it will not be valid if unreasonable. In *Mason* v. *Provident Clothing Co. Ltd.* (1913) for example it was held that a contract that restrained a canvasser from working within twenty-five miles of London for three years was illegal because it covered an area wider than was necessary to protect the former employer.

Contracts illegal by statute.—Some contracts that contravene statutes are illegal, but this is not a universal rule. The situation will depend upon the intention of the statute as interpreted by the court. The Moneylenders Act 1927 provides expressly that contracts made by moneylenders who have no licence will be illegal.

Contracts void by statute.—Contracts that are void by statute are not enforceable in court. In this they are similar to illegal contracts. They differ from illegal contracts however, in that an illegal contract invalidates any other contract that depends on it, while a contract void by statute does not.

Any contract that a statute declares to be void is a mere nullity. There are two important kinds of contract in this category: first, the Restrictive Trade Practices Acts 1956 and 1968 render void certain contracts that are contrary to the public interest. The Act is directed mainly against contracts between manufacturers and dealers to keep prices up; secondly, the Gaming Act 1845 makes all gaming and wagering contracts void. Wagering is betting and gaming is playing a game of chance for winnings in money or something worth money. Because of this statute a gambler cannot sue a bookmaker who refuses to pay over his winnings.

Generally speaking when there is an illegal contract the courts will do nothing for either party, but there are some exceptional cases. In particular if the parties are not equally to blame, or to use a legal phrase not *in pari delicto* (equally at fault), the law may help the less guilty to get back any property he may have handed over under the contract.

EXAMPLE OF A CONTRACT TO PROVIDE CURTAINS

AN AGREEMENT made the 15th day of January 1981 between Jane Doe of "Laburnum House", Dukesthorpe Road, Sydenham, London SE26 (hereinafter called "the supplier") of the one part and Jackie Atkins of 10, Crumpton Road, Chiswick, London W5 (hereinafter called "the purchaser") of the other part.

WHEREBY IT IS AGREED AS FOLLOWS

1. The supplier agrees to provide red velvet curtain material of the best quality.
2. The supplier agrees to make from the said material two curtains to fit and together cover the window in the front downstairs room of the said "Laburnum House".
3. The work shall be completed by 1st March 1981.
4. The purchaser shall, on delivery of the curtains as specified, pay the supplier the sum of £300.

Signed by the said supplier   JANE DOE
Signed by the said purchaser   JACKIE ATKINS

DISCHARGE OF CONTRACTS

When a contract comes to an end it is said to have been discharged. There are various ways in which a contract may be discharged. These are, first, performance, which means carrying out the contract to completion; secondly, agreement, which signifies that the parties have agreed with one another to end the contract; thirdly, frustration, which means that it has become impossible to carry out the contract, and lastly, breach, which is a situation where the contract has been broken by a failure to adhere to its terms. It is necessary to consider each of these types of discharge a little more closely.

Performance

In order to discharge a contract by performance it is usually necessary to carry out *exactly* all the terms of the contract. This rule could lead to injustice, however and there are some exceptions. For example, if part of the work contracted for is carried out in such a way that the party for whom the work is executed is in a position to accept or reject what has been done, then if he accepts the part done, he will have to pay for it. On the other hand, partly finished work which is forced on somebody cannot be used to demand payment. Thus in *Sumpter* v. *Hedges* (1898) Sumpter agreed to put up some buildings on the land of Hedges, but did not finish the work. Hedges was forced to accept the work done, and so Sumpter was unable to recover any money for his unfinished job.

In some contracts performance cannot be achieved without the co-operation of both parties; the delivery of goods that have been ordered is an example of this. If the party due to deliver the goods offers them, but the other refuses to accept them, there is said to have been "tender of performance". A party who has tendered performance need do nothing more, and his part of the contract is considered to have been carried out.

Agreement

There is more than one way of discharging a contract by agreement. If neither party has carried out his part of the bargain there is a bilateral discharge of the contract. The agreement by each party to end the contract will be consideration for the agreement of the other. If one party has carried out his obligations under the contract and it is agreed that the contract be ended, then the position will be different. There will be a unilateral discharge of the contract. The one who has carried out his obligations can give up his right to insist that the other performs his side of the contract, and by giving up this right he gives consideration. The party who has done nothing cannot give consideration in the same way; he cannot give up a right to insist on something being done after it has already been done. Therefore, if he is to be able to enforce the agreement to end the contract, he must give some other consideration instead; this will usually be a sum of money. There is one exceptional case in which no consideration is required; this occurs where the agreement is made in the form of a deed (see p. 195).

Frustration of Contract

There are a number of circumstances in which a contract may be discharged by frustration. For example a pianist who has contracted to play may become ill, a concert hall which was to have been hired may be burned down, or there may be a change in the law that makes performance of the contract illegal. In circumstances such as these the common law rule was that the rights of the parties were frozen as from the date of the event that frustrated the contract. The effect of this was that payments due before the frustrating event took place had still to be made, but payments due after that date no longer had to be handed over. Any property handed over under the contract before it was frustrated could not be recovered.

In certain instances these rules led to unfair results, and so the Law Reform (Frustrated Contracts) Act 1943 was passed; this regulates the position today. The Act lays down that where a contract is frustrated, money paid under the contract may be recovered and money payable at the date of frustration ceases to be payable. The court has a discretion under the Act to permit a party who has incurred expenses under the contract to recover or keep a sum of money in respect of those expenses. There are certain other provisions in the Act. Contracts of insurance and contracts for the sale of specific perishable goods (see p. 201) do not come within the Act.

Breach of Contract

Some breaches of contract will entitle the aggrieved party to treat the contract as discharged. Whether the breach will discharge the contract will depend on what sort of term in the contract has been broken. The more important terms in a contract are called conditions, and the less important terms are called warranties. A breach of a condition by one party gives the other party the option to treat the contract as discharged, or, if it suits him better, of treating it as continuing and suing for damages for the breach. A breach of a warranty does not discharge a contract. The remedy of the party suffering from the breach of warranty is to sue for damages.

Sometimes before the date fixed for performance, a party to a contract will say something or do something to show that he intends to break a contract. For example, in *Frost* v. *Knight* (1872) the defendant promised to marry the plaintiff when his father died, but in fact he married somebody else while his father was still alive. He could not therefore carry out his contract to marry the plaintiff. A breach of contract of this kind is called an anticipatory breach; the party suffering from the breach has the alternative of suing immediately the breach occurs or waiting until the date fixed for performance arrives and then suing. In *Frost* v. *Knight*, therefore the plaintiff could have sued as soon as the defendant married or could have waited until the father died before suing.

REMEDIES FOR BREACH OF CONTRACT

The remedy for breach of contract at common law is an action for damages. A plaintiff who has suffered from a breach of contract will not necessarily be awarded damages in respect of all the loss he has suffered. No compensation will be given in respect of any loss that is regarded as not being sufficiently closely connected with the breach of contract. A loss that is not connected closely enough with the breach of contract is said to be a consequence that is "too remote" from the breach of contract. The most important case on remoteness of damage is *Hadley* v. *Baxendale* (1854). A broken crankshaft belonging to a mill was handed to the defendants for carriage. They were late in delivering it and the plaintiffs suffered a loss of profits since they had no other shaft and their business was held up in its absence. The miller sued the carriers for the loss sustained but were unsuccessful because the carriers had not been told that they were delivering the only shaft, and had no reason to suppose that their delay would cause such a loss of profits as occurred. The present rules as to remoteness of damage in contract which may be gathered from *Hadley* v. *Baxendale* and subsequent cases are as follows: first, a party who is in breach of contract will be liable in all cases for losses that can be expected to follow performance (see p. 193), which is used mainly in connection with contracts for from the breach in the ordinary way. Secondly, the party in breach of contract will only be liable for special losses if he knows of the circumstances which may give rise to a special loss and contracts on the basis that he will be liable for that special loss. A plaintiff must mitigate his loss as far as possible. He will be awarded damages only in respect of unavoidable loss.

Other less usual remedies for breach of contract are the equitable remedy of specific performance (see p. 220), which is used mainly in connection with contracts for the sale of land, and the equitable remedy of injunction (see p. 70) that is used to restrain a threatened breach of contract.

WRITING IN RELATION TO CONTRACTS

Generally speaking, there is no particular requirement as to how a contract shall be made. In most cases it is possible to make a valid contract by speaking, by writing or by conduct. An example of a contract made by conduct is one made at an auction sale. If the auctioneer asks "will anyone bid £100?" and Jack nods, Jack has made an offer. When the auctioneer brings down his hammer he accepts the offer and the contract is complete. In certain instances, however, writing is necessary to a contract, and these instances are considered below.

Deeds

Deeds are also called specialty contracts to distinguish them from simple contracts which have already been considered. Contracts made by deed differ from simple contracts in one main respect. No consideration is required to make a contract by deed valid. In a deed the important thing is that the correct procedure should be complied with. If the deed takes the right form and is made in the right way it will be valid. The rules are as follows:

(i) a deed must be in writing;
(ii) it must be written, printed or typed on paper, parchment or vellum;
(iii) it must be signed;
(iv) it must be sealed;
(v) it must be delivered.

The requirement of a signature was introduced only in 1926. To seal a deed it is only necessary to touch it with the intention of sealing it, although it is customary to stick a red wafer on it to show that sealing has taken place. Delivery means handing the deed over to the other party to the contract. Sometimes two copies of a contract made by deed are prepared. Each party signs and seals one copy and delivers it to the other. The rule that no consideration is required for a contract made by deed means, for example that if in a deed Alice contracts to give her car to Jack for nothing, he can sue on the contract and recover the price of the car if Alice fails to carry out her promise. If it is intended to transfer title to land by conveyance (see p. 220) or to create a lease of land for more than three years, a deed must be used or else the transaction will have no effect.

Contracts Needing Written Evidence

Two types of contract are made subject to a special statutory rule. They may be made by word of mouth, by ordinary writing, or by deed in the usual way, but they cannot be proved to exist in a court of law without some evidence in writing. The first type of contract coming within the rule is a contract of guarantee, which is regulated by the Statute of Frauds 1677. This statute lays down that if anybody promises to pay a debt in the event of the debtor himself failing to do so, this promise must be proved by written evidence, if the case should come to court. The other type of contract within the rule is a contract for the sale of land. This is regulated by the Law of Property Act 1925, s. 40, which provides that no action can succeed in respect of a promise to sell land unless the plaintiff can produce written evidence of the contract.

If a contract of guarantee or a contract for the sale of land is made by deed or in writing without the use of a deed, no difficulty arises; the deed or written contract can be produced in court. If however, the contract is made by word of mouth, the position is different. In the case of both a contract of guarantee and a contract for the sale of land the plaintiff must, if he is to succeed, produce to the court a "note or memorandum" in writing which sets out the essential terms of the contract. This is in contrast to the usual situation where the existence of a contract may be proved by giving spoken evidence. It is not necessary for the note or memorandum to set out all the terms of the contract, but it must show who are the parties to the contract, the property to which the contract relates, what has been promised, and the consideration except in the case of a guarantee; lastly it must be signed by the defendant. The note may be made out and signed at any time between the making of the contract and the date of the trial. If the parties have made a contract by word of mouth, and then written to each other about it, a letter, or two or three letters read together may show all the essentials required for a note or memorandum, and if so the court will accept the letters as providing the necessary evidence. It should be noted in conclusion that if there is a contract coming within this category and there is no note or memorandum of it, the contract is valid like any other, and things done under the contract are validly done. Any disadvantage is felt only when the contract becomes the subject of litigation.

Equity will not permit unfair advantage to be taken of the

provisions of the Law of Property Act 1925, s. 40 and under the equitable doctrine of part performance, it will grant the equitable remedy of specific performance to a contracting party even in the absence of a sufficient note or memorandum if the following conditions are fulfilled:

  (i) if it would be fraudulent for the other party to go back on the promise;
 (ii) if there is proper oral evidence of the contract;
(iii) if it is a contract of the type in respect of which specific performance may be granted (e.g. it will not be granted if either party to the contract is an infant);
(iv) if the promise made could have referred only to the contract in question.

Chapter 13

Some Important Contracts

BUYING GOODS

A contract is created by the buying and selling of goods but this is a specialised field and the law on the subject is largely governed by the Sale of Goods Act 1979; any points not covered by the Act are governed by the general rules of the law of contract. The Act defines precisely what is meant by a "sale of goods"; s. 2(1) defines it as "a contract whereby the seller transfers or agrees to transfer the property in goods to the buyer for a money consideration called the price". There are several points to notice in connection with this definition: (i) the words "the property in the goods" mean the ownership of the goods; (ii) the consideration (see p. 181) must be wholly or partly money; in the absence of money consideration the transaction will not amount to a sale of goods, and the Act will not apply to it. If for example Jack handed over goods to Alice and she did some work for him in return, there would be a valid contract, but not a sale of goods, and the ordinary rules of contract would apply instead of the Sale of Goods Act; (iii) the seller may pass the ownership of the goods to the buyer immediately the contract is made, in which case the transaction is called a "sale". On the other hand he may instead agree to pass the ownership to the buyer at some later date, in which case the transaction is called an "agreement to sell": both of these arrangements come within the definition.

The Sale

An agreement to sell becomes a sale when the agreed date

arrives and the goods become the buyer's; it is for these reasons that the words "transfers, or agrees to transfer the property in goods" have been put into the definition.

The main purpose of the Sale of Goods Act is to lay down a series of rules so that everybody who buys or sells goods will know exactly what are his rights and duties. As far as buyers are concerned, the most important rules are those concerning what are called the "implied conditions" laid down in the Act. Normally these implied conditions are automatically incorporated into every contract for the sale of goods, without any action by the parties and even without their knowledge of the Act. The conditions are contained in ss. 12–15 of the Act and are detailed below. They place a number of duties on sellers, for the protection of buyers.

At one time the parties to a contract, especially sellers, were free to exclude any or all of the implied conditions of agreement between themselves.

This led to some sellers taking unfair advantage of buyers. Nowadays the Unfair Contract Terms Act 1977 assists persons dealing as consumers when they make a contract to buy goods. Such contracts are the subject of a definition which has three main elements: (a) the seller sells in the course of business, (b) the purchaser does *not* buy in the course of business, and (c) the goods are of a type ordinarily bought for private consumption. We are concerned here only with this type of sale. The Act makes it impossible to exclude or vary any of the terms implied in a contract of sale of goods by those sections. As regards non-consumer sales, ss. 13–15 may be excluded by the contract but only in so far as such an exclusion is reasonable.

The Implied Conditions

(i) It is an implied condition of the contract that the seller has a right to sell the goods (s. 12). If it turns out that the goods do not belong to the seller, and the buyer has to give them up to the true owner, the effect of the implied condition is to make the seller liable in damages for the price of the goods to the buyer. This was held to be the case in *Rowland* v. *Divall* (1923) where a car was sold by a vendor who did not own it.

(ii) Where goods are sold by description, there is an implied condition that the goods will correspond with the description (s. 13).

(iii) Where the seller sells goods in the course of a business, there is an implied condition that the goods supplied are of merchantable quality except (a) as regards defects drawn to the buyer's attention before the contract is made or (b) if the buyer examines the goods before making the contract as regards defects which that examination ought to reveal (s. 14(2)). Section 14(6) of the Act lays down that "Goods of any kind are of merchantable quality within the meaning of subsection (2) above if they are as fit for the purpose or purposes for which goods of that kind are commonly bought as it is reasonable to expect having regard to any description applied to them, the price (if relevant) and all the other relevant circumstances."

This definition introduces the idea of reasonableness. For example, the words "the purpose or purposes for which goods of that kind are commonly bought" would make it impossible to claim that a dish cloth is not of merchantable quality if it makes a poor handkerchief. The definition also has the effect of making it necessary to consider such facts as whether the goods were sold second-hand, or at a very cheap price, when a decision has to be made, for example by a judge, on the question of whether or not goods sold were of merchantable quality.

(iv) Where the buyer makes known to the seller any particular purpose for which the goods are being bought, there is an implied condition that the goods are reasonably fit for that purpose whether or not that is a purpose for which such goods are commonly supplied, except where the buyer does not rely, or it is unreasonable for him to rely on the seller's skill and judgment (s. 14(3)).

Thus a person who, when buying a dish cloth says he wants it to dry his dog after giving it a bath, may have a right of action if the seller says, wrongly, that the dish cloth will make a good towel for a dog.

(v) Where goods are sold by sample there are implied conditions that the bulk shall correspond with the sample, that the buyer shall have a reasonable opportunity to compare the bulk with the sample, before accepting the bulk, and that the goods shall be free from any hidden defect rendering them unmerchantable (s. 15).

Passing of Ownership

Sometimes it is important to know the exact time at which the ownership of goods passes from the seller to the buyer because under s. 20 of the Act, the goods are at the risk of the owner unless the parties agree otherwise. There are a number of rules laid down by the Act to deal with the time of the passing of ownership in various eventualities, and for the purposes of these rules goods are divided into two main categories, "ascertained goods" and "unascertained goods". Ascertained goods (which are also called specific goods) are those identified and agreed on at the making of the contract, *e.g.*, "the silver Toyota Crown 4464"; unascertained goods are goods which have not been identified and agreed on.

The main rules are as follows:

(i) The ownership of unascertained goods will pass when goods fitting the agreement are appropriated to the contract by one party with the consent of the other party: *e.g.*, if 1,000 tons of copper are landed by the "Quo Vadis" at the port named by the buyer, or if the motor dealer writes to the buyer saying "two silver Toyota Crowns have arrived, one standard and one de luxe, which do you want?" and gets the reply "I want the de luxe one", and thereupon sticks a "sold" label on the de luxe model, the ownership will pass at that time.

(ii) Where there is a contract for the sale of ascertained goods in a deliverable state, ownership passes when the contract is made. This is the usual situation.

(iii) If something remains to be done to ascertained goods to put them into a deliverable state, ownership will not pass until the thing is done and the buyer has notice of this.

(iv) If ascertained goods are in a deliverable state but have to be weighed, measured or tested by the seller to ascertain the price, ownership will not pass until this is done and the buyer has notice of this.

As an illustration of the working of the rules we may consider the purchase of a tape deck. If the buyer goes into the shop, sees a tape deck to his liking, offers to buy it, and the shopkeeper agrees to sell it to him, then in the ordinary course of events it becomes his at once (see (ii) above). This will be so even if it is agreed that the buyer will collect the tape deck and pay for it the following day. If during the night, the shop is burnt down and the tape deck destroyed, the buyer will have to pay for it. If, on the other hand the buyer agrees with the shopkeeper to purchase the tape deck provided that the head is changed, and that he will collect it when this has been done, then the buyer will not have to pay if the tape deck is destroyed in the night, since ownership will not pass to him until the change has been made and the buyer has been told of this (see (iii) above).

It is always open to the parties to the contract to make a special agreement as to when ownership shall pass, or when payment shall be made, but most people never think of these details, and when goods are destroyed or damaged before delivery the rules laid down in the Act will usually apply.

The Act lays down that it is the duty of the seller to deliver the goods and that the buyer's duty is to accept and pay for them. Unless the parties make any other arrangement the proper place for delivery, under the Act is the seller's place of business, or if he has none, his residence. The seller has a right of action for damages if the buyer does not pay for the goods when payment is due. If the buyer refuses to accept and pay for the goods the seller has a similar right. If the seller still has the goods in his possession on the date of payment, and he is not paid, he has a right of "lien". This means that he can keep the goods in his possession until he is paid, even if the ownership of them has passed to the buyer.

Refusal to Deliver

The buyer has a right of action for damages if the seller refuses to deliver the goods. If there is a breach of a term of the contract, the buyer's rights will depend on whether the term was a condition, *i.e.*, a major term of the contract, or a warranty, *i.e.*, a minor term of the contract. If the broken term is a condition, whether it be one of the implied conditions described above, or some other condition, the buyer is entitled to treat the contract as ended and may sue for damages for non-performance. In practice this right is a limited one, since it is lost if the buyer has accepted the goods, in this case he has only a right to sue for damages. If the seller is guilty of a breach of warranty the buyer has a right to sue for damages. In very exceptional cases the buyer may be able to obtain specific performance (an order of the court) ordering the seller to hand over the goods. In order to obtain specific performance it will probably be necessary to show that the goods in question are unique, *e.g.*, an irreplaceable antique or work of art.

Methods of Sale

Goods may be sold in various ways; by one person offering them to another personally, by putting them in a shop window, by advertising them on a commercial radio station, or by putting them in an automatic vending machine, for example. In order to decide on the legal implications of any particular method of sale it is necessary to look at the facts of the particular case. It has been held that the effect of displaying goods in a supermarket is merely to invite those who enter the supermarket to do business; the putting of goods on the shelves is not an offer. The shopkeeper is saying, in effect "if you offer me the price marked on the goods, I may accept your offer". It is the shopper who makes the offer, and the shopkeeper who accepts, but he is not bound to accept the offer. The same situation applies in respect of goods shown in a shop window. If the advertisement on the commercial radio station says "send £1 to Alice and you will receive a bottle of perfume", this is an offer, which can be accepted by sending the pound. On the other hand, if the advertisement says "send 5p to Alice for her catalogue of perfumes", this is an offer to sell the catalogue but only an invitation to do business in respect of the goods advertised in the catalogue.

The effect of putting an ordinary slot machine full of goods in a public place is to make a standing offer to the world at large that if the appropriate coin is inserted, certain goods will be delivered. The insertion of the coin constitutes the acceptance and the contract is made when the coin goes in; this is a contract made by implication. The world is moving on, however, and there is no reason why an automatic vending machine equipped with a computer should not be devised which will only supply goods in certain events (*e.g.*, beer during licensing hours), and will otherwise return the money. In such circumstances the setting up of the machine would constitute an invitation to do business, and not an offer. The person inserting the coin would be making the offer, which the machine might accept by delivering the goods, or reject, returning the coin.

HIRE-PURCHASE

A hire-purchase contract is a means whereby a person without sufficient money to buy goods outright (or who for some other reason such as a wish to keep his capital intact), is enabled to buy goods by paying the purchase price in instalments. Under the contract the owner usually hands over the goods to the hirer in return for a small sum as soon as the contract is made. The typical agreement of hire-purchase provides that the owner shall let out the goods to the hirer who is to make regular periodical payments, and that the hirer is to have the option of buying the goods. Ordinarily if the hirer pays all the sums agreed in the contract and remains in possession of the goods throughout the agreed period it will be assumed that he has opted to buy, and ownership will pass to him. As the hirer under a hire-purchase agreement has not agreed to buy the goods, he will not have the protection of the implied conditions contained in the Sale of Goods Act 1979.

Hire-purchase agreements are of two types, those governed by the common law, and those governed by statute. Most of the law concerning hire-purchase contracts governed by statute is to be found in the Hire-Purchase Act 1965. Statutory control applies to all hire-purchase contracts other than those where the hirer is a corporation (see p. 97), or where the hire-purchase price exceeds £5,000.

Requirements for the Agreement

The Hire-Purchase Act 1965 s. 1(1) defines a hire-purchase agreement as "an agreement for the bailment of goods under which the bailee may buy the goods, or under which the property in the goods will or may pass to the bailee". A bailment is the handing over of goods to another person, without handing over ownership, and a bailee is a person who receives goods under a bailment. The main provisions of the Act are discussed below.

Before the agreement is made the owner must state the cash price of the goods to the hirer in writing. This requirement will be fulfilled if the hirer has inspected the goods with a label attached to them showing the cash price, or if he has selected them from a price list or advertisement (s. 6).

The agreement must contain the following:

   (i) a statement of the cash price, the hire-purchase price (which will usually be higher than the cash price to cover interest charges) and the amounts and dates for payment of the instalments;

   (ii) a list of the goods;

   (iii) a notice setting out the right of the hirer to terminate the agreement;

   (iv) a notice explaining the restrictions on the owner's right to recover the goods (s. 7).

If the hirer signs the agreement at the owner's place of business he must be supplied there and then with (i) a copy of the agreement signed by all parties to it, or (ii) a copy of the agreement, not yet signed by all parties to it, followed by a copy signed by all parties to it sent on to him within seven days (s. 8).

If the hirer signs the agreement elsewhere than at the owner's place of business different rules will apply. This is to meet the situation which arises, for example when the high-pressure salesman persuades a housewife at home to sign a hire-purchase agreement for some luxury and her husband returns home to find the family saddled with an unwanted liability. The Act provides for a "cooling-off" period during which the hirer can change his mind and call the contract off. If anybody is in doubt as to the wisdom of entering into a hire-purchase contract, while he is in a shop, he should tell the shopkeeper to give the agreement to him to take home or to send it on to his home; in this way he will be able to take advantage of the "cooling-off" period. The rules about signing the agreement away from the shop are that when the agreement is presented to or sent to the hirer for signature, it must be accompanied by a copy. This copy is called "the first statutory copy". In addition a copy of the agreement signed by all parties to it must be sent by post to the hirer within seven days of the making of the agreement, this is called "the second statutory copy". Both of the statutory copies must contain a statement of the right of the hirer to serve a notice of cancellation of the agreement and must give the name and address of the person to whom the notice of cancellation must be sent (s. 9).

The reason the Act makes such elaborate provisions as to the supply of copies of agreements to hirers is to ensure that a hirer is not without a copy at any time after he has signed the agreement. It is particularly important for him to have a copy if he is thinking of cancelling an agreement under s. 9.

Right of Cancellation

The hirer (who is called "the prospective hirer" for the purposes of cancellation) who has signed the agreement off the owner's premises in accordance with s. 9 has the right to cancel the agreement at any time after he has signed the agreement and before the end of the period of four days beginning with the day on which he received the second statutory copy. The notice must show the intention of the prospective hirer to withdraw from the transaction, but it need not be in any particular words (s. 11).

A notice of cancellation is regarded as being served on the owner at the time it is posted (s. 12). If the prospective hirer has the goods in his possession he is not under any obligation to deliver the goods to the owner except at his own premises. He is under an obligation to take reasonable care of the goods for twenty-one days from the date of service of notice of the cancellation unless he refuses to hand them over after a request in writing from the owner, in which case his obligation to take care of them is extended until he does so (s. 13).

Right of Hirer to Terminate Agreement

At any time before the final payment is due the hirer can end the agreement by written notice, and should then send the goods back. The ordinary rule is that on terminating the agreement he must pay what is necessary (if anything) to make up what has been paid to half the hire-purchase price. However, if in an action in court the court is satisfied that the owner has lost less money than half the purchase price on the deal, it may order the payment of some smaller sum than would be due under the ordinary rule.

Owner's Right to Recover Possession

At common law when a hirer has fallen into arrears in making payments, the owner is entitled to take the goods back, *e.g.*, by driving away an unattended motor car on which instalments are outstanding. No particular proportion of the hire-purchase price need be unpaid to give the owner this right. Under the Act the owner's right to recover goods by taking them back himself is lost as soon as one-third of the hire-purchase price has been paid or tendered, *i.e.*, offered; goods coming into this category are given the name "protected goods" by s. 33, and if the owner wishes to recover possession of them he must bring an action in the county court.

CREDIT-SALE AGREEMENTS

Hire-purchase agreements must be distinguished from credit-sale agreements which are also dealt with in the Act. A credit-sale agreement is an agreement for the sale of goods under which the purchase price is payable by five or more instalments. As it is an agreement for the sale of goods it differs in two main respects from a hire-purchase agreement. First, the Sale of Goods Act 1979 applies to it, and secondly the ownership of the goods passes to the buyer when the contract is made. This means that a purchaser under a credit-sale agreement, unlike a hirer under a hire-purchase agreement can pass on ownership of the goods to somebody else before he himself has paid the full price except in respect of motor vehicles under the Hire-Purchase Act 1964, s. 27. Some provisions of the Hire-Purchase Act 1965 apply to credit-sale agreements.

REFORM OF THE LAW ON FAIR TRADING AND CONSUMER CREDIT

The Fair Trading Act 1973, in order to assist consumers, created the office of Director General of Fair Trading, and set up a Consumer Protection Advisory Committee. Under the Act it is the Director General's duty to keep under review commercial activities relating to goods supplied to consumers and to collect information about practices which may adversely affect consumers in any way.

Following the report of the Committee on Consumer Credit, the Consumer Credit Act 1974 was passed. This Act heralds a great change in consumer protection and the hire of goods. Parts of the Act came into force in 1974, and the rest of it will be introduced gradually by means of Statutory Instruments over the next few years. The Director General of Fair Trading who was appointed under the Fair Trading Act 1973 has already been given extended duties, and eventually the Hire Purchase Act 1965 will be repealed and replaced by the provisions of the new Act.

The new Statute is concerned with lenders and borrowers and as far as possible treats all lenders and types of credit alike. In the first place the businesses of creditors and owners of goods as well as of others engaged in the credit industry have to be licensed by the Director General of Fair Trading. These other businesses include credit brokers, who introduce those wanting to obtain credit to lenders; debt adjusters who negotiate terms for the discharge of a debt; debt counsellors who give advice to debtors on paying off debts; debt collectors and credit reference agencies which collect information about people's financial standing and sell it to lenders. In 1978, 62,897 licences were issued.

There are numerous definitions in the Act, which governs, in the main the type of agreement known as a *regulated consumer credit agreement*. There are three conditions to be fulfilled if an agreement is to come within this category. Firstly, it must not be an exempt agreement. There are various types of exempt agreement; examples are house purchase, weekly newspaper and milk bills, cash loans at low rates of interest, and hire of gas and electricity meters. Secondly, the credit granted to the debtor must not exceed £5,000. (This sum is now under review.) The third condition is that the credit is granted to an individual and not to a corporation. A hire-purchase agreement comes within these conditions. Also falling under the provisions of the Act is the *consumer hire agreement* which is similar to the agreement mentioned above, but which is not a hire-purchase agreement and which is a hiring for more than three months.

The Act makes provision for Regulations (by way of a Statutory Instrument) to be made about the form and contents of agreements for credit so that the consumer is told his rights and duties, the genuine rate of interest he has to pay, and the protection he has under the Act. In many cases the consumer will have a five-day cooling-off period during which he can change his mind after signing an agreement.

If a credit reference agency has a file about a consumer, it must when requested and paid a fee of 25 pence give the consumer a copy of the file, and if the consumer considers that the file is incorrect he can ask the agency to rectify it. If it does not, the consumer can put the matter before the Director General for appropriate action to settle the dispute.

THE TRADING STAMPS ACT 1964

When buying goods purchasers are often given trading stamps, and this Act was passed to regulate their use and to assist and protect the public. The first important provision of the Act is that every stamp issued by a trading stamp company must have on its face, the money value of it. Secondly, the Act lays down that if the holder of any number of trading stamps having a total face value of not less than 25 pence requests the company promoting the trading stamp scheme to do so, the company shall redeem them by paying over their cash value. The holder may exercise his right by presenting the stamps at the promoter's registered office or by sending them by post to that office. Thirdly, in every shop or other place in which a trading stamp scheme is operated there must be kept posted a notice stating the cash value of the stamps issued under the scheme, and giving such particulars as will enable customers readily to ascertain the number of trading stamps, if any, to which they are entitled on any purchase.

If any current catalogue has been published for the trading stamp scheme by the promoter, a copy of it must be kept where it can be conveniently consulted by customers. If the shop does not comply with these provisions, the person having control of the shop shall be liable on conviction to a fine of twenty pounds.

It should be noted that there are certain shops which give metal tokens or stamps which may be exchanged for goods or cash only by the proprietors of the shop where the tokens or stamps were given. Tokens and stamps falling into this category do not count as "trading stamps" for the purposes of the Act, and consequently the Act does not apply to such arrangements.

CONTRACTS OF EMPLOYMENT

There are two main types of contract of employment, each giving rise to a different legal relationship. The first type of contract is sometimes described as a contract of service, and it gives rise to the relationship of master and servant. The characteristic of this type of contract is that the master controls the manner in which the servant does his work and is vicariously liable for any torts committed by the servant in the course of his employment (see p. 157). Most contracts for employment in offices, shops, and industry are contracts of service and it is this type of contract that is considered in this chapter. The second type of contract is called a contract for services, and it gives rise to the relationship of employer and independent contractor. The characteristic of a contract of this type is that the employer does not control the manner in which the independent contractor does his work and is entitled only to a satisfactory final result. Contracts with architects, solicitors and accountants are generally within this category, and with some exceptions the employer is not responsible for the torts of his independent contractor.

Characteristics of the Contract

The general law of contract applies to contracts of employment. Generally speaking no particular form is required for the contract; it may be oral or written. The Employment Protection (Consolidation) Act 1978, however, provides that the employer must within thirteen weeks of the beginning of employment give the employee a written statement containing particulars of the terms of employment. The thirteen-week rule assists employers by making it unnecessary for them to prepare written statements for casual workers. The items to be included in the statement are:

(i) the scale of remuneration and the intervals at which payment is made (*e.g.*, weekly or monthly);
(ii) hours of work;
(iii) holidays and holiday pay;
(iv) sick pay and pension scheme;
(v) the length of notice the employee must give, and the length of notice the employer must give, to end the contract;
(vi) whether an employment is or is not pensionable.

It is not necessary for the employer to give a statement to any employee who is employed normally less than twenty-one hours weekly, or to any employee who is his parent, child or spouse.

Employment of Minors

Minors have a limited capacity at common law to enter into contracts of employment (see p. 177). In addition to the rules of common law, there are a number of restrictions laid down by statute. For instance under the Children and Young Persons Acts 1933 to 1963 as amended no person under the age of seventeen years may be employed in street trading unless over fourteen years and employed by his parent under a local authority by-law. Under the same Acts, no child under sixteen shall take part in a performance for entertainment where a charge is made for admission, or where the performance is broadcast or recorded unless a licence has been granted by the local authority permitting the child to take part. The Acts do not seek to control occasional performances, and no licence is required if the child has not taken part in other performances on more than three days in the six months prior to the performance in question. Other employments for children which are forbidden or restricted are factory work, employment on ships and employment below ground in a mine. A contract of apprenticeship is not strictly a contract of employment, although the Employment Protection (Consolidation) Act 1978 applies to it. Usually, it is an agreement under which the master agrees to teach the apprentice his trade or profession and the apprentice agrees to learn and to serve the master. It must be made in writing if it is to be enforceable, and it is often made by deed.

Duties of Employer and Employee

The employee has various duties towards his employer, and unless the parties agree to the contrary, the following will be implied by the law as arising from the relationship of master and servant. The employee's implied duties are to go to the place of work, to carry out his work with care and skill, to obey orders from his master, to behave properly at work, and to behave towards his master with good faith. It will be a breach of this last duty to give away any of his master's secrets, or to try to take away any of his master's customers.

The implied duties of the employer are to pay the wages agreed upon in the contract, to take reasonable care for the employee's safety by providing proper premises and appliances, a competent staff of men and a safe system of work, and in certain cases where the opportunity for the employee to work is a vital factor in the contract (*e.g.*, in the case of an actress) the employer must provide work; payment of wages alone will not be enough.

The duty to pay the agreed wages is regulated to a certain extent by the Truck Acts and the Payment of Wages Act 1960 as amended. This type of legislation began during the industrial revolution when it became the practice of some employers to make their employees accept goods instead of money as wages. The Truck Acts, the first of which was passed in 1831, were intended largely to prevent various malpractices by employers, and the 1831 Act laid down that workmen must be paid in the current coin of the realm. In this context "workmen" means manual workers. With the passage of time and the growth of banking facilities, the payment of employees in cash came to be regarded by some as cumbersome and old-fashioned, and so the Payment of Wages Act 1960 was passed. This Act permits an employer who has received a request in writing from his employee to make payment in one of a number of ways instead of in cash. He may pay the wages directly into the employee's bank account, or give him a cheque, postal order or money order, but must also let the employee have a statement showing how the amount paid is arrived at, by indicating what deductions have been made for income tax, national insurance, or other reasons.

Statutory Duties

In addition to duties placed on the employer expressly by the contract, and by implication, statutes and statutory instruments may place extra duties on employers either generally or in particular trades. Thus, under a statutory instrument the employer will have to deduct from the employee's pay the appropriate sum (if any) that the employee must give to the collector of taxes through the "pay as you earn" income tax scheme; this money must be sent by the employer to the collector. It is the duty of the employer under the Social Security Acts to buy from a post office national insurance stamps for his employees (with certain exceptions), and to stick these stamps on a card. He must send completed cards to the appropriate government department. The price of the stamps is paid partly by the employer and partly by the employee through deductions from his pay made by the employer. The money raised in this way is used to pay for the national health service, and for benefits given under the national insurance scheme to those injured at work, their dependents, and others.

Since the coming into force of the Redundancy Payments Act 1965 (see below) employers have had to make contributions to a redundancy fund through extra national insurance contributions. The Industrial Training Act 1964 provides for the establishment of training boards for particular industries as a step towards making better provision for the training of persons who are over compulsory school age in industry and commerce. The Act obliges employers to pay a levy towards the expenses of the training board for their own industry.

The Factories Act 1961 lays many duties on employers to secure the health and safety of factory workers, and in particular contains rules designed to protect young persons, that is those under eighteen years of age. There are rules concerning, for example, maximum hours of work and meal intervals. The Offices, Shops and Railway Premises Act 1963 as amended sets up similar standards to be observed by employers in offices and like premises, and this Act too contains certain provisions designed to protect young persons.

The Termination of the Contract of Employment

The contract will terminate automatically, if it is entered into for a fixed period, when that period ends. If no particular period is laid down the contract may be terminated by either party giving reasonable notice. What amounts to reasonable notice will depend on the employment in question and may be dependent on the custom of a particular trade; sometimes the length of notice that is reasonable corresponds to the period between payments, *e.g.*, a month's notice for monthly paid employees. Generally the more exalted the employment, the longer the period. The Employment Protection (Consolidation) Act 1978 lays down minimum periods of notice, but these will not apply if a longer period is given by custom or by express agreement. The minimum periods do not apply unless the employee has been continuously employed for at least thirteen weeks. An employee who has been employed for twenty-six weeks or more must give at least one week's notice, although the employer can put into the contract a term that longer notice be given. The minimum periods to which employees are entitled are: one week for an employee with between thirteen weeks and two years continuous employment; two weeks for an employee with two years or more but less than five years continuous employment; and so on up to eight weeks for employees with fifteen or more years' continuous employment. A schedule to the Act lays down how periods of employment are to be computed.

Redundancy Payments

Under the Redundancy Payments Act 1965 as amended by the Employment Protection (Consolidation) Act 1978 an employee who has been continuously employed by the same employer for at least two years since attaining the age of eighteen years and is under sixty-five years of age if a man, or under sixty years if a woman is entitled in certain circumstances to be given a redundancy payment by his employer if he is dismissed by reason of redundancy. He will be paid nothing if dismissed because of his own fault. Certain classes of employees such as civil servants are excluded from the scheme.

Documents

When an employee leaves his employment it is the duty of the employer to hand to him his national insurance card stamped up to date, together with an income tax form showing the amount he has earned during the current income tax year (which ends in April), and the amount that has been deducted by the employer under the "pay as you earn" scheme and sent to the collector of taxes. The employee hands these documents to his next employer.

Restrictions on Re-employment

Sometimes a contract of service contains a clause restricting the employment that can be taken by the employee on changing jobs. Usually the agreement will be valid, and the employer will be entitled to institute proceedings against a former employee who disregards the restriction. Occasionally, however the clause is invalid because it is too restrictive (see p. 189). The former employee's duty to act in good faith continues after he has left his previous employment, and he is even then not entitled to give away his former employer's trade secrets, or to take away his customers.

Testimonials

There is no obligation on an employer, except in the case of a merchant seaman, under the Merchant Shipping Act 1970, to give a testimonial to an employee. If however, he decides to give one, it should be accurate because if it is better than the employee deserves, and induces somebody else to employ him thus causing loss, the employer may be held liable for the loss of the person relying on the testimonial. If, on the other hand the testimonial is defamatory of the employee, he may be able to bring an action for defamation; in such a case the employer will be able to set up the defence of qualified privilege, which can only be overcome by proof that the employer acted maliciously (see p. 172).

Remedies for Breach of Contract of Employment

The employer has the right to dismiss an employee instantly in certain cases where he is guilty of conduct that amounts to a fundamental breach of contract. Whether the conduct of the employee is such as to justify the dismissal is a question of fact, but if, for example, he steals his employer's money or is often too drunk to carry out his duties instant dismissal may well be justified. In the event of a justified dismissal the employer need not give any notice or wages in lieu, and there are situations where the employee may even lose his right to wages in respect of work already done by him. In some cases the employer may have the right to suspend an employee for a time; the employee will not be allowed to work, and the employer will not be liable to pay wages during the period of suspension.

Another remedy available to the employer is an action for damages for breach of contract, and in appropriate cases the employer may be able to obtain an injunction (order of the court) against the employee to restrain him from committing a breach of contract, *e.g.*, if an actor has contracted not to work for any other employer for a certain time.

If the employer commits such a fundamental breach of the contract as to show that he no longer intends to be bound by it, the employee may leave and sue for damages. He has the right to an action for damages for other breaches, and in particular a right to sue for damages for wrongful dismissal, where he has had his employment terminated without proper justification. Of course if either the employer or the employee bring the contract to an end by serving the proper notice, no action for damages will succeed.

BUYING A HOUSE

Houses are considered in law as being a part of the land on which they stand, and land differs from everything else that can be bought or sold, in various ways. In the first place, land is much more permanent than anything else, and usually one can be confident that it will still be in existence in say, a hundred years time. Secondly, a number of people may have rights over the same piece of land; thus Jack may own it, and Alice may have a right of way across it, which entitles her to use it, but which does not make her in any sense the owner. Thirdly, because of being different from other things that can be owned, land has become the subject of special rules of law. We will consider the usual steps that lead to the ownership of a house and the "parcel" of land, as it is called, on which it stands.

The Estate Agent

A landowner wishing to sell a house usually places the task of finding a purchaser in the hands of an "estate agent", whose business it is to bring vendors and purchasers together for a fee. Although many estate agents have professional qualifications, these are not necessary, and anybody can set himself up in business as an estate agent. It is best, if possible, to deal with an agent who has a professional qualification, because he has to conduct his business fairly in accordance with the rules of his professional organisation. The fee paid by the vendor to an estate agent for finding a purchaser varies, usually, with the value of the land or house to be sold.

Let us suppose that Jack and Alice have just married and are looking for a house. They see a house they like and go to the estate agent who is acting on behalf of the vendor to say that they want to buy it. The estate agent will then ask them to pay a deposit, which will usually be something between five and twenty pounds. This is a very important stage in the transaction and the intending purchaser should insist on receiving a proper receipt from the estate agent; if he does not, he may find himself in the most serious difficulties. The purchaser should insist the the receipt for the deposit includes the words "subject to contract and survey". If he obtains such a receipt, he has not made a contract to buy the house, and remains free to withdraw and demand his deposit back. By the same token, however, the vendor is free to send the deposit back and sell to somebody else, although this would be unusual. The paying of a deposit shows that the intending purchaser is serious and after having received a deposit, an estate agent will normally not offer the house to others. At the time of paying the deposit Jack and Alice should ask for the name and address of the vendor's solicitor.

Consulting a Solicitor

The next step that Jack and Alice should take is to consult a solicitor. They should not go to the solicitor who is acting for the vendor, even if it is suggested that there will be a saving of money, since this will be false economy, for even a solicitor may find it difficult to serve two masters, particularly in the event of a dispute arising at some later stage in the transaction. At their first consultation with their solicitor they should tell him the names and addresses of the estate agent and the vendor's solicitor, and should show or hand over to him their receipt.

From this stage onwards, Jack and Alice should not communicate with the vendor, his solicitor or his estate agent about the sale except after consulting their solicitor. This is not a rule of law, but merely a commonsense precaution. If, for example, they wrote a letter without considering the legal implications, it might have some adverse effect on the negotiations being conducted by their solicitor on their behalf. Jack and Alice should have the house inspected by a competent surveyor before deciding finally to buy. The words "Subject to Survey" in the receipt allow them to call off the purchase if the surveyor advises this.

The solicitor acting for Jack and Alice will write to the vendor's solicitor saying that he is acting for Jack and Alice, and will ask a number of questions about the house. These questions are called "enquiries before contract". He will also write to the county council and the borough council asking them to search various registers to find out whether or not there are certain difficulties affecting the land in question, and he will also ask them a number of questions. These enquiries are designed to find out a number of facts about the land, including, for example, whether the council is intending to purchase it compulsorily in the foreseeable future. If the solicitor discovered this to be the case he would probably advise Jack and Alice not to buy the house.

Next the two solicitors will decide on the terms of a contract of sale which will be in writing, and so will satisfy the Law of Property Act 1925, s. 40 (see p. 196). The vendor will sign one copy, and Jack and Alice (if they are buying the house jointly) will sign the other copy, and return it to their own solicitor.

The Contract

Generally the contract will not come into existence until copies have been exchanged and usually the contract provides that exchange will have taken place when the vendor's part of the contract is delivered at the offices of the purchaser's solicitor; (in exchange for the purchaser's part of the contract which will have been received by the vendor's solicitor before he posted his client's part). It is important to know at what moment exchange has taken place, since from this moment the house really belongs to the purchaser because he gets the equitable interest immediately, although the vendor can continue to occupy the house until the whole of the purchase price has been paid. It is therefore clear that from the moment of exchange of contracts the purchaser must insure the property because he will have to pay for it even though it may be destroyed by fire. The legal interest passes to the purchaser on completion.

Specific Performance of the Contract

The remedy for a purchaser whose vendor refuses to complete the transaction by handing over the legal title, is to apply to the court to exercise its equitable jurisdiction and to order "specific performance", which is a remedy for injustice that was developed in the old Chancery courts. A vendor who refuses to obey a decree of specific performance can be sent to prison by the civil court that made the decree.

The Deposit

It is usual for the contract to provide that 10 per cent of the purchase price shall be paid as a deposit by purchasers on exchange of contracts, *i.e.* in the case of a £40,000 house, £4,000. Allowance is made for the deposit paid originally. It is best to pay the deposit to the vendor's solicitor rather than to the estate agent. The reason for this is that in the unlikely event of the money being misapplied by an estate agent who disappears, there might be no compensation available to the purchasers, whereas in the equally unlikely event of a solicitor disappearing with the money, the Law Society would make full compensation from a special fund held for this purpose.

Completion

After exchange of contracts the solicitors will have further correspondence on various technical matters of which space does not permit description, and the details of the document that will transfer ownership will be decided. Some land is identified and transferred by title deeds, and for this type of land a document called a "conveyance" is used to transfer ownership. All other land is identified by a registration number and a map at the Government Land Registry, and is transferred by filling in a form. It is easier and cheaper to transfer registered land than unregistered land, and registration is being extended gradually to cover all land. The final stage in process is called "completion" which takes place usually at the office of the vendor's solicitor. Here the money outstanding is handed over in exchange for the conveyance.

In most cases where land is bought the purchasers have not the capital to pay outright, and borrow the money from a local authority, a building society, an insurance company, or privately through their solicitor. A mortgage is an arrangement whereby in exchange for a loan of money towards the purchase price, the purchaser agrees to pay interest, and gives the lender a right to sell the house if the loan repayments are not kept up. The purchaser's solicitor has to do certain legal work in connection with a mortgage if there is one.

RENTING A FLAT

The principles mentioned here apply equally to the renting of houses. When anybody is considering renting a flat or house he should first consult a solicitor. It will be quite obvious to anybody who has glanced at this book that the smiling gentleman who pushes forward a document saying, "sign there; it is a mere formality" is quite mistaken. Much time and money may be lost by entering too hastily into a contract.

Chapter 14

Family Law

MARRIAGE

The family is the basic unit in our system of social organisation, although the individual is the basic unit of our legal organisation. Ordinarily a family can be regarded as coming into existence on the occasion of a marriage. Marriage is closely connected with the family and the social organisation of the state, and religious significance is also attached to it. Because of this, marriage is closely regulated in all societies both by legal and moral rules. In England there is an established church and for this reason there are two sets of legal rules relating to marriage, those of the general law which apply to everybody, and those governing the Church of England in relation to marriage. Although the Church of Wales has been disestablished, there are nevertheless legal rules that apply to it, and these are similar to those regulating the Church of England.

We are here concerned only with those rules of the law of England and Wales that apply to everybody. The attitude of English law towards the marriage customs and rules of those who are not members of the established church is one of tolerance up to a point; for example the law recognises marriages celebrated according to the customs of the Society of Friends (sometimes called Quakers), but does not recognise any purported marriage by a person who is already married, even though that person may profess some religion which allows or even encourages him or her to take more than one spouse.

Marriage has been defined as a voluntary union for life by one man and one woman to the exclusion of all others: *Hyde* v. *Hyde* (1866). A marriage is usually preceded by an engagement to marry. Prior to the coming into force of the Law Reform (Miscellaneous Provisions) Act 1970, on the 1st January 1971, an engagement constituted a legally binding contract, but by virtue of that Act, this is no longer so, and it will no longer be possible for a broken engagement to be followed by an action in contract for breach of promise of marriage. Section 3 of the Act lays down that gifts between engaged couples may be claimed back if the engagement is broken off irrespective of which party terminated the engagement. It goes on to state that an engagement ring shall be presumed to be an absolute gift, but that it may be reclaimed if the giver presented it on condition that it must be returned if the marriage did not take place. No particular formalities are required for an engagement, which may be made orally or in writing, and an engagement ring, although customary, is not a necessity.

Requirements for a Valid Marriage

There are a number of essential requirements that must be fulfilled to enable a couple to enter into a valid marriage, these are as follows:

Minimum Age

The minimum age at which anybody can marry is sixteen years. If a person under eighteen years wishes to marry he or she must in normal circumstances first obtain the consent of both of his or her parents if alive and living together. If the parents are separated or divorced the consent of the parent who has custody is required. An orphan requires the consent of his or her guardian (if any), while an illegitimate child requires only the mother's consent. If consent is refused the minor may apply to a magistrates' court, a county court, or the High Court for permission to marry. The magistrates' court is the one most often used. After hearing the views of both the minor and those refusing consent, the court may, if it thinks fit, grant permission to marry.

It may be mentioned in passing that the reason why young

people go to Gretna Green to be married is that in the law of Scotland no parental consent is required for the marriage of those aged over sixteen years, and that English people may marry in Scotland after establishing a few weeks' residence and complying with the requirements of Scots law. Gretna Green is traditionally chosen because it is the first town north of the border, but the same rules apply all over Scotland.

Unmarried Status

A married person cannot validly marry again in England even if his religion or nationality would allow this in some other country.

No Close Relationship

Persons who are too closely related cannot intermarry. The prohibited degrees of relationship are set out in the Marriage Act 1949. Under the 1949 Act a man may not marry his stepdaughter but it is possible to avoid this prohibition by having a private statute passed. The Edward Berry and Doris Eilleen Ward (Marriage Enabling) Act 1980 allowed a couple to marry, and the main parts of the Act are set out below:

Whereas—

> Mr. Berry is now aged 62 years and Mrs. Ward is now aged 58 years and, after the late Mrs. Berry died, they formed the wish to be married to each other but a marriage between them would be void as falling within section 1(1) of the Marriage Act 1949, in that they stand in the relationship of stepfather and stepdaughter:
>
> Mr. Berry and Mrs. Ward regard the legal impediment to their marriage as imposing hardship on them, and as serving no useful purpose of public policy, in the particular circumstances of their case:
>
> They accordingly desire that the impediment should be removed in their case:
>
> The object of this Act cannot be attained without the authority of Parliament:
>
> Therefore, Mr. Berry and Mrs. Ward most humbly pray

that it may be enacted, and be it enacted, by the Queen's most Excellent Majesty, by and with the advice and consent of the Lords Spiritual and Temporal, and Commons, in this present Parliament assembled, and by the authority of the same, as follows:—

1. Power to marry

Notwithstanding anything contained in any enactment or any rule of law to the contrary, there shall be no impediment to a marriage between Mr. Berry and Mrs. Ward by reason of their relationship of stepfather and stepdaughter, and no marriage hereafter contracted between them shall be void by reason of that relationship.

Soundness of Mind

If either of the parties is suffering from mental disorder at the time of the marriage, it will be void.

Consent to Marry

If there is no real agreement to marry by one or both of the parties, the marriage will not be valid; *e.g.*, if the apparent consent were obtained by a threat of violence, or if either (*e.g.*, a foreigner) did not realise the nature of the ceremony.

The Legal Formalities of Marriage

The formalities for a Church of England marriage must be considered separately from those concerned with weddings outside the established church. The procedure to be followed by a couple wishing to have a Church of England wedding must be chosen from one of the following four.

Marriage by Banns

The wedding must be preceded by the reading of banns announcing the intended match, on three successive Sundays in the parish churches of both the parties. If the parent or guardian of an infant party says publicly in the church where the banns have been read, that he forbids the banns, and both parties to the marriage know this, a subsequent wedding ceremony will be void.

Marriage by Common Licence

A common licence may be obtained from a bishop. The licence enables the parties to marry without having any banns called, and authorises the wedding to be celebrated at the church of a parish in which at least one of the parties has had his usual place of residence for at least fifteen days before the issue of the licence.

Marriage by Special Licence

The Archbishop of Canterbury alone is empowered to grant special licences. These are issued in urgent cases and may be obtained quickly. With a special licence the parties may marry anywhere and at any time. It is not necessary for the marriage to be celebrated in a church.

Marriage under the Marriage (Registrar General's Licence) Act 1970

The 1970 Act is intended to assist those who do not intend to be married in accordance with the rites of the Church of England or the Church in Wales, but who wish to marry speedily. Provided that one of the parties is seriously ill and is not expected to recover and cannot be moved, the Registrar General may issue a licence for the marriage to take place at a hospital or other place he names.

Marriage by Superintendent Registrar's Certificate

This certificate is obtained by giving notice to a government official, the superintendent registrar, of each of the districts in which the parties have resided for seven days before giving notice. The notice is put in a book which is open to the public to inspect, and if after twenty-one days no objection has been taken, the certificate is issued. If a minor wishes to get married, and declares that he has the requisite consent of any person, the superintendent registrar is entitled, by the Family Law Reform Act 1969, s. 2 to require written evidence of this. The superintendent registrar's certificate furnishes sufficient legal authority to a Church of England clergyman to conduct a marriage in church, but such a clergyman is not bound to accept such a certificate.

In all the circumstances mentioned above, the procedure leads up to a wedding ceremony according to the rules laid down for the Church of England. The most important rules are that the wedding ceremony shall be conducted by a man in Holy Orders before two witnesses between 8 a.m. and 6 p.m. (except in the case of a special licence, when the wedding may take place at any time).

Marriage Outside the Church of England

A wedding outside the Church of England requires either a superintendent registrar's certificate, described above, or a superintendent registrar's certificate and licence. To obtain a superintendent registrar's certificate and licence, notice must be given to one superintendent registrar at least, of a district in which at least one of the parties has resided for fifteen days previously. The notice is put in the book which is open to the public, and provided that no entry is made in the book forbidding the marriage, the certificate and licence is issued on the second working day after the giving of notice.

A valid superintendent registrar's certificate and licence enables a wedding to be solemnised outside the Church of England in one of the four following manners:

In a Superintendent Registrar's Office (popularly called a "Registry Office").—The wedding is celebrated before a registrar and at least two witnesses, in the office which must have its doors open, and certain prescribed words must be used. If Jack Black is marrying Alice White for example, he would have to say, "I call upon these persons here present to witness that I, Jack Black, do take thee, Alice White, to be my lawful wedded wife." Alice would say similar words.

In a Registered Building.—Religious denominations other than the Church of England may register their places of worship for the solemnisation of marriages, and may use any ceremony they think fit provided that the doors are left open and the wedding takes place in the presence of a registrar or an authorised person (such as a priest). In some part of the ceremony the parties must use words identical with those used in a registry office wedding, or, if the wedding is conducted in the presence of the authorised person instead of the registrar, the parties may say, to each other such words as "I, Jack Black, do take thee, Alice White to be my wedded wife".

Quaker Marriage.—The Society of Friends are entitled by statute to celebrate marriages according to their own usages.

Jewish Marriage.—If both parties to a marriage profess the Jewish religion they are entitled to celebrate their marriage according to the usages of the Jews.

Most of the law relating to marriage is to be found in the Marriage Acts 1949 to 1970.

Void and Voidable Marriages

A marriage that appears on the surface to be entirely valid may in fact be either void or voidable. A void marriage is one that despite appearances, is never legally brought into existence. A voidable marriage is one that begins as a valid marriage, but which is liable to be pronounced void by a court on certain legal grounds. There are various grounds in which a court may pronounce a marriage void, some arising before the wedding, some at the time of the wedding, and others after the wedding. The Matrimonial Causes Act 1973, ss. 11 and 12, deal with this matter.

Void Marriages

A marriage will be void if any of the following circumstances apply to it:

(a) If either of the parties were under sixteen years of age;
(b) if either party was already married;
(c) if the parties were within the prohibited degrees of relationship;
(d) if the parties were not respectively male and female;
(e) if either party had not genuinely consented to marry, *e.g.*, if a foreigner thought it was a ceremony of engagement, or in the case of a "shotgun wedding".

The position concerning the legal formalities is somewhat complicated. The law is that if certain of these formalities are not observed the wedding will be valid although the parties may have to face a prosecution, while if others are not observed, the marriage will be void. The following are the most important examples of the formalities which if neglected, will render a marriage void.

With reference to a Church of England marriage:

(f) if the wedding was not solemnised by a person in Holy Order;

(g) if the banns (in the case of a marriage by banns) were not properly published;

(h) in the case of an infant, if the infant's parent or guardian forbade the banns;

(i) in the case of a marriage by a licence or certificate, if the licence or certificate had not been duly issued;

In the case of a marriage outside the Church of England:

(j) if the certificate or licence had not been duly issued;

(k) if the wedding was not celebrated in the presence of a registrar or an authorised person.

A marriage will only be void under paragraphs (f) to (k) above if both parties knew at the time of the wedding of the irregularity.

Because a void marriage is no marriage, there is no need to apply to a court to set it aside, since nothing exists which can be set aside. This is obvious, but there remains the practical difficulty that people other than the parties to the marriage may be affected; and there are cases where it is doubtful whether the marriage is valid or void. For these reasons, and to make the position clear once and for all, the court is sometimes asked to declare a marriage void. If on looking into the circumstances, the court reaches the conclusion that the marriage is void, it will make a declaration to this effect. It must be borne in mind, however that the court is not making the marriage void, it is just telling everybody in the community that the marriage which has been examined is a void one. After such a declaration there can be no doubt, and it will be plain that the parties have never been married for a single instant. Of course the parties to a void marriage may have had children, and the effect on them, as children of unmarried parents will be considered below.

Voidable Marriages

A court may annul an existing marriage by making a decree of nullity in the following cases:

(a) if a party is unable to consummate the marriage it may be annulled at the request of either spouse;

(b) if a party wilfully refuses to consummate the marriage it may be annulled at the instance of the other party;

(c) if at the time of the marriage either party:

    (i)   was of unsound mind, or

    (ii) was suffering from mental disorder within the meaning of the Mental Health Act 1959, of such a kind or to such an extent as to be unfitted for marriage, or

    (iii) was subject to recurrent attacks of insanity or epilepsy;

(d) if a party was at the time of marriage suffering from venereal disease in a communicable form;

(e) if the wife was at the time of the marriage pregnant by some person other than the husband.

The grounds (a) and (b) above, on which a marriage may be annulled have been part of the law of England for centuries, but the grounds (c), (d) and (e) were introduced for the first time in 1937, and are now regulated by the Matrimonial Causes Act 1973. The Act lays down that the court shall not grant a decree of nullity unless it is satisfied that:

    (i)   the party requesting a decree of nullity was at the time of marriage ignorant of the facts alleged, and

    (ii) proceedings were instituted within three years from the date of marriage, and

    (iii) (a) that the petitioner, knowing that it was open to him to have the marriage annulled, behaved in such a way as to make the other party reasonably believe he would not try to get a decree of nullity, and

(b) that it would be unjust to the respondent to grant the decree.

The court terminates the marriage by a "Decree *Nisi*" followed usually three months later by a "Decree Absolute", as for divorce (see p. 233). Under the Matrimonial Causes Act 1973, s. 16, the marriage ends on the date of the Decree Absolute.

The Effect of Void and Voidable Marriages on the Children of Such Marriages

The Legitimacy Act 1959, s. 2 lays down that the child of a void marriage shall be treated as the legitimate child of his parents if at the time of the act of intercourse resulting in the birth (or at the time of the celebration of the marriage if later) both or either of the parties reasonably believed that the marriage was valid.

The Matrimonial Causes Act 1973 lays down that where a decree of nullity is granted in respect of a voidable marriage, any child who would have been the legitimate child of the parties to the marriage if at the date of the decree the marriage has been dissolved instead of being annulled shall be deemed to be their legitimate child. This means that the child of a voidable marriage which is annulled will be deemed to be legitimate only if born or conceived between the date of the marriage and the date of the decree of nullity.

The Ending of Marriage

If either a husband or a wife dies, this of course ends the marriage. If one party to a marriage disappears for a long time and the other party believes that his spouse is dead, he may under the provisions of the Matrimonial Causes Act 1973, s. 19, present a petition (request) to the court to have it presumed that the other spouse is dead and to have the marriage dissolved. One important type of evidence of death is mentioned particularly in s. 14. If the petitioning spouse proves that the other spouse has been continually absent for seven years or more, and that there is no reason to believe that he or she is living, this will be regarded as evidence of death until the contrary is proved. Other types of evidence if available would be accepted. If the court makes a decree of presumption of death and of dissolution of marriage the petitioning spouse is free to remarry.

DIVORCE

A married person may make an application to a court to have the marriage dissolved. All such applications must be commenced in a county court, but if the other spouse indicated that he intends to defend the marriage, the case must be transferred to the High Court. For the purposes of the legal proceedings the party applying is called the "petitioner", and the other party is called the "respondent". The application is commenced by presenting a document called a "petition" to the court.

Divorce is regulated by the Matrimonial Causes Act 1973. This lays down that the sole ground for divorce is the irretrievable breakdown of the marriage. In order to show such breakdown the petitioner must satisfy the court of one or more of the following:

(a) that the respondent has committed adultery and the petitioner finds it intolerable to live with the respondent
(b) that the respondent behaved in such a way that the petitioner cannot reasonably be expected to live with the respondent
(c) desertion by the respondent for two years
(d) that the husband and wife have lived apart for two years, and the respondent consents to a decree being made
(e) that the parties have lived apart for five years.

It is the duty both of the petitioner's solicitor and of the court to help effect a reconciliation between the parties. The Matrimonial Causes Act 1973 Part II makes detailed provisions for payment by one former spouse to the other after the divorce, and for the custody and education of the children.

If, after hearing any evidence that the petitioner and the respondent wish to put forward in court, and taking all relevant matters into consideration, the court considers that the marriage ought to be terminated, it has power to bring it to an end. It does this in two stages. At the hearing the court makes a "Decree *Nisi*" (unless). This entitles the successful party to apply for a "Decree Absolute", usually after 3 months, ending the marriage completely. Neither party can re-marry until the Decree Absolute is granted.

Ordinarily a petition cannot be presented within three years of marriage, but in cases of exceptional hardship suffered by the petitioner or of exceptional depravity on the part of the respondent, it will be allowed. Even though a petitioner is able to satisfy the court of the truth of the allegations in the petition, it does not automatically follow that a divorce will be decreed. The court will take into account the conduct of the parties, the possibility of hardship to the respondent, and the interests of the children.

If the parties have lived apart for two years and the respondent consents to a decree and there are no children, a divorce can be granted by a judge with no public hearing. The petitioner can practically get a divorce "by post" without the help of a solicitor if he applies to his local county court for the proper forms.

Matrimonial Jurisdiction of Magistrates' Courts

The High Court, or a county court in addition to its jurisdiction to grant decrees of divorce can give other types of matrimonial relief; for example it can, on the application of one spouse, make an order for judicial separation, the effect of which is to relieve the parties of their ordinary married duty to live together, and it can order a husband who is not doing so, to pay money to his wife for her and the maintenance of the children. In practice the great bulk of applications for matrimonial relief short of divorce are made to magistrates' courts which have wide powers.

Under the provisions of the Domestic Proceedings and Magistrates' Courts Act 1978 either party to a marriage may apply to a magistrates' court for an order that the other party, known as the respondent, should pay the applicant periodical payments or a lump sum. The applicant must prove that the respondent:

    (a) has failed to provide reasonable maintenance for the applicant, or

(b) has failed to provide, or to make a proper contribution
     towards, reasonable maintenance for any child of the
     family, or
(c) has behaved in such a way that the applicant cannot
     reasonably be expected to live with the respondent, or
(d) has deserted the applicant.

When deciding whether to make an order or not the
magistrates must have regard to a number of matters including
the income and property of each party, their financial needs, their
standard of living, their ages and the duration of the marriage,
any disabilities of either and any contributions by either to
looking after the home or family. The court may in addition to an
order for payment make one concerning the custody of and access
to children of the marriage. It must also consider the possibility of
a reconciliation between the parties. In most cases an appeal lies
from the decision of the magistrates to the Family Division of the
High Court.

The Mutual Duties of Husband and Wife

It is the duty of each spouse to live with the other and to
consummate the marriage. Both spouses have the right to sexual
intercourse during the marriage, but if one party insists on
restricting or demanding intercourse to an unreasonable degree,
this conduct may amount to behaviour of a sort that the other
party cannot reasonably be expected to live with the guilty spouse,
so as to be the foundation for a divorce petition. It is a husband's
duty to let his wife have children.

A husband must provide his wife with the necessities of life such
as lodging, food, clothes and medical attention, although he need
not provide luxuries.

If a husband's illness or old age reduces his earning capacity it
becomes his wife's duty to support him if she can. Spouses are
entitled to use force to protect one another from attack.

If one spouse owns the matrimonial home, the Matrimonial
Homes Act (1967) prevents him or her from selling it and turning
out the other in case of desertion. The non-owner spouse who

remains has a right to stay in occupation until death or until the marriage ends.

PARENTS AND CHILDREN

Our system of social organisation assumes that in normal circumstances children will be born to parents who are married to one another either at the date of the child's conception or at the date of the child's birth. Children born in such circumstances are termed legitimate children. The ordinary rules concerning duties and rights as between parents and children are intended to apply to legitimate children. A child whose parents were not married to one another either at the date of conception or birth is said to be illegitimate and does not fit into the usual pattern of social organisation; because of this, special rules apply concerning rights and duties as between illegitimate children and their parents. An illegitimate person can become legitimate through the subsequent marriage of his parents, and as from the date of the marriage will be treated as if he had always been legitimate. Legitimation is governed by the Legitimacy Act 1976. If there is doubt as to a person's legitimacy he may present a petition to the High Court or a county court asking the court to make a decree declaring him legitimate; the procedure for doing so is laid down in the Matrimonial Causes Act 1973, s. 45.

Parental Rights and Duties

The basic right of parents is to have the children in their keeping, or in legal language, to have custody of their children. Normally parents are jointly entitled to custody but there are circumstances such as death or divorce which can result in only one parent having custody. In divorce proceedings the court usually awards the custody of the children of the marriage to one of the spouses; ordinarily the mother. If a child has no parents or has for some reason nobody to look after him, the local authority may take over custody. Magistrates' and other courts have power to decide who shall have custody of children in various eventualities; if, for example a child is beyond parental control a court may commit the child to the custody of some fit, *i.e.* suitable, person or send him to a school approved by the Home Secretary. If a child has committed a crime the court may, on taking into account his age and all the circumstances, send him into the custody of a detention centre (which takes offenders for short periods), a prison, or some other institution. If the child who has committed the crime is found to be suffering from mental disorder, the court may in a proper case commit him to the custody of a mental hospital.

A father has a duty to protect his children physically and morally and must provide them with the necessities of life; if a man deserts his wife and children the wife may pledge the husband's credit for necessaries for the children (see p. 234), and may apply for a maintenance order against the husband on behalf of the children. A father must see that his children receive education between the ages of five and fifteen years either by attending school or by some other means. Parents have a right to correct children by moderate corporal punishment, and are entitled to enjoy services, such as domestic duties, rendered by their children. The right to decide on the religion of children belongs to the parents, who can insist on their choice of religion being followed even if the child has been committed to the custody of some other person or institution.

Parental Rights and Duties in Respect of Illegitimate Children

The mother of an illegitimate child will ordinarily have custody of the child. It is her duty to protect the child physically and morally. She must see that the child is educated and has a right to decide on the child's religion. The mother of an illegitimate child may apply to the magistrates' court for an "affiliation order" against the father of the child. This means that if the court is satisfied that the man named in the application is the father of the child, it may order him to pay a weekly sum for the child's maintenance.

Adoption

The relationship of parent and legitimate child may be created artificially by means of adoption. The rules concerning adoption are contained in the Children Act 1975 and the Adoption Act 1976. Only a person under the age of eighteen, and who has never been married may be adopted. It is possible for a parent to adopt his or her illegitimate child. An adopter must be either a parent of the child, a person over twenty-one years of age, or a relative of the child who is over twenty-one years of age. A married couple may adopt jointly. The effect of adoption is to place the adopting parent and adopted child in the same position legally as a parent and legitimate child and to break the child's connection with his own parents.

LAW OF SUCCESSION

The law that governs inheritance to the property of a person who has died is known as the law of succession. A person succeeds to property by becoming owner of it on the death of another. There are two branches of the law of succession: testamentary succession and intestate succession. If a person dies after having made a valid will, which as described below, is a document setting out how he wishes his property to be distributed after his death, the rules of testamentary succession are applied. Nowadays the words "testament" and "will" are used interchangeably, but in times past a will was a document in which directions were given for the distribution of land, while a testament was a document in which directions were given for the distribution of moveable property. For this reason a will, even today, often starts with the words "This is the last will and testament of ...", so that the same document can contain directions for the distribution of both land and moveable property. If a person dies without having made a will, the rules of intestate (without a will) succession are applied.

Wills

The most important statute relating to wills is the Wills Act 1837. This lays down much of the detailed law, but there is besides, a considerable body of case law and there are also a few less important statutes. In order to make a valid will, a testator (person who makes a will) must be over eighteen years of age unless he comes within the provisions of the Wills Act 1837, s. 11 and the Wills (Soldiers and Sailors) Act 1918. These provisions, together with certain others permit soldiers and airmen in actual military service and mariners who are at sea to make a valid will despite the fact that they may be under eighteen years of age provided that they have attained the ages, if male, of fourteen, and if female, of twelve. It should be noted that the Act also permits those in the above mentioned classes to make an informal will. That is to say, a soldier or airman in actual military service or a mariner at sea need not comply with the requirements mentioned below as to the form a will must take, for example, although a will must usually be in writing, a mariner at sea may make a will by word of mouth by telling someone how he wishes his goods to be disposed of.

In *Hodson* v. *Barnes* (1926) a testator who was a pilot on the Manchester Ship Canal attempted to make a will by writing "17–1925. Mag. Everything i possess—J.B." on an eggshell. The President of the Probate, Divorce and Admiralty Division, Lord Merrivale, in his judgment, said that the act of writing on the egg was one of the most grotesque proceedings conceivable on the part of a man in a responsible position, holding that the writing was not meant to be a will, and furthermore that there was no evidence that the testator was at sea when he made it, although his work took him into the tidal reaches of the Mersey.

If a testator makes a will while suffering from mental disorder, or while acting through fear, fraud or force it will be invalid.

Example of a valid sailor's will

This will does not conform to the requirements of the 1837 Act for two reasons. Firstly, the testator is only 17, and secondly, the will is not witnessed. It is valid, however, because the sailor making it was at sea when he did so, and it is saved by the Wills (Soldiers and Sailors) Act 1918.

> *I, Jack Tar, born on 24th February 1964, an ordinary seaman on the M.V. Quango, now in mid-Atlantic, give all my property to my wife Bridget Tar on my death.*
>
> *Jack Tar*
> *24th February 1981*

The Form of a Will

The Wills Act 1837, s. 9 lays down that a will shall be in writing, but does not make any rules as to the language to be used or the writing materials to be employed. Section 9 goes on to make it a requirement of a valid will that it shall be "signed at the foot or end thereof". The courts are liberal in their interpretation of "signed" and have accepted wills as validly signed by means of a mark, and in other ways. In *In the Estate of Finn* (1936) a thumb print made by an illiterate testator was accepted as a signature by the court, although without enthusiasm. Section 9 continues by requiring that the will shall be signed "by the testator, or by some other person in his presence and by his direction". This means for example, that a testator who is ill and too weak to sign his will himself by writing his name on it, may make a valid will if he tells somebody else to do it while he looks on. Another requirement of s. 9 is that the testator's signature "shall be made or acknowledged by the testator in the presence of two or more witnesses present at the same time". The effect of this is that the testator may sign the will in front of two witnesses, or if he prefers it, sign the will while alone and then to produce it to two witnesses saying that he acknowledges the signature on it to be his. Finally s. 9 requires that the witnesses "shall attest and shall subscribe the will in the presence of the testator". To attest is to witness the signature of a document, while to subscribe is, literally, to write underneath. Here subscribing means signing so as to show that the person who subscribes has witnessed the signature, or the acknowledgement of the signature, of the testator.

It should be noted that there is a rule laid down by the Wills Act 1837, s. 15 which nullifies benefits given in the will to those who witness it. Section 15 lays down that if a will makes a gift to a person who attests and subscribes the will, or to his or her spouse, there shall be a good attestation and subscription, but the gift to the witness and the spouse shall be void. If therefore a person knows he is to receive some benefit under a will, or that his spouse is to receive a benefit, he would be wise to refuse to witness the testator's signature, if asked. The Wills Act 1968 provides that if there are more than two witnesses to a will, gifts to one or more of them will remain valid provided that there are at least two witnesses who take no benefit.

The following example of a will conforms to the requirements of the Wills Act 1837. The testator gives all his property to his wife.

I, John Doe, of "Laburnum House", Dukesthorpe Road, Sydenham, London SE26, hereby revoke all former testamentary dispositions made by me.

I give all my real and personal property whatsoever and wheresoever to my wife Jane Doe of the above address absolutely and appoint her sole executrix of this my will.

IN WITNESS whereof I have hereunto set my hand this 19th day of January 1981.

Signed by the above-named John Doe as his
last will in the presence of us present at the
same time who at his request in his presence
and in the presence of each other have
hereunto subscribed our name as witnesses.   *JOHN DOE*

D. M. M. Smith	*M. C. Cerise*
The Firs	Sharp House
Salisbury Court	Knife Street
Southampton	Sheffield
Solicitor	Solicitor

The Revocation of a Will

A will does not come into effect until the testator dies, and he is free to change it, or replace it by another will as often as he wishes, and he may, if he likes, destroy his will altogether and die intestate. There are a number of ways in which a will may be revoked. First, a testator may revoke a will by making another one in which the previous will is declared to be revoked. Secondly, the testator, without making another will, may revoke his will by means of a document signed, attested and subscribed in the same manner as a will, which just declares the will to be revoked. Thirdly, he may, in accordance with the Wills Act 1837, s. 20 revoke the will by "burning, tearing, or otherwise destroying" it, or by getting some other person to do this in his presence. Fourthly a testator will, under the Wills Act 1837 s. 18, automatically revoke his will by subsequently getting married, although there are certain exceptions to this rule. One exception is laid down in the Law of Property Act 1925, s. 177 which provides that a will made expressly in contemplation of a marriage, will not be revoked by that marriage.

Executors and Administrators

An executor is ordinarily a person who is appointed by a testator in a will to carry out his wishes in distributing his property after the testator has died. An administrator is a person appointed by the court to distribute the property of a deceased person when no executor is appointed or available to do the work. Both executors and administators are also known as "personal representatives". There are a number of reasons why no executor may be available. The executors named in the will may be dead, particularly in cases where the testator has lived for many years after making his will, or may be sick. Even though a person named as executor is in good health, he will not be compelled to act as executor if he does not wish to do so since the work of personal representatives is often onerous and time-consuming.

Probate and Letters of Administration

An executor derives his authority to carry out his duties from the will, but he will not be recognised as being the executor until he has proved that there is a valid will appointing him. He must "prove the will" to the satisfaction of the appropriate court or other authority as described below. When the will is proved the executor will be relieved of the original will and given instead a certified copy. After proof, a copy of every will is open to public inspection for a small fee. The executor may produce the certified copy if his authority to do anything in connection with the property of the deceased is questioned. The procedure by which the will is proved and the executor is recognised is known as granting "probate", and the copy of the will given to the executor is called the probate copy.

An administrator is not appointed by a will and usually the spouse of the deceased or some close relative applies to be appointed administrator, although if the deceased dies owing a large sum of money, and none of the relatives wish to become administrator, the court has power to appoint a creditor of the deceased as administrator. The administrator is appointed by being given a document known as "Letters of Administration".

Probate or letters of administration may be granted to one person or to not more than four persons jointly. Minors are not eligible for a grant. If there is a dispute as to who shall be appointed the matter will be decided, in the case of a deceased who left less than £15,000 after allowing certain deductions, such as funeral expenses, by the local county court, and in the case of a deceased who left £15,000 or more, by the Chancery Division of the High Court.

Application for Probate or Letters of Administration

If the deceased lived in the London area, application should be made to the Principal Probate Registry of the Family Division, which is an office at Somerset House in the Strand, London, or if application is made in the provinces, to a local District registry.

Proving the Will

There are two methods of proving a will. It may be proved in common form or in solemn form. To prove a will in common form it is necessary only to make application to Somerset House, a probate registry or sub-registry, although at least one interview will be necessary, and to fill in certain forms, which are mentioned below. To prove a will in solemn form is to prove it by means of a full-scale action in court to the satisfaction of either a Chancery Division judge, or a county court judge according to the amount involved. Most wills are proved in common form, and this is the quicker and cheaper method. It should be used where there is a well-drawn will, with no question of family disputes as to whether the testator was of sound mind, whether the will was properly witnessed, or any similar question. An executor who believes that the will is going to lead to a dispute concerning such matters would be well advised to prove in solemn form, provided that a sufficiently large sum of money is at stake.

Contentious Proceedings

If anybody with an interest under the will, or a close relative of the deceased wishes, he can make the executor prove in solemn form by instituting an action himself. It should here be emphasised that we are now concerned only with the question of whether or not the will is valid. We are not concerned with what the wording of the will means. To take an example, if Jack is named as executor in a will, and Alice maintains that the will was not witnessed in accordance with the Wills Act 1873, s. 9, the dispute will, if the sum involved is substantial, have to go to the Chancery Division. If the case is finally settled in Alice's favour, that is the end of the matter; the will is pronounced invalid, the deceased has died intestate, and an administrator must now be appointed instead of the executor. Of course Jack could apply to be appointed administrator, but he might find Alice applying too, in which case the court would decide whom to appoint. If, on the other hand the case was finally settled in Jack's favour, the will would have to be accepted by everybody including Alice as valid. However, if the will was badly drawn up so as to have, for example, two possible meanings, Alice could then take Jack to the Chancery Division to get a ruling on what it really meant.

Common Form Procedure

The executor must lodge at the probate registry the following documents:

(a) *An Inland Revenue Affidavit.*—This is a list of all the deceased's assets and debts, and is required by the Estate Duty Office of the Inland Revenue department to enable them to calculate the actual value of the deceased's estate. The net estate is the gross estate (total amount left by deceased) less debts. Included in the debts are funeral expenses and payment for mourning clothes. The document is called an affidavit because the executor must sign it before a commissioner for oaths and swear that the information it contains is true as far as he knows.

(b) *The will.*—If the will is in Welsh an English translation must be lodged as well.

(c) *The executor's oath.*—This is another affidavit in which the executor swears that he will deal with the estate according to the law and will produce accounts when called upon. After these documents have been found satisfactory probate is granted.

(d) *The death certificate.*—It must be realised that this is an account of an absolutely straightforward probate application, and that in practice various snags may occur which will be dealt with as they appear. For example, if the executor comes across the will in such a condition that it looks as if it has been tampered with, he is obliged to declare to the probate registry that he was not responsible for the apparent interference. He has to submit, in addition to the usual documents, an Affidavit of Plight in which he swears that the will is in the same plight, *i.e.* condition, as it was when he found it. Because of the complications that can arise it is advisable in all but the simplest cases for an executor who is not a lawyer to employ a firm of solicitors to make application for probate.

The Grant of Administration

An application for letters of administration is made in a similar manner to that used for common form probate. The person applying must lodge with the probate registry the following: (a) an Inland Revenue Affidavit; (b) the administrator's oath, in which must be included, among other information, the place and time of the deceased's death; (c) possibly a guarantee from an insurance company that he will carry out his duties properly. This will not always be necessary under the Administration of Estates Act 1971.

Again, it is probable that there will be an interval of time and that some correspondence will be entered into before the arrangements are settled and letters of administration are granted. The two main types of grant are a grant of "administration with the will annexed", which is made when there is a valid will but no available executor, in which case the administrator has a duty to carry out the instructions laid down in the will, and a grant of "administration in case of intestacy", in which case the administrator has to distribute the estate in accordance with statutory rules set out below.

Cases where Probate and Administration are Unnecessary

Although the usual rule is that nobody can claim any money which represents a debt due to the deceased at his death, unless he is a personal representative, there are a number of important exceptions to the rule where small sums are concerned. These exceptional cases are governed by the Administration of Estates (Small Payments) Act 1965. The idea behind the Act, which amends certain prior legislation, is that persons who become entitled to the payment of small sums by such organisations as building societies and provident societies on the death of another, shall not be put to the bother of applying for probate or administration just in order to obtain a few pounds. The Act has no application to sums payable by private persons, so that, strictly speaking, no private individual can discharge a debt due to a deceased person unless he pays it to an executor or administrator who has been appointed in the proper way.

The Administration of Estates (Small Payments) Act operates in the following manner. Before the passing of the Act, there were two types of situation in which organisations were allowed to pay out money owing to a deceased person to somebody who was not a personal representative of the deceased. First, certain statutes allowed, and still allow, depositors in such organisations as provident societies to nominate some person to receive whatever funds stand to the credit of the depositor on his death. Nomination entitles the person named to demand payment without having to bother about any question of executors or administrators. Secondly, certain statutes allowed, and still allow, certain organisations such as building societies to pay money standing to the credit of a deceased member or depositor to any person who appeared to be entitled to it, without there being any grant of probate or administration.

The Act confirmed the existing arrangements, made certain modifications, and raised the limit. It is now £1,500. In view of this, any person who is considering applying for probate just in order to be able to obtain from an organisation, a sum of money payable on the death of another, should pause and find out from the organisation whether or not it has power under the Act to pay out without having to insist on handing the money to a personal representative appointed in the regular manner.

The Duties of a Personal Representative

Although there is a good deal of law concerning the subject, it is not necessary here to do more than mention in outline what are the functions of personal representatives. They must pay any estate duty that may be due. As the Estate Duty Office might, through being supplied with wrong information, or through taking a wrong view of the law, initially ask for more than is legally due, the actual amount owed may not be the sum originally requested. Usually some friendly correspondence will put the matter right, but in proper cases it may be the duty of the personal representative to engage in litigation.

Personal representatives must obtain control of the assets belonging to the estate, pay the debts of the deceased, and distribute the remaining estate to those entitled. Distribution of the assets will be postponed until the other duties have been carried out, and personal representatives are allowed what is popularly called the "executor's year" dating from the date of death of the deceased before they are bound to distribute any assets. The question arises as to who should be appointed an executor. The choice lies between a relative, a personal friend, the Public Trustee (a government official), a bank, and a solicitor. A relative or friend might die before the testator. The Public Trustee, being a corporation sole (see p. 97) will not die, and is a good choice where large sums of money are involved, but since the Public Trustee runs a large organisation those entitled under wills cannot expect such quick service as may be obtained from a smaller unit. Banks tend to be rather expensive and if faced with a tricky point of law, are too apt to play for safety and spend the money of the estate on making an application to the court for directions as to what ought to be done. On the whole, for small estates, it is best to choose a local firm of solicitors with a good probate department; it is possible for any solicitor to act as executor, but the work is best done by a specialist. Many banks employ local solicitors to do certain kinds of work for them, and enquiries at a bank or a personal recommendation will usually lead to a reliable firm which will give sympathetic and quick service at a moderate cost.

The Construction of Wills

Where a will has been admitted to probate and there is a dispute as to the meaning of the words, the dispute is resolved by the Chancery Division of the High Court. The old Court of Chancery and its successor have developed over the centuries, a sophisticated battery of legal rules for determining the meaning of obscure wills, and these have been patiently developed to give a uniformity of treatment to all the wills that come before the court. These rules can sometimes work justice in a surprising way; an example of this is the case of *Re Jackson* (1933), where a testatrix left some property in her will to "my nephew Arthur Murphy". It turned out that she had two nephews of that name, and so there came into operation a rule which provides that when two persons fit the same description, evidence may be called to show what the intention of the person making the will actually was. The evidence showed that in addition to the two nephews who were entitled to be considered under the normal rules, there was also an illegitimate nephew called Arthur Murphy, who normally would not be entitled to consideration at all, and, further that this illegitimate nephew was the one the testatrix actually had in mind, so that he was awarded the property. Had there been one legitimate Arthur Murphy and one illegitimate one, no ambiguity would have arisen and the legitimate nephew would automatically have been given the property. Of course, if the testatrix had been careful enough to describe the person intended to receive the property as "my illegitimate nephew", he would immediately have been awarded the property.

The Rules of Intestate Succession

Where a person dies without making a will, and an administrator is appointed to distribute his estate, the rules governing who shall be entitled to benefit are governed by the Administration of Estates Act 1925 as amended by the Intestates' Estates Act 1952 and the Family Provision Act 1966 and certain statutory instruments. These rules were drawn up after an investigation designed to discover the way an average testator drew up his will, and they are intended, as far as possible, to distribute the estate of a deceased intestate in a manner that is as close as possible to the way an average man would wish it to be done. The rules are rather complicated and only the more important features of them will be mentioned. These are as follows: (a) first, the expenses of the funeral, and of administration, including any estate duty, must be paid together with the debts of the deceased; (b) if the intestate dies leaving a spouse, but no parents, no issue, *i.e.*, children, grandchildren, etc., no brothers, sisters, nephews or nieces, the spouse will be entitled to the whole of the remaining estate (called the residuary estate); (c) if the intestate left a spouse, and issue, the spouse will take the personal chattels (household goods), the first £25,000 out of the remaining estate and the rest will then be divided into two equal portions, one of which is divided among the deceased's issue. The surviving spouse will receive a life interest in the other portion which means that he or she is entitled to any income accruing from it, but is not entitled to the capital which on his or her death is also divided among the issue of the intestate deceased; (d) if the intestate leaves a spouse but no issue, and one or more parents, brothers, sisters or their issue, the spouse will take the personal chattels, the first £55,000 of the remaining estate, and half what is then left. The other half of what is then left goes to the parents. If there are no parents the half is divided equally among the deceased's brothers and sisters or their issue; (e) if the intestate leaves issue but no spouse the whole of the residuary estate will go to the issue; (f) if the intestate leaves no spouse, or issue, but one or both parents, the parents will take the whole of residuary estate; (g) if the deceased leaves no close relatives, the whole residuary estate goes to the Crown, and is called by the latin name *bona vacantia* (goods without an owner). If however the deceased has been supporting any person who might be expected to benefit in any will the deceased might have made, the Crown may pay such persons a proper sum out of the *bona vacantia*. In most cases if a child of the deceased has died before the testator leaving children of his own, they will take any share which their parent would have taken had he been alive. The Family Law Reform Act 1969, s. 14, entitles an illegitimate child to share in the intestate estate of his parents (but not of his grandparents or remoter ancestors) on the same footing as his legitimate brothers and sisters.

Family Provision

Until 1938 a person was completely free to leave his property to any person or organisation without restriction even if this left his or her family destitute. There is still no restriction on how an estate may be disposed of by will, but the Inheritance (Provision for Family and Dependants) Act 1975 permits certain classes of persons who have not been provided for by a will, or under the rules of intestate succession to apply to the court for an order that they be given reasonable financial provision out of the estate of the deceased. The following may apply: a spouse; a former wife or former husband who has not remarried; a child of the deceased including an adopted or illegitimate child; any person who was treated as a child of the family by the deceased; and any other person who immediately before the death of the deceased was being maintained wholly or partly by the deceased. The application must ordinarily be made within six months of a grant of probate or letters of administration. The court has to decide whether or not any payment shall be made taking into consideration a number of factors including the size of the estate, the applicant's financial position, any disability of the applicant, the deceased's reasons for making the will he did, or his reason for making no will, and the way the applicant behaved towards the deceased during his lifetime. The main object of the legislation is to provide an annual income for applicants. The court may order the payment of a lump sum instead of annual income. The courts are not inclined to be over-generous in the payments they authorise. For example in *Re Greenham* (1964) a testator left a gross estate of £400,000. Of the net estate the Estate Duty Office took £263,000, and the rest was left to charity, the testator saying in his will that he had provided amply for his wife some years before. He had paid his wife £65 a month under a separation agreement and given her a house before he died, and since his death she had received £952 a year from an insurance policy paid for by him in 1928. It was held by the Chancery Division that the wife was entitled to an annuity of £1,000 a year.

Index

CONTRACT—*cont.*
sale of goods, for
See SALE OF GOODS
specialty
See DEED
Statute of Frauds, effect of, 196
uberrimae fidei, meaning, 188
undue influence, 187, 188
unfair contract terms, 199
utmost good faith, when required,
188
writing, when necessary to prove,
195, 196

CONTRACT OF EMPLOYMENT
breach of—
damages, employee's right to, 216,
217
dismissal, when justifying, 216
remedies for, 216, 217
contract of apprenticeship, whether
regarded as, 212
implied duties of parties to, 212
infant, limited capacity to make, 211,
212
notice—
Contracts of Employment Act
1972, under, 214
reasonable, what is, 214
termination by, 214
redundancy
See REDUNDANCY PAYMENTS
restrictions on re-employment, how
far valid, 215, 216
statement of, 211
termination of, methods of, 214
types of, 210

CONTRIBUTORY NEGLIGENCE
defence to action for negligence, as,
176
reduction of damages where, 176

CONVENTION
British Constitution, as constituent
of, 4
meaning, 4

CONVERSION
tort of, 177

CORONER
duties of, 68
jury, when summoned, 68

CORONER—*cont.*
majority verdict, when accepted, 68
qualification for appointment as, 68
suspect must not be named, 68

CORPORATION
aggregate
See CORPORATION AGGREGATE
chartered
See CHARTERED CORPORATION
contract by, validity of, 185
crime, how far punishable for, 127,
128
existence separate from its members,
97
land, ability to hold, 97
legal capacity of, 97
limited company
See COMPANIES
local authorities
See LOCAL AUTHORITY
nature of, 97
sole
See CORPORATION SOLE
statutory, powers, definition and
limitation of, 98

CORPORATION AGGREGATE
chartered corporation as, 98
nature of, 98
statutory corporation as, 98

CORPORATION SOLE
bishops of Church of England as, 97
cannot die, 98
creation of, 98
Crown as, 97
nature of, 97, 98

COSTS
civil proceedings, in—
discretion of court as to, 87
general rule as to, 87
successful party, when deprived of,
87
taxation of, 87
criminal proceedings, in—
acquitted person, of, when payable
from public funds, 88
convicted person, power to order
payment by, 88
discretion of court, 88